SELECTED CHAPTERS FROM WEIL:

HANDBOOK OF COST MANAGEMENT

A Wiley Canada Custom Publication

Prepared for:

York University
AK/ADMS3510

WILEY

Wiley Canada Custom Services

JOHN WILEY & SONS CANADA, LTD.

Printed and bound in Canada
10 9 8 7 6 5 4 3 2 1

John Wiley & Sons Canada, Ltd
6045 Freemont Blvd.
Mississauga, Ontario
L5R 4J3
WILEY   Visit our website at: www.wiley.ca

HANDBOOK OF COST MANAGEMENT

SECOND EDITION

ROMAN L. WEIL
MICHAEL W. MAHER

WILEY

JOHN WILEY & SONS, INC.

Published by John Wiley & Sons, Inc., Hoboken, New Jersey
Published simultaneously in Canada

Portions of the FASB Concepts Statement No. 2, *Qualitative Characteristics of Accounting Information,* and FASB Statement No. 107, *Disclosures about Fair Value of Financial Instruments,* copyright by the Financial Accounting Standards Board, 401 Merritt 7, Norwalk, CT 06856-5116, USA, reprinted with permission. Complete copies of these documents are available from the FASB

For general information on our other products and services, or technical support, please contact our Customer Care Department within the United States at 800-762-2974, outside the United States at 317-572-3993 or fax 317-572-4002.

Wiley also publishes its books in a variety of electronic formats. Some content that appears in print may not be available in electronic books.

Library of Congress Cataloging-in-Publication Data

Handbook of cost management / [edited by] Roman L. Weil, Michael W. Maher.--
2nd ed.
     p. cm.
  Rev. ed. of: Handbook of cost management. c1978.
  Includes index.
  ISBN-13 978-0-471-67814-4
  ISBN-10 0-471-67814-7 (cloth)
  1. Cost accounting--Handbooks, manuals, etc. 2. Managerial
accounting--Handbooks, manuals, etc. I. Weil, Roman L. II. Maher, Michael,
1946- III. Handbook of cost management.
  HF5686.C8H237 2005
  657'.42--dc22

Printed in the United States of America

TABLE OF CONTENTS

Chapter 7   243
Target Costing for New Product Development

Chapter 8   271
Kaizen Costing for Existing Products

Chapter 11   329
Logistics and Marketing Costs

Chapter 16   465
Allocations of Cost and Revenue

Chapter 18   503
Forecasting Pro Formal Financial Statements

Chapter 20   573
Theory of Constraints

Chapter 28   697
A Managerial Accounting Guide for Nonprofit Managers

TARGET COSTING FOR NEW PRODUCT DEVELOPMENT*

ROBIN COOPER, DBA
Emory University

REGINE SLAGMULDER, PhD
INSEAD

CONTENTS

7.1 INTRODUCTION 243

7.2 MARKET-DRIVEN COSTING 245

    (a) Setting Long-Term Sales and Profit Objectives 246
    (b) Structuring the Product Mix 248
    (c) Setting the Target Selling Price 248
    (d) Establishing the Target Profit Margin 250
    (e) Computing the Allowable Cost 252

7.3 PRODUCT-LEVEL TARGET COSTING 253

    (a) Setting the Product-Level Target Cost 254
    (b) Designing the Product 256

    (c) Application of Disciplining Mechanisms of Product-Level Target Costing 257

7.4 COMPONENT-LEVEL TARGET COSTING 259

    (a) Selecting and Rewarding Suppliers 260
    (b) Setting the Target Costs of Major Functions 261
    (c) Setting the Target Costs of Components 265

7.5 SUMMARY 267

APPENDIX 7A TARGET COSTING EQUATIONS AND GLOSSARY 269

7.1 INTRODUCTION

Target costing is a structured approach to establish the cost at which a firm must manufacture a proposed product with specified functionality and quality to generate the desired profitability over its life-cycle at its anticipated selling price.[1] It is a tool of profit

---

*   This chapter is based on material contained in *Target Costing and Value Engineering*, Robin Cooper and Regine Slagmulder, Portland, Ore.: Productivity Press; 1997.

1.   Target costs should include any costs that are driven by the number of units sold. For example, if the firm accepts responsibility for disposing a product at the end of its useful life, the target cost would include these costs.

management as well as cost management. In Japan, where the lean enterprise[2] evolved, firms view target costing not as a stand-alone program, but as an integral part of their product development process. These firms have developed target costing to bring the competitive challenge of the marketplace to both the product designers and the firm's suppliers. When applied effectively, target costing creates a discipline that harmonizes the labor of disparate participants in the product development effort, from designers and manufacturing engineers to market researchers and suppliers.

At the heart of target costing lies a deceptively simple equation:

$$\text{Target cost} = \text{Target selling price} - \text{Target profit margin} \qquad (1)$$

According to this equation, the firm need only select the price at which its future products will sell, subtract the required profit margin, and then design products so that it can manufacture them at their target costs. In fact, the process is more complicated than the equation suggests. First, before a firm can establish the target selling price, it must define the proposed product's quality and functionality. These product characteristics establish the value that the customers associate with the new product. Second, the firm must set the target profit margin so that the product will generate an adequate return on the up-front investment throughout its life. Before the firm can establish the target profit margin, however, it must estimate the product's sales volume. Thus, embedded into the target costing equation is an assumption about the proposed product's sales volume.

Target costing is the critical first step in managing product costs because once a firm locks in a product's design, many of the costs become immutable. For example, a product's design determines the number of components, the different materials used and the time required for assembly. Some authorities estimate that design drives as much as 90 to 95 percent of a product's costs–costs the firm cannot avoid without redesigning the product. Exhibit 7.1 shows that the level of committed costs increases as the design process advances with approximately 66 percent of costs committed at the end of the product planning stage, approximately 85 percent by the end of the preliminary design stage and approximately 95 percent by the end of the detailed design stage. Once a firm has

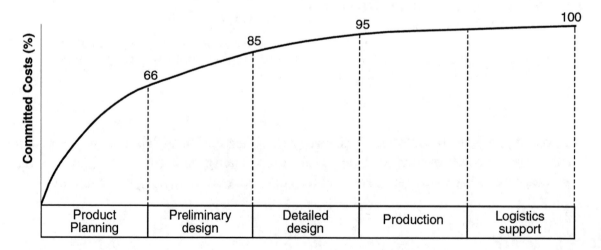

Source: Adapted from B.S. Blanchard, *Design and Manage to Life-Cycle Cost* (Portland, Ore.: Dilithium Press, 1978)

EXHIBIT 7.1 COMMITTED COSTS

---

2. Lean manufacturing is characterized by manufacturing a single part just-in-time for its incorporation into the product.

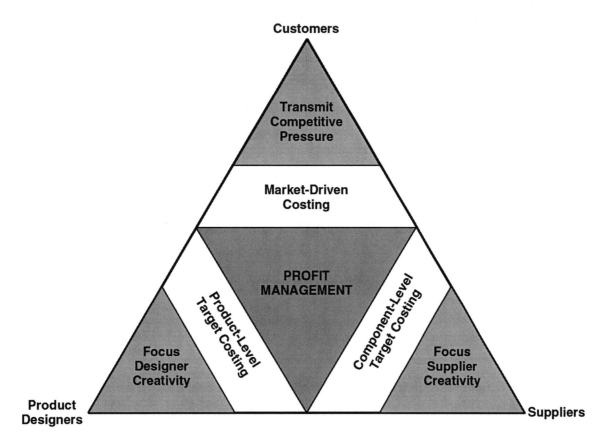

EXHIBIT 7.2   THE TARGET COSTING TRIANGLE

designed a product, it has little freedom to manage costs. Consequently, effective cost management programs must begin at the design and continue into the manufacturing phase of a product's life cycle.

Target costing's simple equation also masks the sophistication required to effectively use it. At many firms, the target costing process contains three major segments (see Exhibit 7.2).

- *Market-driven costing* identifies the allowable cost of the proposed products. It reflects the target selling price (driven by market conditions) and the firm's desired target profit margin, but ignores the cost management capabilities of the firm and its suppliers.

- *Product-level target costing* establishes the product's target cost that reflects more practical considerations (i.e., the firm and its suppliers' capabilities to affect cost) than does market-driven costing.

- *Component-level target costing* establishes the component-level target costs derived from product-level target costing.

We next discuss the elements of these three target costing segments and how they drive profit management.

7.2 MARKET-DRIVEN COSTING

The market-driven costing portion of target costing focuses on customers and their requirements and uses this information to transmit the competitive pressure to the product designers and suppliers (Exhibit 7.3).

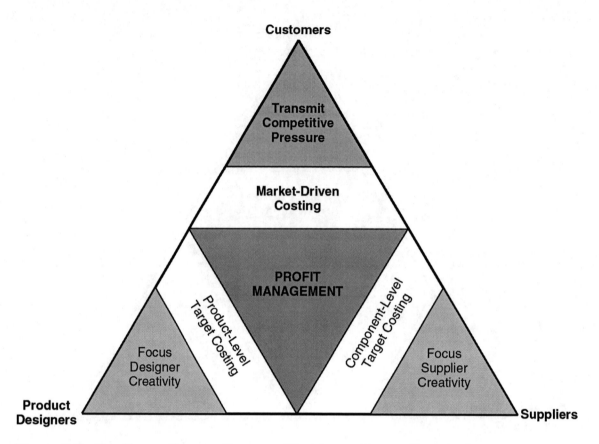

EXHIBIT 7.3   THE TARGET COSTING TRIANGLE: THE MARKET-DRIVEN COSTING STAGE

Market-driven costing consists of five major steps, illustrated in Exhibit 7.4. We list them here and offer an expanded explanation in the subsequent sections.

1. *Set long-term sales and profit objectives.* This step highlights the primary role of target costing as a technique for profit management.

2. *Structure the product mix to achieve maximum profitability.* This step highlights the importance of broad market analysis to effective target costing.

3. *Set the target selling price of the proposed product.* This step relies heavily on analysis of both customer and competitor behavior.

4. *Establish the target profit margin.* This step requires a life-cycle analysis of the product's profitability. This analysis should include the magnitude of the up-front investment, as well as estimates of the product's sales price, production costs and sales volumes over the product's life.

5. *Compute the allowable cost.* This step simply subtracts the target profit margin from the target selling price (Exhibit 7.5). The allowable cost is the product's theoretical target cost; the firm must manufacture the product at this cost to generate its target profit margin. As mentioned previously, it may not reflect a practical target cost, which is the function of product-level target costing, discussed in Section 7.3.

(a) SETTING LONG-TERM SALES AND PROFIT OBJECTIVES. Target costing begins with the firm's long-term sales and profit objectives. Target costing's primary objective is to ensure that, over its life, each product contributes its share of profits to the firm's

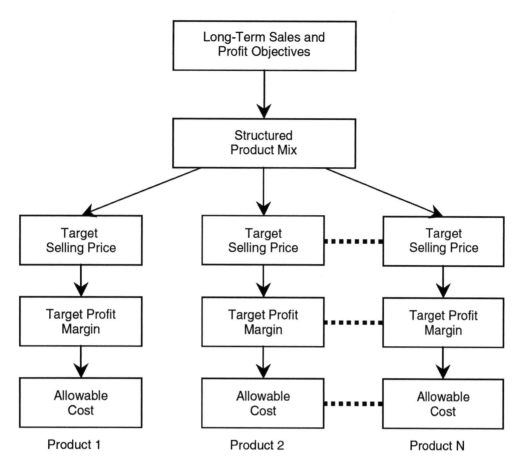

EXHIBIT 7.4 MAJOR STEPS OF MARKET-DRIVEN COSTING

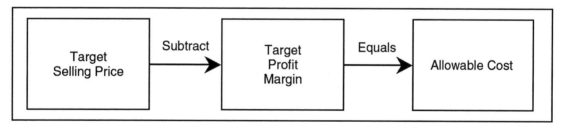

EXHIBIT 7.5 MARKET-DRIVEN COSTING

long-term profit objective. The credibility of the long-term plan becomes paramount in establishing the target costing discipline. The plan achieves credibility in three ways:

1. *It results from analysis of all relevant information that the firm collects.* The credibility of the analysis influences the degree of reliance that individuals in the firm place on the target costing process.

2. *The firm approves only realistic plans.* Whereas analysts may have a natural temptation to set optimistic sales and profit objectives, an effective target costing system must constrain optimism so that the firm approves only achievable long-term plans. If the firm approves unrealistic plans, the target sales volumes and profit margins will in turn reflect undue optimism. Experience has shown, however, that target costing proves effective only when the firm establishes realistic and achievable target costs.

3. *The firm should test the plan's robustness.* Plans that rely heavily on the success of a single product prove less robust than plans that rely on more moderate success of multiple products.

(b) STRUCTURING THE PRODUCT MIX.   Products typically exist within the context of a product line. Any product's success comes from both its individual quality and functionality, and its relation to other products in the line. To ensure successful product lines, firms must first design them to satisfy diverse customer tastes without an unprofitably large number of different products. Too many products may confuse the firm's customers by giving them too many choices. Second, the product development costs become too high and the product line fails to achieve its profitability objectives.

Conversely, having too few products in the line can make customers dissatisfied with the firm's product offering, and they may purchase competitors' products. Consequently, structuring product lines reflects a cost–benefit trade-off. Only with well-designed product lines will every product sell sufficient volume to ensure that it remains profitable over its life cycle.[3]

Target costing helps discipline the structuring of product lines in two ways. First, it evaluates each product according to its ability to earn an adequate profit. If a proposed product cannot earn an adequate return, the target costing process includes an analysis of whether to launch the product. Second, it evaluates the proposed products' levels of quality and functionality to ensure that the firm can justify the costs of manufacturing at such levels. Target costing thus helps control undue increases in product functionality that product engineers may propose.

(c) SETTING THE TARGET SELLING PRICE.   The target costing process requires that the firm establish a specific target selling price (Exhibit 7.6). A number of factors come into play when establishing the target selling price. These factors include the relative functionality and selling price of any competitive offerings that the firm anticipates will be available when it launches its new product. If the firm expects that the competitive offerings will have differing functionality and price than the proposed product, then its target selling price will have to take these differences into account. The target selling price should also reflect the firm's strategic objectives for the new product. The firm also needs to consider other factors, such as the desired market share for the new product and impact that the new product might have on corporate image. If the firm wants to aggressively pursue target market share, then the firm might have to lower the target selling price to make the new product more attractive on launching. Similarly, if the product plays an important role in establishing a corporate image (such as the Coca-Cola score boards in high school gyms), the firm might lower the price to make the new product more attractive. Finally, the selling price needs to reflect the perceived value that the customers associate with the product and their loyalty to the firm. The higher the perceived value or the higher the loyalty to the firm, the higher the potential selling price.

Since the target costing formula (equation 1 in Section 7.1) uses a single target selling price, when firms sell the same product at different prices—for example, in different countries—they must use a weighted average selling price.[4] Similarly, if the firm anticipates changing the selling price across the product's life, then it adopts the anticipated

---

3.   The only exceptions should be strategic products designed to create a corporate image.
4.   The weighted average would be computed by summing the product of each selling price and its associated volume, and then dividing by the total volume expected to be sold.

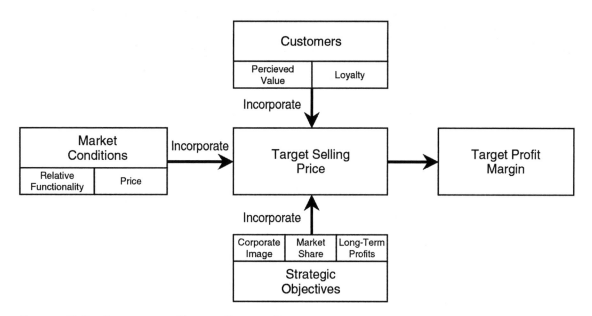

EXHIBIT 7.6 SETTING THE TARGET SELLING PRICE

selling price at launch. The firm uses the launch selling price rather than an estimated average price across the life of the product because of the high degree of uncertainty about that average and the ability to reduce costs through *kaizen* costing and other activities.[5]

Most firms work hard to set a realistic target selling price. Target selling prices reflect the market conditions that the firms anticipate at the product's launch date. Internal market factors include the position of the model in the firm's product line and management's strategic and profitability objectives for that model. External market factors include the corporation's image and level of customer loyalty, the product's expected quality level and functionality compared to competitive offerings, the product's expected market share, and, finally, the expected price of competitive products.

(i) Customers: Perceived Value and Loyalty. Perceived value lies at the heart of the price setting process. Customers will pay more for a product than they did for its predecessor only if they perceive an increase in value. Rather than undertake the analysis *de novo*, many firms take an incremental approach. They start with the predecessor product's actual selling price and adjust it accordingly, based on incremental perceived value. They then calculate the selling price of a new model as the selling price of the equivalent existing model plus any incremental value attributable to improved functionality. For example, adding air conditioning to an automobile's standard version will increase its price by the perceived value of air conditioning. To assess this incremental value of a new model, the firm must analyze market conditions. In a mature industry, such as the automobile industry, most new features already exist in some form on other models. For example, if the standard version will include air conditioning, the firm can evaluate its added value using the list price of optional air conditioners for other models. If no equivalent option existed—a rare event—then the firm's design engineers and market specialists estimate how much customers will pay for the added feature.

(ii) Competitive Offerings: Functionality/Price Tradeoff. The firm examines the interaction between functionality and price during the market-driven costing process. It considers

5. See Chapter 8, "Kaizen Costing for Existing Products."

perceived value when setting the product's functionality, and the product's functionality when setting prices. The firm aims to design a product that will sell at its target price and achieve the desired sales volume while generating its target profit margin. Thus, the availability of competitive products and their perceived value temper the price increases associated with incremental perceived value. Selling prices can increase only if the new product's perceived value not only exceeds that of the product's predecessor but also that of competing products.

The complexity of the task that the firm faces in setting target selling prices depends primarily on the similarity or difference between product generations. This becomes particularly difficult for a product that has no direct predecessor. In contrast, the task becomes relatively simple when the new products resemble those they will replace.

Some industries have little latitude for setting prices because the industry competes at defined price points. For example, a relatively simple point-and-shoot camera might sell in retail stores for $49.99, and the next model might sell for $59.99. Essentially, no cameras sell between these two prices in retail camera stores. Therefore, the firm must simply identify at which price the product will sell. Sometimes the product's specific or distinctive functionality establishes the price. For example, a camera's distinctive feature (e.g., the magnification capability of the zoom lens or the camera's small size) establishes its price. The competitive analysis and technology review used in developing the product plan drives the relation between distinctive features and prices. The product plan thus describes cameras only in terms of their distinctive feature. Product designers may add other features as the camera design nears completion.

In some markets, such as that for cameras, the price/functionality trade-off changes over time and the price for a given level of functionality falls. The reduced cost of camera technology allows the functionality of the camera sold at a given price to improve over time. Therefore, the functionality that previously defined the $59.99 price is now available at the $49.99 price. Such firms face the challenge of introducing new levels of functionality to maintain the high prices, while simultaneously decreasing the costs of existing levels of functionality sufficiently to generate adequate profits as prices fall. For example, the price at which a camera with given functionality sells tends to decrease over time with improvements in technology. Manufacturers typically hold prices constant for as long as possible by adding functionality to the cameras offered—for example, by adding a quartz date/day feature. Typically, a manufacturer introduces a given camera model at one price. The camera stays at that price for several years but with increasing functionality. Eventually, there is no incremental functionality that the firm can add so it simplifies the next generation of that distinctive functionality and issues it at the next lower price point. This process generates new price points at the low end. For example, the price point for the simplest compact camera was $150 in 1987 and $100 in 1990. The lowest price point by 2004 was down to $60.

Setting target selling prices requires analysis of how the customer perceives value and how competitive offerings deliver value. Given the importance of the target selling price to the target costing process, most firms aim to maximize the realism of their assumptions regarding target selling prices.

(d) ESTABLISHING THE TARGET PROFIT MARGIN.   Firms set target profit margins at levels that will ensure that they can achieve their long-term profit plan, as Exhibit 7.7 illustrates. Responsibility for achieving the overall profit target typically rests with the division responsible for the product line. The division needs to set realistic target profit margins that will also prove sufficient to offset the product's life-cycle costs.

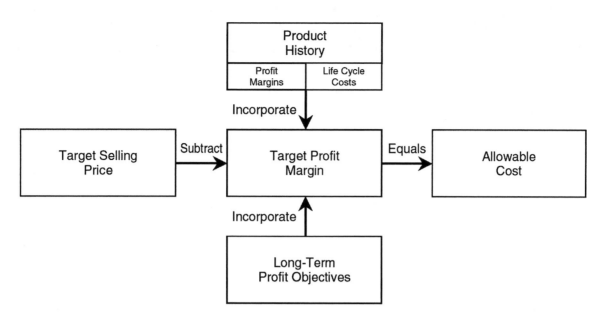

EXHIBIT 7.7   SETTING THE TARGET PROFIT MARGIN

(i) Setting Realistic Target Profit Margins.   Firms can use one of two methods to set target profit margins. The first method starts with the actual profit margin of the predecessor product and then adjusts it for changes in market conditions. The other method starts with the target profit margin of the product line (or other grouping of products) and adjusts the target profit margin for each product based on the realities of the market place. The choice between the two approaches depends on several factors, including the diversity in the products. Firms often apply the second approach when the product line has similar products. As product diversity increases, the first approach typically dominates because the profit level of one product less well predicts the profitability of other products in the line.

The firm bases the target profit margin on historical profit levels (either of the individual product or its product line), the relative strength of competitive offerings, and its long-term profit objective. If the firm perceives the profit objective as unrealistic, it should reduce the target profit margin and thus increase the allowable cost. Setting target profit margins in this manner causes the allowable costs to reflect the firm's competitive position. An efficient firm will set target profit margins that exceed those of less efficient firms and hence have lower allowable costs for products selling at the same price. Similarly, a firm that has products with higher functionality than its competitors will typically have higher profit margins because it can sell its products at a premium price.

(ii) Adjusting the Target Profit Margin for Life Cycle Costs.   To make target costing operational, the firm sets the target cost of a new product at the cost level that the firm expects the product to reach some time after product launch (this time period is often three months). It does not set it at the time of product launch because the production process needs time to settle down and the higher costs encountered directly after launch do not indicate the product's long-term manufacturing cost. The firm has to adjust target profit margins when products require high investments to launch, when the firm discontinues products, or when it expects selling prices and costs to change significantly during the products' lives. A firm would expect a product that requires higher up-front investment to generate higher margins than one that does not, *ceteris paribus*. These adjustments ensure that the product's expected profitability across its life will prove adequate.

If the firm decides that the product will make a satisfactory contribution throughout its life cycle, the conceptual design process will continue. An evaluation of unsatisfactory profit margins will induce the firm to redesign the product. When the product has a long development cycle, the firm may use multiple life-cycle analyses. Typically, the firm performs such life-cycle analyses at each major design step to ensure that the product will support the firm's profit objectives. Toward the end of the conceptual design stage, the firm often conducts a major review of the new product. This review includes an updated profitability study and an analysis of the model's performance characteristics. In the profitability study, the firm compares the product's expected profitability (i.e., target price minus target cost) to the latest estimates of the capital investment and remaining research and development expenditures required to complete the product's design and begin production.

Firms that can substantially reduce the cost of their products during the manufacturing stage use a different life cycle analysis. This analysis reflects any anticipated savings in production costs during the manufacturing phase in the target costing profitability analysis. Consequently, a firm will use a lower initial target profit margin for a product whose costs it expects to fall more rapidly than the selling price, and a higher initial margin for a product whose costs it does not expect to fall as fast as the selling price, *ceteris paribus.* Thus, the life-cycle adjustment ensures that the analysis considers all costs and savings when setting the target profit margin. Without such adjustments, the firm risks either launching products that do not earn an adequate return or not launching products that, over their lives, will earn an adequate return.

(e) COMPUTING THE ALLOWABLE COST.   Once the firm has established the target selling price and profit margin, it can calculate the allowable cost using the following formula:

$$\text{Allowable cost} = \text{Target selling price} - \text{Target profit margin} \qquad (2)$$

The allowable cost reflects the firm's competitive position. In competitive environments, efficient firms will have higher target profit margins and, hence, lower allowable costs than their less-efficient competitors. Consequently, to use allowable costs as a benchmark, the firm must set target profit margins that reflect the capabilities of the most efficient competitor. Such margins give benchmark profits, not the firm's lower, realistic long-term profit objectives. Firms at a significant competitive disadvantage will benefit most from estimating benchmark costs and calculating the difference between them and allowable costs. If the firm faces a significant disadvantage, it might not be possible to reach the benchmark costs in a single generation of product design. Such firms will have to adopt a multigenerational strategy of product design, setting ever more aggressive targets for each generation. The narrowing gap between the benchmark and allowable costs would monitor the achievement of competitive parity.

Thus, the allowable cost represents the cost at which, according to top management, the firm must manufacture the product to achieve the target profit margin when it sells the product at its target price. To all involved in the target costing process, the allowable cost signals the magnitude of the cost-reduction objective that the firm must eventually achieve. The allowable cost, however, reflects only the market's demands and the firm's profit requirements. It does not reflect the actual capabilities of the firm and its suppliers. Product-level target costing will incorporate those capabilities into the target cost, as explained next.

7.3 PRODUCT-LEVEL TARGET COSTING

Once the firm has calculated the allowable cost—the cost level that matches the firm's prices with its desired profit margin—it needs to decide whether or how it will achieve the allowable cost level. Product-level target costing provides such a method. Firms use product-level target costing to establish aggressive but achievable product-level target costs. These target costs should press the firm's product engineers to find ways to reduce the manufacturing costs of the products they design. Target costs differ from allowable costs because they incorporate the capabilities of the firm and its suppliers into the target costing process. In practice, the designers cannot always find ways to achieve the allowable cost and still satisfy the firm's customers; consequently, product-level target costing increases the product's allowable cost to a level that the firm can reasonably expect to achieve, given its capabilities and those of its suppliers (see Exhibit 7.8).

Product-level target costing consists of three major steps (see Exhibit 7.9). We list them here and provide an expanded explanation in the subsequent sections.

1. *Set the product-level target cost.* This step incorporates the capability of the firm and its suppliers into the allowable cost to establish an achievable product-level target cost.

2. *Design the product* so that the firm can manufacture it at its target cost. Achieving the target costs in most competitive settings requires considerable engineering. This engineering needs to take customer expectations into account, as well as cost.

3. *Apply the disciplining mechanisms of target costing* to ensure that the firm achieves the product-level target cost. These mechanisms include progress monitoring and validation and application of the cardinal rule of target costing.

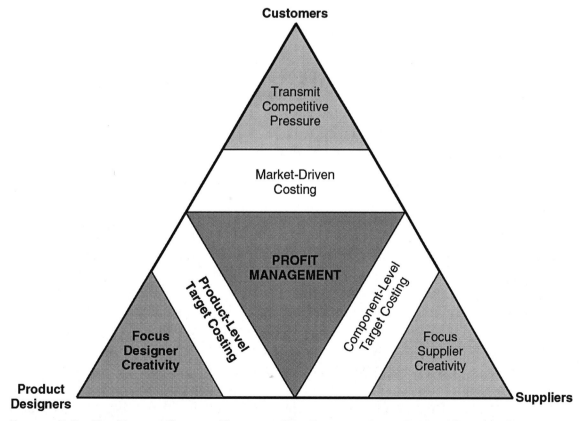

EXHIBIT 7.8 THE TARGET COSTING TRIANGLE: THE PRODUCT-LEVEL TARGET COSTING STAGE

Product-Level Target Costing

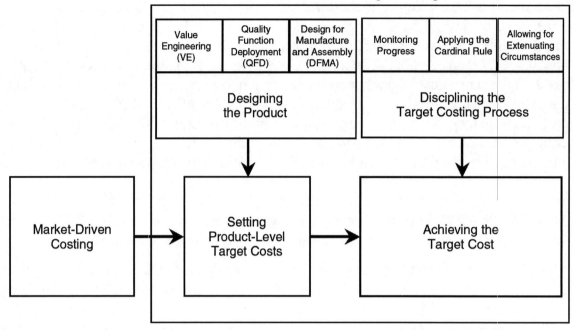

EXHIBIT 7.9   PRODUCT-LEVEL TARGET COSTING

The monitoring and validation process helps ensure that the firm achieves savings identified through value engineering. Application of the cardinal rule of target costing—namely, "Do not launch a product above its target cost"—maintains the discipline of target costing. If the designers know that violating the target cost does not lead to serious consequences, they feel less pressure to achieve the target costs.

(a) SETTING THE PRODUCT-LEVEL TARGET COST.   In competitive markets, customers expect each generation of products to provide more value per dollar of price than do its predecessors. The firm can increase value by improving the quality or functionality of the products, or by reducing its prices, or by a combination of both actions. Any of these improvements or some combination thereof requires that the firm reduce costs to maintain its profitability. The cost reduction required to achieve the allowable cost is called the *cost-reduction objective,* calculated by the following formula:

$$\text{Cost-reduction objective} = \text{Current cost} - \text{Allowable cost} \qquad (3)$$

Current cost is the cost of a proposed product if it were manufactured today using existing components or variants thereof. When computing the product's current cost, firms do not assume any future cost-reduction activities. To calculate a meaningful current cost, the components used in its estimation have to closely resemble those that the firm will eventually use in the proposed product. For example, if the existing model uses a 1.8 liter engine and the proposed model uses a 2.0 liter engine, the current cost should reflect the cost of the most similar 2.0 liter engine the firm produces or purchases.

Since the allowable cost reflects the market's demand rather than the firm's design and production capabilities, the firm runs the risk of not achieving the allowable cost. To maintain the discipline of target costing, the firm has to identify the achievable and the unachievable part of the cost-reduction objective. Analyzing the ability of the product designers and suppliers to remove costs from the product drives the achievable or target

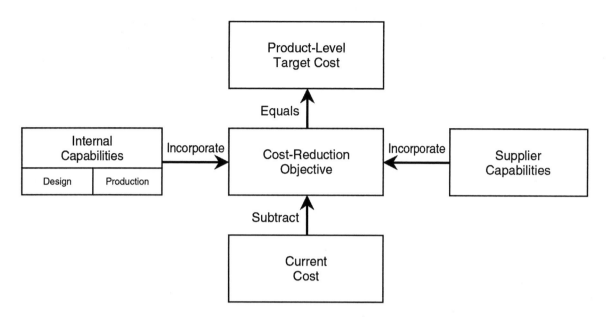

EXHIBIT 7.10   SETTING THE TARGET COST REDUCTION OBJECTIVE

cost-reduction objective. Thus, the target cost reduction objective reflects the internal capabilities of the firm's engineers to design and produce the internally manufactured items in the new product at a lower cost and of its suppliers to provide externally sourced items at a lower cost (see Exhibit 7.10).

The unachievable part of the cost-reduction objective is the *strategic cost-reduction challenge*. That is:

$$\text{Strategic cost-reduction challenge} = \text{Cost-reduction objective} - \text{Target cost reduction objective} \quad (4)$$

It identifies the profit shortfall that will occur because the designers cannot achieve the allowable cost, and it signals that the firm falls short of the efficiency demanded by competitive conditions. A firm with a well-established target costing system will achieve all or almost all of its cost reduction objective and will pressure its design team to ensure that the strategic cost-reduction challenge reaches or remains at zero.

For the most efficient firms, the achievable cost reduction for a product might exceed the cost-reduction objective. Such firms do not face a strategic cost-reduction challenge. They can take advantage of their superior efficiency either to increase market share by reducing the product's selling price or increasing its functionality while keeping the price constant or to increase profits by keeping both the price and functionality at their targeted levels.

To maintain the discipline of target costing, the firm must manage the size of the strategic cost-reduction challenge so that it reflects the firm's inability to match its competitors' efficiency. To ensure that the strategic cost-reduction challenge meets this requirement, management must set the target cost-reduction objective so that the firm can achieve the objective only if the entire organization makes a significant effort to reach it. If management consistently sets the target cost-reduction objective too high, the workforce will face excessive cost-reduction objectives, risking burn-out, and the firm will lose the discipline of target costing as it frequently exceeds target costs. If management sets the target cost-reduction objective too low, the firm will lose competitiveness because new products will have excessively high target costs.

The firm calculates the product-level target cost by subtracting the proposed product's target cost-reduction objective from its current cost:

$$\text{Product-level target cost} = \text{Current cost} - \text{Target cost-reduction objective} \qquad (5)$$

The firm measures the strategic cost-reduction challenge by subtracting the allowable cost from the target cost

$$\text{Strategic cost-reduction challenge} = \text{Target cost} - \text{Allowable cost} \qquad (6)$$

Note that this means that the firm can calculate the product-level target cost by adding back the strategic cost reduction challenge to the allowable cost

$$\text{Product-level target cost} = \text{Allowable cost} + \text{Strategic cost-reduction challenge} \qquad (7)$$

Differentiating between the allowable cost and the target cost creates discipline in cost-control efforts. Most firms will—at some time—face an allowable cost too low to achieve, given the capabilities of the firm and its suppliers. Target costing systems derive their strength from the cardinal rule: Never allow manufacturing costs to exceed target costs.

The distinction between allowable and product-level target costs thus plays two roles. First, it identifies the strategic cost-reduction challenge, which pressures the design team of the product's next generation to become even more aggressive about cost reduction. In this way, the failure to achieve the allowable cost for the current product becomes a challenge for the future, not a current defeat. Second, it avoids weakening the cardinal rule, which applies only to target costs (which management can set), not allowable costs (which management cannot set). The firm must have a disciplined process to establish the strategic cost-reduction challenge. Otherwise, target costs will be too easy to achieve, thereby reducing the effectiveness of target costing. In most firms, top management approves the strategic cost-reduction challenge before the chief engineer sets the product-level target cost.

Technically, a product's target cost equals the target selling price, less the target profit margin, plus the strategic cost-reduction challenge. Many firms blur the distinction between the allowable cost and the target cost by stating that the target cost equals the target profit margin minus the target selling price, as we did in equation 1 in Section 7.1. This simplification helps people understand the price-driven nature of target costing. Obviously, if the strategic cost-reduction challenge equals zero, the allowable and target costs are identical.

(b) DESIGNING THE PRODUCT. Once planners have identified the target cost-reduction objective, product designers work toward achieving it. In this second stage of product-level target costing, several engineering techniques can help product designers reduce product costs (Exhibit 7.9). They include value engineering (VE),[6] design for manufacture and assembly (DFMA),[7] and quality function deployment

---

6. Value engineering can be defined as an organized methodology that identifies and selects the lowest life-cycle cost options in design, materials and processes that achieves the desired level of performance, reliability and customer satisfaction. It seeks to eliminate unnecessary costs in the above areas and is often a joint effort with cross-functional internal teams and relevant suppliers.

7. DFMA includes activities such as product simplification, should costing (should costing establishes a benchmark for what the product "should cost." Central to the should costing approach is accumulating real information about manufacturing costs), and supplier bid verification.

(QFD).[8] Value engineering, the most important of the three techniques, has the primary objective of maximizing customer value—it focuses on increasing functionality and quality while reducing cost. In contrast, DFMA focuses on reducing costs by making products easier to assemble or manufacture, while holding functionality at specified levels. Finally, QFD provides a structured approach to ensure that the design process does not compromise customer requirements.

Value engineering begins with the product's conceptualization and continues through the design process until the product advances to manufacturing. Even then the process continues, but under the name *value analysis (VA)*. VA and VE differ not in the approach taken or the tools used but the point at which they occur in the product's life cycle. In particular, the functionality of the product is considered a variable under VE, but is a constant under VA. The firm uses VE during the product design and development stages, and VA during the manufacturing stage and when purchasing parts. For this reason, target costing and value engineering become concurrent activities, as do *kaizen*[9] costing and value analysis.

One should not view VE as just another cost-reduction program. VE focuses primarily on product functions and only secondarily on cost. Firms use VE to ensure that the product achieves its basic function in a way that satisfies the customer at an acceptable cost. Consequently, VE programs occur in the product engineer's domain, not that of the accountant.

(c) APPLICATION OF DISCIPLINING MECHANISMS OF PRODUCT-LEVEL TARGET COSTING. Disciplining the product-level target costing process begins with monitoring and validating the progress of the design engineers toward reaching the cost-reduction objective. It continues to apply the cardinal rule of target costing: Never launch a product above its target cost. Sometimes the firm has to apply the rule in a more sophisticated way than the conventional, single-product perspective. When one product leads to increased sales of other products, the firm must adopt a multiproduct perspective; when it will lead to sales of future generations of products, the analysis requires a multigenerational perspective. The firm can violate the target cost rule only when getting the product to market becomes so imperative that cost merits secondary consideration. Finally, when the firm releases the product for mass production and can measure the actual cost of manufacturing, it may need to reduce those costs to the target level.

Once the firm has established the target cost-reduction objective, it can begin designing the product so that manufacturing will meet the target cost. The discipline of target costing requires that the chief engineer and his superiors continuously monitor and validate the progress the design engineers make toward this objective. This monitoring ensures that the designers can take corrective actions and that manufacturing costs will not violate the target cost rule.

Some firms specify an *as-if cost* at this point in the development process. The as-if cost reflects cost-reduction opportunities identified when the firm was designing or

---

8. QFD is a structured method that employs matrix analysis to link the market requirements with the development efforts that they dictate. This method is most valuable during the stage of development when a multifunctional team agrees on how customer needs relate to product specifications and features which deliver those. By explicitly linking these aspects of product design, QFD limits the chance of omitting important design characteristics or interactions across design characteristics. QFD is also an important mechanism in promoting multifunctional teamwork.

9. *Kaizen* is the Japanese term for continuous improvement. We refer the reader to Chapter 8, "Kaizen Costing for Existing Products."

manufacturing the product's previous generation. It is the cost at which the firm could manufacture the product if it did so today. The as-if cost usually exceeds the target cost of the new product. Therefore, the additional cost reduction that the firm must achieve equals the difference between the target cost and the as-if cost.

As the design process reduces costs of the major functions,[10] the estimated manufacturing cost gradually falls toward the target cost. Many firms call the updated estimate the *drifting cost.* Exhibit 7.11 shows the relation among current cost, as-if cost, drifting cost, target cost, and target cost reduction objective. Thus, the product design process starts with a current cost higher than the target cost, and across the design process reduces the expected or drifting cost until it reaches the target cost. At most firms, once the drifting cost equals the target cost, cost-reduction activities cease. The firm will reap no reward for achieving greater savings than those required to achieve the target cost. The engineers should instead devote efforts toward decreasing the drifting cost of other products to equal their target costs.

The firm will continue to compare the drifting cost to the target cost throughout the design process. For example, product designers often make a final review of the target cost's feasibility just before releasing the product to production. If the estimated production cost exceeds the target cost, designers will need to undertake additional analyses. Frequently, they need to make only relatively minor changes in the product's design to reduce the cost estimate to the target cost level. As long as these changes do not alter the product's selling price, then the design engineers decide to reduce the product's functionality (thereby reducing cost) and submit the product for approval. If the design changes will reduce the selling price, the research and development group typically redesigns the product.

For products that feature various options, the firm makes small adjustments to the target cost by specifying the features that the standard product will contain. For example, faced with excessive manufacturing cost, design engineers might convert one or more standard features to options for which the customer now has to pay. Converting features

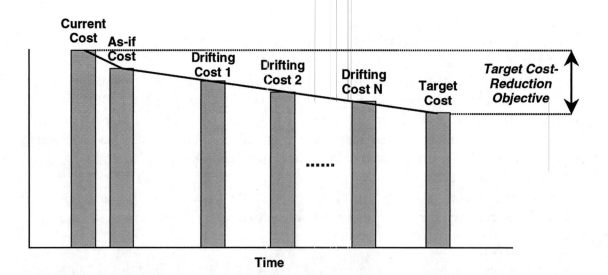

EXHIBIT 7.11   ACHIEVING THE TARGET COST

---

10.   Major functions are the subassemblies that perform a critical function that supports the product in its ability to perform its primary function. For example, an engine cooling system is a major function of an automobile. The engine cooling system performs a major function, keeping the engine cool and hence running so the automobile can achieve its primary function—transporting people.

to options both reduces the cost of manufacturing the standard product, allowing the firm to achieve target cost, and increases the selling price of the originally specified product, allowing the firm to achieve target profit.

The firm should use market analysis to ensure that the customers will accept the reduction in the standard model's functionality. For example, the firm might convert the side-impact air bags from a standard feature to an optional one. Customers will accept this reduction in functionality as long as competitive offerings treat the side-impact air bags in the same way. This fine-tuning process allows firms more leeway to achieve target costs set several years in advance. Similarly, the firm does not fix actual selling price until just before it launches the product. Delaying these two critical decisions significantly reduces the uncertainty that a firm faces in a multiyear product development process.

The cardinal rule (abandon a product if manufacturing costs exceed target costs) plays an important role in maintaining the discipline of target costing. Engineers ensure that the sum of the component target costs does not exceed the product's target cost. Often, an increase in the cost of one component causes the engineers to explore ways to reduce the costs of other components by an equivalent amount. In addition, to help ensure enforcement of the cardinal rule, most firms have a policy against launching unprofitable products. After completing the design phase, the product moves to manufacturing. As part of this transition phase, the firm compares the target cost to the standard cost of production. If the analysis shows excessive standard cost, the firm usually takes steps to reduce manufacturing costs to the target level. If the standard cost lies at or below the target cost, the design engineers freeze the product's design for the rest of its life and the firm takes no further actions, other than general *kaizen* costing (see Chapter 8), to reduce the cost of the new product.

As with any rule, firms occasionally violate the cardinal rule. This occurs when a broader analysis indicates that doing so will benefit the firm. Target costing, by its nature, takes a single-product orientation. Sometimes this view proves too restrictive because the product may generate revenues beyond that attributed directly to sales of that product. Such products include flagship products that create high visibility for the firm, products that introduce the next generation of technology, or products that fill a critical gap in the product line. For such products, the firm often relaxes the target cost rule to allow for the hidden revenues. Typically, however, the firm continues to apply cost-reduction pressures during the early stages of manufacturing until it achieves the target cost.

7.4 COMPONENT-LEVEL TARGET COSTING

We now come to the third and final stage of the target costing process, component-level target costing (see Exhibit 7.12). This stage decomposes the product-level target cost to the component level. The component-level target costs identify the firm's acceptable cost for the components that it purchases. Thus, component-level target costing sets the selling prices of the components manufactured by the firm's suppliers and forces suppliers to design components at low cost. It uses interorganizational costing to achieve this objective by opening new communication channels among suppliers, customers, and product designers. (Chapter 9 discusses interorganizational costing.)

Component-level target costing consists of three major steps, illustrated in Exhibit 7.13. We list them here and offer an expanded explanation in the subsequent sections.

1. Select and reward suppliers.
2. Set the target costs of major functions.
3. Set the target costs of components.

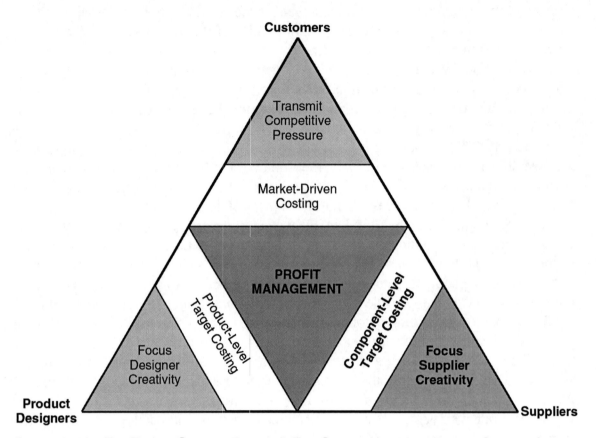

EXHIBIT 7.12   THE TARGET COSTING TRIANGLE: THE COMPONENT-LEVEL TARGET COSTING STAGE

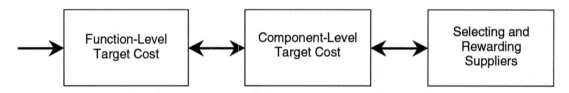

EXHIBIT 7.13   COMPONENT-LEVEL TARGET COSTING

(a) SELECTING AND REWARDING SUPPLIERS.   The firm uses two sets of criteria to select suppliers. The first set of criteria deals with selecting the suppliers that will make up the firm's supplier base and the second set deals with rewarding individual suppliers for superior performance (see Exhibit 7.14).

The supplier-base objectives include maintaining supplier relations, extending the supplier base, and inducing supplier creativity. When a long-term supplier fails to make the lowest bid or develop the most innovative solution, the firm may still award it part of the contract. In this situation, the firm wants to create a stable buyer-supplier relation. (See also Chapter 9.) To increase the rate of innovation and enable the firm to adopt new technologies and production processes, the firm must continuously look for new suppliers. The firm needs to identify creative and innovative suppliers or suppliers that have developed considerable expertise in technologies that the firm wants to incorporate in its products. Finally, the firm uses contracts to reward suppliers for their innovations.

The firm rewards suppliers based on three major criteria: the competitiveness of their bids, their reputation, and the degree of innovation they have brought to the component.

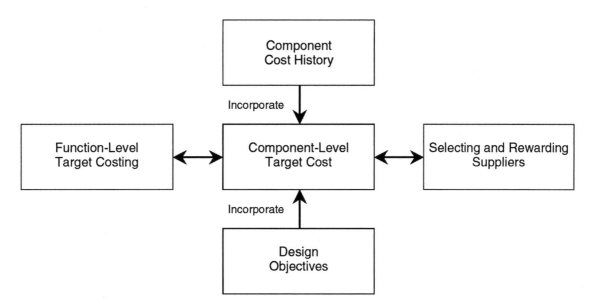

EXHIBIT 7.14 SETTING THE TARGET COSTS OF COMPONENTS

The firm collects the bids as early as possible in the target costing process and incorporates them through an iterative process into the component-level target costs. This process ensures that the firm can achieve individual component-level target costs that sum to the product's component-level target cost.

Supplier reputation for innovation influences the firm's willingness to accept slightly higher prices or lower levels of innovation for a particular order and still grant some of the business. The firm should retain innovative suppliers in the supplier base. For example, although the supplier rated with the highest value generally will win an order, firms will award at least part of that order to reputed good suppliers even if the suppliers' products do not have the highest value.

For a given component, the degree of innovation that the supplier introduces influences the value that the firm associates with the component. The higher the degree of innovation, the higher the value, all else being equal. Since the firm wants to reward innovation, it will typically select the most innovative design.

(b) SETTING THE TARGET COSTS OF MAJOR FUNCTIONS. Once the firm has established a product's target cost, it begins to disaggregate it to identify the target costs of the components that it contains. This process begins with developing target costs for the product's major functions and continues with developing component-level target costs. These steps enable the firm to achieve the second objective of target costing: transmitting the competitive cost pressure that the firm faces to its suppliers. This objective becomes critical in lean enterprises,[11] which have horizontal rather than vertical integration. Such firms purchase a significant portion of the parts and materials required to manufacture their products from external instead of internal suppliers. Thus, the horizontal integration that gives lean enterprises their flexibility and responsiveness creates a heavy reliance on suppliers. Target costing provides a powerful mechanism to discipline suppliers by allowing the firm to set the selling prices of the suppliers' products. With

11. Lean manufacturing is characterized by manufacturing a single part at a time just-in-time for its incorporation into the product (see Chapter 9.)

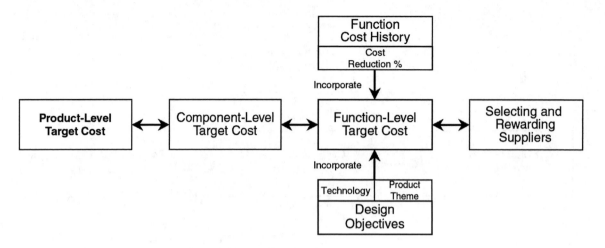

EXHIBIT 7.15   SETTING THE TARGET COSTS OF MAJOR FUNCTIONS

complex products,[12] the firm often sets target costs for externally acquired components by first establishing the target costs of the major functions and then, in a separate step, of the components they contain. Major functions are the subassemblies that provide the functionality that enables the product to achieve its purpose.

The process of establishing function-level target costs takes into account two major factors: the cost history of the major function and the design objectives for the product (Exhibit 7.15). The cost history of the function captures the historical rate at which the firm has reduced the cost of the major function. The firm uses this historical rate as the basis for estimating the likely cost reduction that it will achieve for the next generation. It adjusts the historical rate for the design objectives of the new product. For example, the new product might require a higher capacity engine cooling system (because the product theme was "A more powerful driving experience"), and, hence, the function-level target cost should increase compared with the previous generation (after allowing for the historical cost reduction rate). Alternatively, the firm might adopt a new technology, such as the shift from copper/brass radiators to aluminum, which would invalidate all historical cost information. Consequently, the firm should use the rate for aluminum radiators instead of the function cost history of copper/brass radiators.

Identifying major functions allows the engineers to organize the design process in multiple, somewhat independent tasks. Typically, a dedicated team has responsibility for the design of each major function. Design teams usually include representatives from a number of disciplines such as product design, engineering, purchasing, production engineering, manufacturing, and parts supply.

(i) Matrix Structure.   Most firms using target costing organize product design around a matrix structure with a design team (responsible for each major function) reporting to the chief engineer (responsible for the entire product) and the head of the appropriate design division. The matrix structure balances each product's unique requirements with the desire to maintain common design philosophies across products. Exhibit 7.16 shows such a matrix. Assume the firm is Toyota and Major Function 1 (top row of vertical axis) is the engine cooling system. Products A through M represent different models (Avalon, Camry, Corolla, Highlander, Sequoia, etc.). The head of the design division for engine

---

12.   A complex product is one that contains numerous components and has a multi-level bill of materials.

	Design Team Product A	Design Team Product B	Design Team Product C	··············	Design Team Product M
Major Function 1 Division	Design Team A1	Design Team B1	Design Team C1		Design Team M1
Major Function 2 Division	Design Team A2	Design Team B2	Design Team C2		Design Team M2
Major Function 3 Division	Design Team A3	Design Team B3	Design Team C3		Design Team M3
				⋮	
Major Function n Division	Design Team An	Design Team Bn	Design Team Cn		Design Team Mn

EXHIBIT 7.16   MAJOR FUNCTION DESIGN TEAMS

cooling systems will control the relative functionality and quality of the engine cooling systems across the different models. Each model will have a dedicated design team for each of its major functions and a chief engineer. The chief engineer or product manager has overall responsibility for selecting the distinctive theme of the new product and coordinating the integration of all of the major functions into the vehicle so that it achieves it desired functionality and quality at its target cost. A relatively small team of design engineers usually supports the chief engineer.

This matrix approach has several advantages. First, the chief engineers have responsibility for coordinating the design process at the design divisions. The relatively autonomous design divisions need the chief engineers to develop a concept for the new vehicle that spans multiple design divisions. Keeping the design divisions autonomous is considered important as it allows expertise sharing across all design projects. For example, the firm quickly incorporates design advances in engine cooling systems for the Camry into future generations of other models. If the Camry design teams reported only to the chief engineer of that vehicle, they would possibly not share their innovations with the design teams of other models.

(ii) Setting the Cost-Reduction Rate.   Most firms set different cost-reduction objectives for each major function. As Exhibit 7.17 shows, these different objectives acknowledge that the firm can reduce costs for some major functions (for example, Major Function 5 in the exhibit) more easily than it can for others (such as Major Function 6). For example, major functions that rely on new technologies and new designs often provide more opportunities for cost reduction than major functions that rely on mature technologies and designs.

The chief engineer has responsibility for setting the target cost of each major function, usually through an extended negotiation process with the design teams. The target costs typically reflect historical cost-reduction rates. If the cost of a major function historically has decreased by 5 percent a year, then the target cost will usually use that rate.

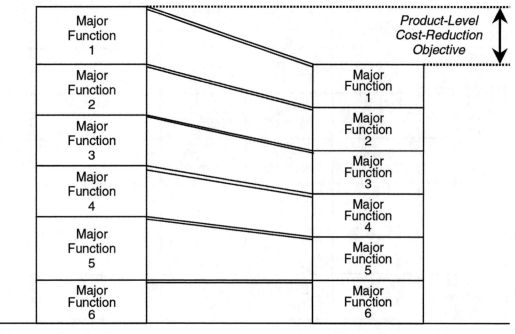

EXHIBIT 7.17 DECOMPOSING THE TARGET COST TO THE MAJOR FUNCTION LEVEL

Not all firms rely solely on historical cost-reduction rates. Some use market analyses to help set the target costs of new products. These market-based approaches apply particularly when the firm introduces new forms of product functionality. For example, Isuzu uses monetary values or ratios to help set the target costs of major functions, and asks customers to estimate how much they would pay for a given function. These market-based estimates, tempered by other factors such as technical, safety, and legal considerations, often lead to adjustments to the prorated target costs. For example, if the prorated target cost for a component is too low to allow the firm to produce a safe version, the firm increases the component's target cost, and decreases the target cost of the other components to compensate.

The chief engineer will modify the target costs derived either from historical rates or market analysis for three major reasons. First, if the sum of all the historical rates doesn't give the desired cost-reduction objective, the chief engineer will negotiate with the head of the design teams of the major functions for higher rates of cost reduction. These negotiations continue until the sum of the target costs of the major components equals the product's target cost.

Second, if the relative importance of the major function changes from one generation to the next, the chief engineer will modify the target costs accordingly. For example, if the product theme for the new vehicle is "quieter and sportier," the engineer might increase the target cost of the major functions responsible for achieving those objectives to make it easier for the design team to achieve both their functionality objective and target cost (see Exhibit 7.18). However, if the firm does not want to violate the cardinal rule of target costing, then the firm will have to reduce the costs of other major functions so the firm can achieve the overall target costing reduction objective.

Third, when the technology used by the major function changes, the historical cost-reduction rate of the old technology loses relevance. Instead, the firm should use the

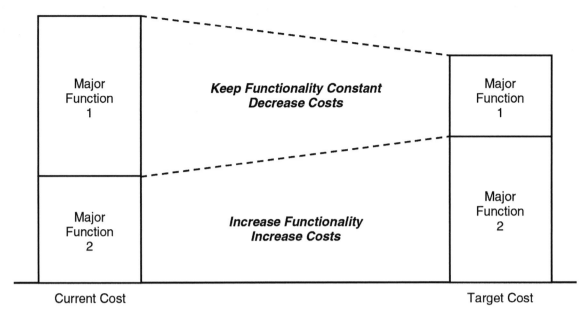

EXHIBIT 7.18 DISTRIBUTING THE TARGET COST ACROSS MAJOR FUNCTIONS

historical rate for the new technology, if available. Entirely new technologies complicate the cost estimation problem because no historical data on cost-reduction trends exist.

Once the firm has established target costs of the major functions, it decomposes the target costs to the group component and parts level as appropriate. The firm needs to set a purchase price for every externally acquired item—whether they are major functions, group components, or individual components.

(c) SETTING THE TARGET COSTS OF COMPONENTS. The process of setting component-level target costs (see Exhibit 7.19) resembles that used to establish function-level target costs (see Exhibit 7.15). The component cost history becomes the basis for estimating the target cost of each component, modified by the design objectives for the product.

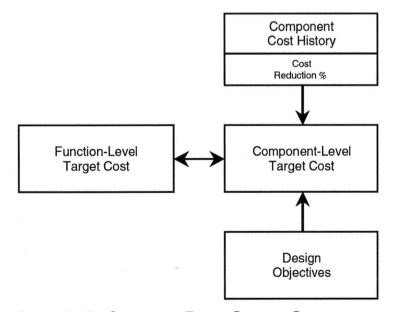

EXHIBIT 7.19 SETTING THE TARGET COSTS OF COMPONENTS

The firm can establish target costs for group and individual components only when the product design has reached the stage at which the design team can identify specific components. For example, many car manufacturers initiate value engineering after they have completed the engineering drawings for trial production to estimate allowable costs for each of the components in every major function of the automobile. The firms derive these estimates by identifying a cost-reduction objective for each outsourced item.

Typically, the major function design teams must decompose the target cost of the major function to the component level, as illustrated in Exhibit 7.20. Sometimes, however, the chief engineer also participates to ensure that the process meets the objectives for the product. If the proposed design requires a higher functionality for the outsourced item, its target costs might increase. In contrast, the firm might ask another supplier to reduce costs because the new part will be smaller or lighter than the old one. The firm might ask a third supplier to maintain the same cost, despite a change in materials, because the firm anticipates no change in performance.

For products with a large number of components, firms have to develop techniques to reduce the cost of developing target costs at the component level. Firms may estimate target costs for similar families of components from a base case. For example, an automobile company may calculate the target cost for the most popular variant of one of its products and then extrapolate the target costs of all of the other variants.

The completion of the target cost setting process for components signals the achievement of a major step in the product design process. The firm can now calculate the anticipated cost of the product by summing the costs of all the components, group components, and major functions either produced internally or acquired externally. The sum of these costs cannot exceed the product's target cost; otherwise, the firm must redesign the product.

Thus, the cardinal rule continues to operate throughout the design process. Even at this late stage, the firm will redesign the product if possible. The interaction between design and manufacturing ensures that the new product's manufacturing cost equals its target cost. Without such interaction, the target cost could significantly differ from the manufacturing cost, rendering the target costing system ineffective.

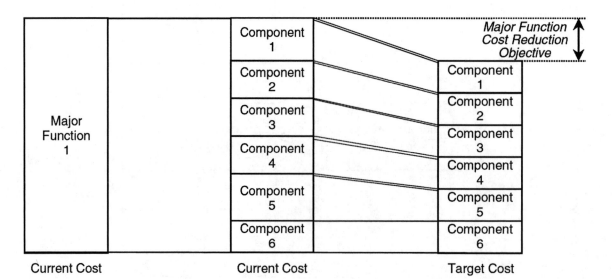

EXHIBIT 7.20   DECOMPOSING TARGET COSTS OF MAJOR FUNCTION TO THE COMPONENT LEVEL

7.5 SUMMARY

Target costing serves as a technique for profit management as much as it does for cost management. The process consists of three major segments: market-driven costing, product-level target costing, and component-level target costing. Exhibit 7.21 shows how these segments fit together. The market-driven costing stage leads to the allowable cost, which analysis converts into a product level target cost during the product-level target costing stage. Finally, the analysis decomposes the product level target costs into costs for the components in the component-level target costing stage.

Market-driven costing captures the external pressure placed on the firm by its customers and competitors and transmits this pressure to the product designers. Market-driven costing takes the anticipated selling price of a product under development and subtracts the desired margin to compute the allowable cost. The firm must manufacture the product at this allowable cost so the product will achieve its profitability objectives when sold at its target volume.

The allowable cost does not reflect the capabilities of the firm's product designers and manufacturing engineers. To develop achievable target costs, the second segment of target costing—product-level target costing—establishes a realistic but stretch (i.e., difficult to achieve) product-level target cost. The firm calculates the target cost by comparing the current cost of the product to its allowable cost. The resulting gap has two elements. The first, the cost reduction objective, captures the level of cost reduction that the firm's engineers believe the firm can achieve. The second element, the strategic cost reduction challenge, represents the unobtainable portion of the overall cost gap. It captures the firm's inability to achieve cost competitiveness. The chief engineer negotiates the split between the cost reduction objective and the strategic cost reduction challenge with senior management. These negotiations aim to keep the strategic cost reduction challenge as small as possible—preferably zero—while setting achievable cost reduction objectives.

Product-level target costing develops the product-level target cost. The firm expects to manufacture the product at this cost in the early days of the manufacturing stage of a

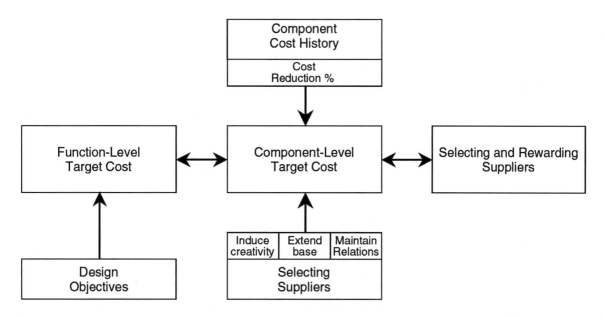

EXHIBIT 7.21 SETTING THE TARGET COSTS OF COMPONENTS

product's life cycle. Product designers can use various engineering techniques—including value engineering, design for manufacture and assembly, and quality-function-deployment—to try to ensure that the product achieves its target cost.

The firm should use the cardinal rule of target costing to maintain the discipline of target costing by canceling new product development projects that the firm does not expect to meet the product-level target cost.

The product-level target cost implicitly reflects anticipated supplier savings. The third phase of the target costing process—component-level target costing—explicitly addresses these savings. Component-level target costs define the suppliers' selling prices and thus, the level of savings the suppliers must achieve to meet their own target costs. Thus, target costing begins the interorganizational cost management process by extending the umbrella of cost management beyond the firm's boundaries.

APPENDIX 7A

TARGET COSTING EQUATIONS AND GLOSSARY

The fundamental equation of target costing identifies the *target cost*—the cost at which the firm must manufacture the product to generate a specified return if sold at its target selling price:

Target cost = Target selling price – Target profit margin

This equation appears in almost all of the discussions of target costing. Unfortunately, this fundamental equation is too simplistic to apply in practice because the market sets the target selling price and the realities of the economics of the product set the target profit margin. Consequently, one cannot guarantee that the firm can achieve the target cost defined in this way. Because we want the firm to rarely modify the target cost once it is set, we define a new term, *allowable cost*:

Allowable cost = Target selling price – Target profit margin

The allowable cost is the same as the conventional definition of the target cost. We can now define a new target cost that has the added property of being achievable about 80 percent of the time. To calculate this target cost, we identify the current cost--the cost at which the firm could build the new product today if it were already designed and the manufacturing facilities were ready. The current cost exceeds the allowable cost, because the firm has not yet pursued a low cost design of the new product or ways to reduce the costs of the manufacturing processes required to produce it.

The level of cost reduction required to achieve the allowable cost is called the *cost-reduction objective:*

Cost-reduction objective = Current cost – Allowable cost

Some firms set overly aggressive cost reduction objectives. They must then split the cost-reduction objective into two parts, one achievable and the other unachievable.

Cost-reduction objective =

Target cost-reduction objective + Strategic cost-reduction objective

The firm can achieve the *target cost-reduction objective* portion, but cannot achieve the *strategic cost-reduction challenge* portion.

The firm calculates the target cost by subtracting the proposed product's target cost-reduction objective from its current cost:

Target cost = Current cost – Target cost-reduction objective

One can also calculate the product-level target cost by adding the strategic cost reduction challenge to the allowable cost:

Target cost = Allowable cost + Strategic cost-reduction challenge

Simple algebra leads to the following observations. First, one can estimate the strategic cost-reduction challenge by subtracting the target cost-reduction objective from the cost reduction objective, as follows:

Strategic cost-reduction objective =

Cost-reduction objective – Target cost-reduction objective

Second, the firm can also estimate the strategic cost-reduction challenge by subtracting the allowable cost from the target cost

Strategic cost-reduction challenge = Target cost – Allowable cost

CHAPTER 8

KAIZEN COSTING FOR EXISTING PRODUCTS

ROBIN COOPER, DBA
Emory University

REGINE SLAGMULDER, PhD
INSEAD

CONTENTS

8.1 INTRODUCTION 271

    (a) Achievability 272

    (b) Controllability 273

8.2 GENERAL KAIZEN COSTING 273

    (a) Kaizen Costing for Direct Costs 273

    (b) Kaizen Costing for Indirect Costs 280

8.3 ITEM-SPECIFIC KAIZEN COSTING 283

    (a) Product-Specific Kaizen Costing 283

    (b) Component-Specific Kaizen Costing 286

8.4 SUMMARY 287

8.1 INTRODUCTION

Kaizen is the Japanese term for continuous improvement. It connotes a continuous process, in which the entire firm participates, of finding ways to become more efficient. Successful kaizen programs can do more than reduce costs; they also increase the quality of products and the safety of production processes. Kaizen costing is the application of continuous improvement principles to reduce costs in the manufacturing stage of a product's life. Kaizen costing should seamlessly integrate with the firm's target costing system.[1] Target costing applies to the design stage and kaizen costing to the manufacturing stage of the product life cycle. Two types of kaizen costing interventions occur, general and item-specific. Each of these has two additional categories.

> **1.** *General kaizen costing* reduces the costs of the products that the firm produces. General kaizen costing consists of period-by-period programs that reduce direct costs and multiperiod programs that reduce overhead or indirect costs, as shown in Exhibit 8.1. Firms use *kaizen costing for direct costs* to continuously reduce the material and labor content of the products in their manufacturing phase. For this type of program, the firm sets cost reduction objectives for each period. Each

---

1. See Chapter 7, Target Costing for New Product Development.

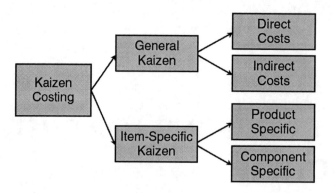

EXHIBIT 8.1   THE VARIOUS KAIZEN COSTING APPROACHES

budgetary period has modest savings objectives, but the savings accumulate over time. *Kaizen costing for indirect costs* reduces the demand for production support activities. The firm typically achieves these savings across multiple budgetary periods.

2. *Item-specific kaizen costing* reduces the costs of individual products and the components that they contain. *Product-specific kaizen costing* increases the rate of cost reduction for individual products that face particularly intense price competition in the marketplace. The firm uses the technique to ensure that the product will earn its life-cycle profit objectives. Firms apply *component-specific kaizen costing* to significantly and rapidly reduce the costs of components that have excessive costs. Savings from these interventions add to those achieved by the general kaizen costing programs.

Two principles govern the setting of effective cost-reduction objectives for any form of kaizen. The achievability principle deals with the commitment to the cost reduction objectives. The controllability principle deals with the individual or group's ability to influence the costs included in their cost-reduction objectives.

(a) ACHIEVABILITY.   The achievability principle states that a firm should set challenging and realistic cost reduction objectives. Firms with successful kaizen costing programs typically expect about 80 percent achievement of goals. High achievement percentages ensure a high level of commitment to achieving the cost-reduction objectives. If the individual or group failed to achieve the last 10 objectives, they will have little motivation to achieve the next objective. Furthermore, a high failure rate means that failure has little or no stigma, even if success enjoys prestige. In contrast, high achievement will engender a strong stigma associated with failure while retaining significant prestige related to success. Achievable cost-reduction objectives must also ensure that the firm remains cost competitive. Consequently, a natural tension arises between setting achievable and adequate cost-reduction objectives. A firm can use two mechanisms to resolve this tension. First, it can translate the cost-reduction pressure imposed by the marketplace into the corporate cost-reduction objective. The decomposition process should maintain this pressure as the firm sets its cost-reduction objective at the material and labor level.[2] Second, it can ensure that knowledgeable individuals establish each level of cost-reduction objectives. If the higher-level negotiator has detailed knowledge about the lower-level negotiator's production processes and cost-reduction capabilities,

---

2.   See Chapter 7, "Target Costing for New Product Development."

the lower-level negotiator will have less temptation to introduce slack into the process. The higher-level negotiator must set cost-reduction objectives that, while achievable, will also challenge. Some firms refer to these as *tiptoe objectives*, signifying that the firm can realize them only if everybody stretches to achieve them.

(b) CONTROLLABILITY. The controllability principle also governs the cost-reduction objective setting process. This principle states that cost-reduction objectives should include costs only if the group or individual can control them. For example, a kaizen program for blue-collar workers might exclude the costs of utilities, purchased parts for maintenance, office supplies, and white- and blue-collar wages. In contrast, a white-collar program might include these costs. Furthermore, the controllability principle governs the range of activities that the kaizen program considers. For example, it might expect white-collar workers to change the production processes to make them more efficient. In contrast, it wouldn't expect blue-collar workers to change the production processes, but rather, to accept them as given and make them more efficient. Given the different constraints on the two groups, the white-collar cost-reduction objectives often exceed the blue-collar objectives.

8.2 GENERAL KAIZEN COSTING

General kaizen costing has two categories. The first deals with direct costs, such materials, direct labor, and equipment maintenance. The second deals with the indirect costs. These costs include interactions with vendors, parts administration, and other costs that relate to the acquisition of externally sourced items.

(a) KAIZEN COSTING FOR DIRECT COSTS. Kaizen costing for direct costs aims to remove unnecessary inefficiencies from existing product designs and production processes. As the firm removes these inefficiencies, the overall direct costs of production—and hence, product costs—decline. In most settings, kaizen costing for direct costs is the responsibility of small groups of individuals who have responsibility for a distinct part of the production process. It creates a continuous pressure on these groups to reduce direct costs by a specified amount in the current period.

The process of setting direct cost-reduction objectives typically starts with the corporate profit plan. These plans incorporate assumptions about the level of cost-reduction objectives that the firm will achieve each period. The level of cost reduction demanded over time reflects the long-term cost-reduction pressure that the firm faces in the marketplace and top management's belief in the firm's improvement potential. The corporate cost-reduction objective incorporated into the profit plan identifies the level of cost reduction that the entire firm must achieve in the period. The plan typically does not, however, specify how the firm will achieve those savings. The process of establishing detailed cost-reduction objectives begins with identifying and then decomposing the corporate-level objective to the material and labor level. This is accomplished in four steps:

Step 1. Identify a corporate level objective.
Step 2. Decompose the corporate-level objectives to the divisional and then plant level. A predominately top-down negotiation process between corporate and plant management will identify these plant-level objectives.

Step 3. Decompose the plant-level objectives to the production group level. Typically, a more balanced negotiation process between plant management and group leaders establishes these objectives.

Step 4. Distribute the group-level objectives to the material and labor level.

(i) Corporate-Level Cost-Reduction Objective.   Management develops the annual plan based on the corporation's long-term and/or medium-term plans, adjusted for current market conditions. The plan identifies the firm's sales and profit objectives for the coming year. These profit objectives reflect assumptions regarding the level of cost reduction that the firm will achieve during the year. Management then quantifies these assumptions into a specific cost-reduction objective for the corporation for the year.

Firms can use two approaches to setting plant-level cost-reduction objectives: the market-driven approach and the engineering-driven approach. In the market-driven approach, the cost-reduction objectives predominantly reflect the price pressures that the firm encounters in the marketplace. In the engineering-driven approach, the firm establishes cost-reduction objectives based on the savings that it can achieve. The most appropriate approach depends on how consistently the firm can remove direct costs from its products. The more consistent its history, the more effective the engineering-driven approach.

The market-driven approach starts with estimating the cost-reduction pressure that the firm faces in the marketplace and uses that estimate to set a corporatewide cost-reduction objective. Management then decomposes this objective to the plant level as shown in Exhibit 8.2. As denoted in Exhibit 8.2, the primary communication route is top-down, with the bottom-up communication more a reaction to the top-down communication than initiated in its own right. The magnitude of the corporate-level cost-reduction objective reflects the competitive pressure that the firm faces. As the competitive pressure grows, the firm must increase the cost-reduction objective accordingly to maintain its planned

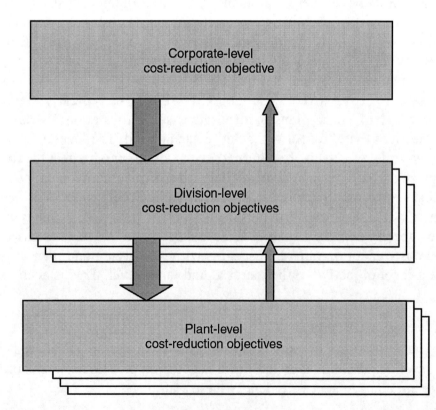

EXHIBIT 8.2   PERIOD-SPECIFIC KAIZEN SUBTRACTION APPROACH: TOP-DOWN PROCESS

profit levels. Typically, the cost-reduction objective reflects long-term anticipated competitive pressures adjusted for current conditions. The corporate planning process, particularly the firm's annual plan, communicates the desired magnitude of the cost-reduction objective.

The engineering-driven approach starts by establishing corporate-wide cost-reduction rates for each major cost element (see Exhibit 8.3). Cost elements include items such as direct material, indirect material, labor, and maintenance. These rates reflect historical experience and provide the basis for computing the plant and corporate-level cost-reduction objective. Management then compares the resulting overall level of cost reduction to the cost-reduction pressure encountered in the market. As Exhibit 8.3 shows, if management decides that the cumulative cost reduction lies below what the market dictates, it will pressure the plant to increase the individual plant-level objectives. These revised objectives begin again at the cost-element level and flow bottom-up. As denoted in Exhibit 8.3, the primary communication route is bottom-up, with the top-down communication more a reaction to the bottom-up communication than initiated in its own right.

The engineering-driven approach calculates the corporate-level cost-reduction objective using corporatewide or plantwide cost-reduction factors for all of the major cost elements of the firm's production processes. While practice varies, corporate planners identify cost-reduction factors for relatively few cost elements—perhaps 10 to 15. The factors reflect historical achievement levels. For example, if the firm has reduced the costs of a class of direct material by 3 percent a year, the planners will begin at 3 percent to estimate the current factor level.

Once the planners have established the cost-reduction factor for each element, they calculate the corporatewide cost-reduction objective for each cost element by multiplying the total quantity of each cost element expected to be consumed in the coming period by the corresponding factor. They then calculate the cost-reduction objective for the corporation by summing all the corporate-level cost-reduction objectives for each cost element. If the firm uses plantwide factors, the planners make the calculations at the plant level and cumulate them to the corporate level. The advantage of plantwide as opposed to corporatewide factors lies in the increased accuracy of the calculations. Plants that

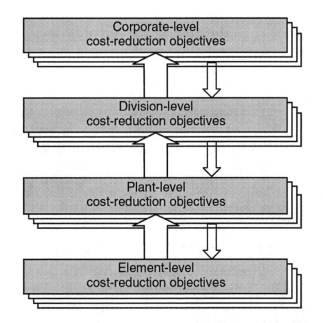

EXHIBIT 8.3 PERIOD-SPECIFIC KAIZEN ADD BOTTOM-UP PROCESS

manufacture new products typically can reduce costs faster than those that manufacture mature products.

In an engineering-driven approach that uses corporatewide factors, management decomposes the corporate-level cost-reduction objective to the plant level—usually by using one of two approaches. The first approach multiplies the corporatewide objective by the ratio of the plants' manageable costs—that is, those subjected to kaizen costing—to calculate the plant-level cost-reduction objective. The second approach multiplies the corporatewide objective by the ratio of the plants' actual costs for the previous periods.

Finally, in the last stage of the process, the planners modify these simplistic estimates to reflect each plant's idiosyncrasies. For example, they will typically increase the cost-reduction objective for plants manufacturing new products and decrease the objective for plants manufacturing mature products.

(ii) Plant-Level Cost-Reduction Objectives.   Corporate and divisional management decompose the corporate cost-reduction objective to the plant level. Each plant-level planning group uses its long-term and/or medium-term plans as the basis for developing the plant-level annual plan under the umbrella of the corporate plan. This plan identifies a number of plant-level annual objectives, including sales, operating profits, inventory levels, investments, personnel levels, and quality targets. These objectives must reflect the plant's cost-reduction objective.

When setting plant-level cost-reduction objectives, the firm wants to maximize those objectives while ensuring that the workforce will commit to them. A pure top-down approach risks setting excessively aggressive cost-reduction objectives that violate the achievability principle. In addition, the individuals involved will likely have a low commitment to the mandated cost-reduction objectives, even with achievable objectives. Thus, a pure top-down process will usually prove ineffective. Alternatively, a pure bottom-up approach risks setting cost-reduction objectives too low to generate the desired level of corporate profits. Plant management will have no insights into the competitive pressures faced by the firm. Therefore, they have no way to benchmark their performance against that of the market. In addition, they will likely develop cost-reduction objectives that they know they can easily achieve. Thus, a pure bottom-up process may also prove ineffective.

A firm might best decide to take advantage of the strengths of the two approaches to reduce the risks. By having a formal top-down process and an informal bottom-up process, the firm ensures that the top-down process dominates and that the cost-reduction objectives reflect the market pressures. The bottom-up process moderates the top-down process to ensure achievable cost-reduction objectives to which the groups will commit.

Although the process functions in a predominantly top-down manner, the corporate and divisional plans incorporate input from the plants. Consequently, annual planning becomes an iterative process that mixes top-down and bottom-up interactions. Although the firm sets corporate, divisional, plant, and group-level objectives in a top-down manner, the process used to establish these objectives relies on a bottom-up information-collection process.

The divisional planning groups typically have daily contact with the individuals in each plant within the division and should develop a detailed understanding of the prevailing conditions. As the planning cycle approaches, the divisional planning groups discuss the magnitude of cost-reduction that each department can achieve. They combine these departmental estimates to develop a divisional estimate of achievable cost reduction. Management will then combine these divisional estimates to give a rough guide to the cost reduction that the firm can achieve for the year.

The information collected from the departments becomes the starting point for the top-down process that culminates in setting the annual cost-reduction objective for each plant. The objectives reflect the information collected, anticipated market conditions, and the firm's long-term profit objectives. Corporate planning typically requires cost-reduction objectives higher than those identified by the informal bottom-up process. Corporate planners increase the informal cost-reduction objectives so that the corporation will achieve its profit objective. Management then communicates the corporate objectives to the divisions and the plants.

(iii) Group-Level Cost-Reduction Objectives. Most production processes contain multiple steps, each performed by a different group. Typically, in lean enterprises[3] these groups have responsibility for producing a family of products or components in a production cell. The production cells start with raw material and end with finished goods using just-in-time (JIT) production methods.[4] The firm usually considers each of these groups as a cost center, but depending on the production process, sometimes the firm has several groups in a cost center. The groups have responsibility for period-specific kaizen costing.

Many firms expect group leaders to negotiate their group's cost-reduction targets. These negotiations occur within a hierarchical negotiation process which mixes top-down and bottom-up communications. Given the informality of some of the process at most firms, one cannot easily describe its exact sequence. The plant manager frequently becomes the critical player in the top-down negotiations of the group-level targets because this individual is the most senior manager who has access to detailed information about the performance on the factory floor. The plant manager acts as the conduit between the factory floor and the divisional manager, helping him or her identify realistic stretch targets for each group. Once the groups identify tentative targets, they enter formal negotiations to fine-tune the targets and commit to them.

Because the work groups set their own cost-reduction targets and then negotiate with senior management, one may not notice the top-down pressure. The negotiations, a mix of top-down and bottom up philosophies, usually result in cost-reduction targets that are more aggressive than those originally planned but still achievable. The power of these negotiations lies in the commitment they create to the cost-reduction targets at every level of the firm, even when senior management strongly influences those targets.

Most kaizen programs base the cost-reduction objective for each group on the anticipated savings potential. The level of savings depends on factors such as how long the group has been making the items, their historical achievements, and the maturity of the technology used. Kaizen programs aim to create the same level of pressure for each group. At some firms, when the cost-reduction objective for a group lies below the average required for the plant, the group must still achieve the average savings for the plant. If the group achieves the average level of cost reduction, then overall savings will exceed the plant-level objectives set by senior management (assuming all of the other groups

---

3. Lean manufacturing is characterized by manufacturing a single part just in time for its incorporation into the product.

4. Under a JIT philosophy, parts are manufactured and delivered just in time to be used in the manufacturing process. No significant inventories of work-in-process are maintained. One can contrast JIT to batch and queue philosophies where firms typically maintain large parts inventories.

also achieve their specified savings levels). Management still holds the group to the average, so that the firm reaps the extra savings if the group achieves the average. However, the plant-level profit plans do not anticipate these extra savings because they will not likely achieve them.

(iv) Selecting Cost-Reduction Objectives.   Most firms use different methods to establish cost-reduction objectives for material and labor. As Exhibit 8.4 illustrates, management typically establishes the objectives for material at the product level; for example, a given product might have an objective of removing X percent of material from its cost. Management typically sets the objectives for labor at the production line level; for example, a given production process might have an objective of reducing labor costs by Y percent. Finally, management sets the objectives for purchased parts for each item purchased; for example, a given purchased part might have an objective of reducing its costs by Z percent. As explained next, these differences reflect how the firm consumes resources as it manufactures products. The nature of the kaizen process and the way it achieves cost reduction therefore differs for the three types of costs.

(v) Material Cost-Reduction Objectives.   Period-specific kaizen costing establishes cost-reduction objectives for material at the product level because a one-to-one relation exists between the product and the material it consumes.[5] We state this relation as follows:

Product X consumes Y kilograms[6] (kg) of Material A.

The firm can change the amount (and hence cost) of material consumed by a product only by changing that underlying relation in one of three ways:

1. Changing the amount of Material A that it consumes (change Y kg to Z kg).
2. Changing the type of material used (change Material A to Material B). This may also affect the kilogram variable.
3. Changing the material's purchase price. Since the cost of material equals the price per kilogram times the number of kilograms consumed, any reduction in the purchase price will automatically lead to an equivalent cost reduction.

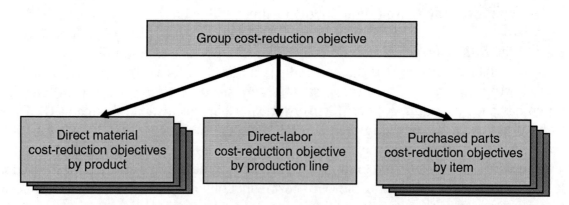

EXHIBIT 8.4   DECOMPOSING THE GROUP-LEVEL COST-REDUCTION OBJECTIVES

---

5.   If the firm uses the material to create a common component (i.e., one that is used in multiple products), then the material cost of all of the products that use that component will be reduced.

6.   We use kilogram in this explanation, but the material's appropriate unit or weight measure would apply here.

Most kaizen costing programs establish cost-reduction objectives at the overall—not individual—material level, leaving it up to the kaizen team to find ways to achieve the objective. This approach leaves the kaizen team with more freedom to identify cost-saving opportunities. Therefore, the firm simply states the material-specific kaizen cost-reduction objective for Product X in Period Y as, "Reduce material costs by A percent." Only as the kaizen intervention identifies individual savings opportunities will the process begin to measure savings at the individual material level. That is, the firm can state savings as follows:

- We can save M percent of Material A (by reducing the quantity consumed)
- We can save N percent of Material B (by substituting Material D)
- We can save P percent of Material C (by reducing the price of the Material C)
- Any combination of the above

To ensure a successful kaizen costing intervention, these savings taken together must equal the product's overall cost-reduction target (in this case, A percent).

Two aspects of material costs make it easy to ensure that resources supplied reflect reductions in the quantity or price of material consumed by a product—that is, in the overall cost of material for the period. First, the reduction occurs at the unit level. Each unit of the product subjected to a kaizen costing intervention consumes less material. Second, as the amount of material consumed drops, the amount supplied automatically drops as well. Therefore, the firm achieves real savings.

(vi) Labor Cost-Reduction Objectives.   Firms establish period-specific kaizen cost-reduction objectives at the production line, not the product level. They cannot set meaningful cost-reduction objectives at the product level because the just-in-time production line is balanced for multiple products. A production line is balanced when every model in the product family that goes through the line takes approximately the same time to manufacture. Consequently, reducing the time it takes to manufacture a single product of the family has no effect. Likewise, the firm will not increase the speed of production because, under single-piece flow, the firm manufactures the products one at a time in random order. Therefore, speeding up the production time of one product simply means that it will have to wait until the preceding product has completed production.

To reduce the number of workers or to increase the speed of the line requires that production achieve a new balance. Such a balance requires that the firm reduce processing times for most, if not all, of the products that the line produces. Consequently, the firm should focus the kaizen intervention on improving the performance of the line as a whole rather than on improving a single product. In such environments, firms set the labor cost-reduction objectives at the product family level.

A firm should not set kaizen cost-reduction objectives at either the individual worker or production step level. Lean manufacturing environments have multiskilled workers who continually change places[7]; therefore, focusing on the individual will focus on the line by default. Focusing on the production step leads to excessively detailed cost-reduction objectives. Such micromanagement will decrease the kaizen team's motivation to identify ways to improve the production process.

---

7.   The conditions inside a manufacturing cell make job specialization virtually impossible. One of the ways to balance the line is by giving individuals multiple tasks to perform. These tasks often vary with the product being produced.

A firm should manage direct labor costs at both the production line and the facility level. At the production line level, the kaizen process manages demands for labor; at the facility level the process manages supply of labor. Stable employment contracts between the firm and the workforce[8] drive the necessity to manage demand and supply separately. For material, a reduction in demand leads to an immediate reduction in supply (the firm simply orders less material); however, matching the supply of labor to the demand requires managerial action. Thus, labor kaizen costing has two elements: one program to reduce demand for labor and another program to bring supply in line with demand.

The kaizen program focuses on reducing the number of workers required to manufacture products. Since most firms with kaizen programs have agreed to no-layoff policies, however, the firms do not lay off these individuals. The firms have four primary ways to offset the resulting excess labor.

1. *Use natural attrition.* When workers retire, the firm does not automatically replace them.

2. *Move displaced workers.* The demand for products varies, and as a line becomes busy because of increased demand, the firm can use displaced workers to increase the number of operators.

3. *Insource products.* The firm could insource products from suppliers to create new jobs.

4. *Expand.* The firm can try to expand into new lines of business to create additional jobs.

(b) KAIZEN COSTING FOR INDIRECT COSTS.   Period-specific and item-specific kaizen costing primarily focus on the direct costs, not the indirect ones. Kaizen costing programs aimed at reducing indirect costs achieve their objectives by reducing any unnecessary complexity in the production support functions. For example, having many unique parts to manage can lead to excessive parts administration costs. The firm can most effectively reduce these costs by decreasing the number of unique parts in its parts list—thus reducing the number of different parts that it has to design, order and process—while removing the need to interact with as many suppliers. If the firm can achieve such simplifications for a number of products, then the indirect costs of production will decrease. Thus, even if the direct costs of products do not change, total product costs will decrease.

Firms that lack a sophisticated cost system will have difficulty quantifying the benefits from an indirect kaizen cost initiative. Traditional cost systems do a poor job of identifying the underlying causes of indirect costs. If they cannot identify the drivers for these indirect costs, these systems cannot predict the savings that will result from a kaizen costing program to reduce complexity. To achieve that objective requires more sophisticated cost systems, such as activity-based costing.[9] Firms that do not have such

---

8. For kaizen programs to be successful, the workforce must believe that the reward for becoming more efficient will not be lay-offs. Therefore, most successive kaizen programs are associated with employment security programs. The same does not hold true of the part time labor force. The supply of part-time workers can be adjusted every time a contract comes up for renewal.

9. Activity-based costing (ABC), discussed in Chapter 6 of this Handbook, is a cost-assignment approach where cost pools represent the major activities performed in the production of products. These activities are hierarchical in nature.

systems must either justify their kaizen programs for indirect costs on faith alone or undertake special studies to try to estimate the likely savings.

The savings in indirect costs become visible only if the reduction in complexity proves sufficient to redeploy the freed-up resources. As Exhibit 8.5 illustrates, the kaizen costing program must typically affect numerous products and extend over several years to have a detectable impact.

The initiative needs to focus on multiple products, because decreasing the number of unique parts required by a single product will lead to a reduced demand for parts administration that is too small to detect. Only when the initiative has reduced the number of parts required by numerous products will the firm convert the decreased consumption of indirect costs into savings.

Similarly, the kaizen costing initiative needs to extend over several years, because the firm can rarely reduce complexity quickly. It may require the redesign of a significant percentage of the firm's products before the number of unique components falls enough for the cost savings to become apparent. Consequently, these programs often contain several phases, with each subsequent phase taking a more aggressive and fundamental approach to complexity reduction until the firm has achieved the objective. At that point, the firm initiates a maintenance program to ensure that the complexity does not return.

Many kaizen programs to reduce indirect costs focus on reducing the number of parts that go into the firms' products. Firms can benefit from such programs because of the high costs associated with parts administration. An aggressive parts reduction program consists of four consecutive stages that focus on both existing and new models:

1. *Increase parts commonality.* Reducing the number of parts through parts commonality requires a careful analysis of all existing parts to assess whether other existing parts can replace them. Such parts commonality programs prove effective in firms that have encouraged design originality and innovation and have low levels of current parts commonality. For example, Olympus Optical designed a new mother camera for the Stylus line that contained components that they expected to become common both across a number of different models and a number of generations of those models.

2. *Eliminate low-volume variants.* This stage focuses on the discontinuance of low-volume models and parts. As stage 1 achieved parts commonality, the remaining low volume items typically relate to low volume end products. Activity-based costing has shown that such products typically cost many times their reported cost and exceed their perceived value. Often, firms should decide to discontinue them.

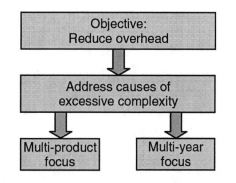

EXHIBIT 8.5 OVERHEAD-SPECIFIC KAIZEN

3. *Reduce the number of parts.* Reducing the number of parts by means of modular design and the purging-of-parts system helps limit the annual increase in the number of new parts. Modular design considers a major portion of a product as a single item, as opposed to a number of distinct components. The parts list no longer contains the components that the modules now subsume. Thus, the product designers have access only to the modules, not the components they contain. The firm then uses these modular designs as widely as possible in all new products. Thus, it amounts to a more sophisticated parts commonality program. A firm can also reduce the number of parts by changing its marketing and sales strategy to introduce fewer new products—particularly, the variants with low sales volume. This reduction can occur at either the product level (no longer support low-volume products) or at the variant level (no longer produce customized components but work from a limited number of standard components to produce effectively equivalent customized products.)

4. *Perform follow-up activities.* This stage includes finishing the stage 3 tasks and setting up some new activities to reinforce the cost-reduction efforts. For example, the emergence of global sourcing might initially increase the number of new parts introduced. A firm can retain reasonable numbers of components by managing the procurement process and aggressively replacing local components that cost more than those obtained globally.

Kaizen costing programs for indirect costs focus on simplifying the complexity of the tasks performed in the production support functions. In addition to parts commonality programs (explained in number 3 above), they include the following:

- *Universal tooling.* The firm designs products and production processes so that the tooling required to make them becomes common across families of products. Such commonality reduces the need to design new tools for each new product.

- *Product line simplification.* The firm uses simplification to eliminate redundant products, especially low volume ones.

- *Matrix tear-down.* The firm removes low-volume components from products. The firm creates a matrix of parts and products. The cell entries are the volume of parts used by that product for the period. The total of all of these volumes equals the total volume for the period of that part. The firm has identified low total volume parts to remove from the product designs, although if it cannot remove a part from all products, this initiative has no payoff.

For all of these projects, the firm will have difficulty assessing how aggressively to set the complexity reduction objectives. Unlike period-specific or item-specific kaizen costing, where the market helps identify the necessary level of cost reduction, kaizen costing for indirect costs offers no obvious guideline regarding optimal cost reduction. Given the lack of activity-based cost systems, the firms typically set the kaizen costing objectives for these programs in nonfinancial terms. These objectives imply an optimal level of complexity. Once the firm has reached this level, the program focuses on maintaining a constant level of simplification. For example, if Isuzu tried to reduce parts count much further, it believes it would lose the ability to increase the functionality of its products at a competitive rate.

8.3 ITEM-SPECIFIC KAIZEN COSTING

Firms initiate kaizen costing interventions to ensure that products in the manufacturing phase of their life cycles achieve their profit objectives. Item-specific kaizen costing initiatives focus on specific products or major functions or group components that the firm has identified as candidates for cost reduction. Firms initiate product-specific programs when the cost problem occurs at the product level and a specific product has a risk of becoming unprofitable or has become unprofitable.

When the firm has an effective target costing system, most product-specific kaizen costing interventions will involve mature products.[10] Although these products earned adequate returns when the firm launched them, changing conditions have reduced those returns to inadequate or at risk of becoming inadequate. Although a steady decrease in profitability over time will trigger aggressive and ongoing general kaizen activity, an unexpected and significant decrease in profitability (current or future) will push the firm to evoke a product-specific kaizen intervention. Consequently, such programs are episodic.

In contrast, component-specific kaizen costing programs have an ongoing time line as the firm's engineers continually look for ways to reduce costs at the component level. Two conditions often lead to component-specific interventions. The first occurs when design engineers identify more cost efficient ways to provide the same functionality. The second occurs when a profitability analysis of the products indicates that the component costs too much.

(a) PRODUCT-SPECIFIC KAIZEN COSTING. Product-specific kaizen costing initiatives focus on individual products. Typically, the firm has established a cost-reduction objective for the product and uses kaizen costing intervention to find ways to achieve it. Product-specific kaizen costing functions as a natural extension of target costing. The primary difference between target costing (which is, by definition, product specific) and product-specific kaizen costing lies in the ability to change product functionality. In target costing, the product's functionality becomes a variable in the costing process. If the firm cannot manufacture the specified product at its target cost, then it can sometimes decrease the product's functionality to reduce its costs. If this results in sufficient cost reduction, then the firm can manufacture the product for its target cost.[11] In contrast, kaizen costing focuses on products with fixed functionality. The functionality of the production line's first unit must be identical to the last unit's functionality. This constraint does not require that the material content and the way the firm manufactures the product cannot change, only that any changes must become invisible to the customer.

A firm initiates a product-specific kaizen costing intervention when a current product has or will have unacceptable profitability unless the firm takes specific actions to reduce the product's cost. Three conditions typically trigger product specific kaizen costing:

1. A product fails to achieve its target cost.
2. The firm has imputed aggressive kaizen cost savings into the target cost and must ensure that it achieves these savings.
3. The relation between a mature product's selling price and its cost deteriorates unexpectedly, and the firm must take steps to bring its costs into line with its revenues. For example, the firm might expect a product's profitability to fall by

---

10. Chapter 7 discusses target costing systems.
11. See Chapter 7, "Target Costing for New Product Development."

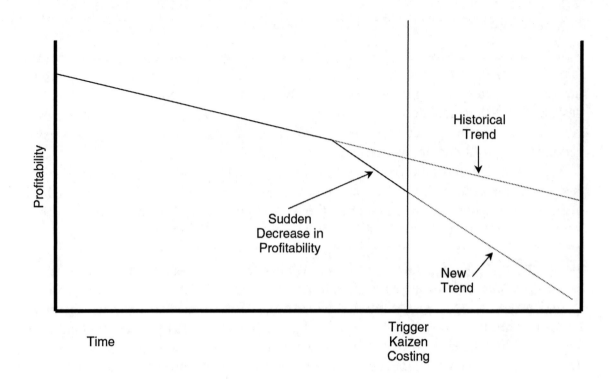

EXHIBIT 8.6   UNEXPECTED CHANGES IN PRODUCT PROFITABILITY AS TRIGGER OF PRODUCT-SPECIFIC KAIZEN COSTING

ten percent per year. In year three, however, it falls unexpectedly to 50 percent of the previous year's level, as illustrated in Exhibit 8.6. The kaizen costing intervention will need to increase the profitability back to the anticipated levels.

No significant difference exists between product-specific kaizen costing interventions for new products and mature ones. For both classes of products, the critical issue becomes whether the firm has enough time to undertake a successful intervention and recoup the cost of that intervention. It takes time to identify a cost problem, identify a solution, and incorporate it into manufacturing. If the new product has a short life, the firm might not have adequate time to incorporate the change and recoup the investment in cost reduction. The same holds true for mature products as they approach the end of their lives. If the firm doesn't have sufficient time, it should expend the cost-reduction effort on the next generation of product. If the firm has sufficient time, then it can justify the cost-reduction effort if a positive cost/benefit trade-off exists. Two factors play a dominant role in this cost/benefit trade-off: (1) the magnitude of the expected volume of product sales and (2) the anticipated magnitude of the investment required to reduce the costs. The higher the expected sales volume and the lower the anticipated magnitude of the investment, the easier it is to justify the program.

If the firm has failed to achieve the target cost for a new product at the time of launch, it might for strategic reasons decide to launch the product anyway. For example, Olympus Optical made a strategic decision to design its first camera to act as a mother camera, to introduce parts commonality. Senior management estimated that the company could derive considerable savings from the parts commonality program and decided to launch the product even though the firm would manufacture it above its target cost. Typically, firms will immediately initiate an item-specific kaizen costing intervention to try to reduce their manufacturing costs back to the level established by their target costing process. The item-specific kaizen intervention must reduce the cost of the new product to its

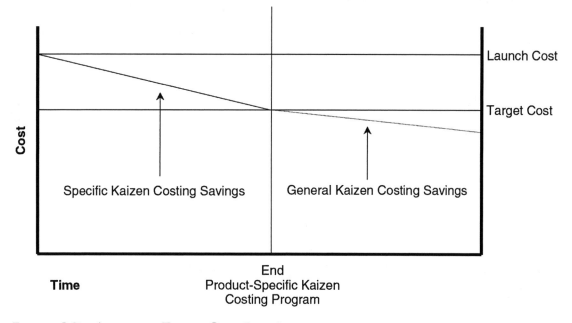

EXHIBIT 8.7   ACHIEVING TARGET COST POST LAUNCH

target cost level, as illustrated in Exhibit 8.7. To maintain the discipline of target costing, management must view such kaizen costing interventions as the exception rather than the rule. Following the cardinal rule of target costing—never launch a product above its target cost—helps maintain the discipline, but the firm may decide to launch some strategic products regardless.

Two primary conditions lead to a firm's failure to achieve target costs: underestimation of the product's costs and overestimation of its revenues.[12] Underestimation of costs typically occurs when the engineers fail to anticipate either technological or engineering difficulties inherent to the new product's design. Cost overruns can occur for many reasons. For example, if an innovative technology fails to work reliably, the firm may need to substitute it with a more expensive solution based on existing technology. Similarly, cost savings that appeared reasonable during the target cost setting process may become impossible to fully realize. Overestimation of revenues occurs when the target selling price or the target volume exceeds actual amounts. If the firm identifies these overestimations before it completes the product development process, it can reduce the product-level target cost, making it more difficult for the engineers to achieve their new higher cost-reduction objectives.

Firms that can significantly reduce the costs of their products through kaizen costing during the manufacturing phase often impute these savings into their target cost calculations. Such imputation makes sense because target costing adopts a life-cycle perspective with respect to adequate profits. Ignoring kaizen savings (or other cost reductions during the manufacturing phase) would lead to unnecessarily aggressive product-level target costs. Including the savings, however, increases the need to achieve them. The firm's long-term profit plan would incorporate a level of kaizen costing savings.

Two conditions lead to the loss of profitability of existing products: (1) the selling price drops faster than the costs and (2) costs increase faster than selling prices. The product-specific kaizen costing intervention aims to return the product to adequate levels

---

12.   We have ignored cost overruns that occur due to poor implementation of target costing.

of profitability. To avoid lost profitability, the firm initiates these product-specific kaizen costing interventions as soon as it detects the decay in profitability. For example, some firms monitor the rate at which selling prices fall for all their products. When the firm expects a product's selling price to fall below its cost in the near future, it subjects the product to an intense product-specific cost-reduction analysis. This analysis consists of identifying the product's major cost components to assess whether the firm can produce them at a lower cost. For example, if the largest costs relate to machining, then design engineers explore ways to replace the machined parts with stamped or plastic components.

For most product-specific programs, the firm can easily establish cost-reduction objectives. For a new product that has exceeded its target cost, the obvious cost-reduction objective becomes that of reducing costs back to target levels. If the problem is imputed kaizen savings, the objective becomes that of achieving those savings. Finally, if a mature product experiences reduced profitability, the usual objective becomes that of returning the product to historical or desired profitability levels or, with a serious cost overrun, assessing whether to eliminate the product. For component-specific kaizen costing programs, the firm should set cost-reduction objectives so that the products that contain the components achieve their profitability objectives.

If the achievable cost reductions identified prove insufficient to reduce costs so that the product will remain profitable, then the firm needs to explore whether to completely redesign the product without changing its functionality. If complete redesign fails to make the product profitable, the firm usually discontinues the product. Thus, kaizen costing carries it own rule similar to that of target costing—namely, that the product mix should maintain only products that can generate an adequate return during manufacturing.

(b) COMPONENT-SPECIFIC KAIZEN COSTING. When it becomes apparent that a major function[13] or group component[14] has a poor design that leads to excessive costs, the firm should subject that component to a specific kaizen costing intervention designed to reduce its costs. The firm can identify such kaizen costing opportunities in several ways:

- All products that contain the item report low profitability. This will hold true if the item represents a significant fraction of the product's total value added.
- Tear-down of a competitive product might indicate a considerable cost-savings opportunity if the firm redesigns the item.
- Cost reductions achieved in previous periods might not suffice, and the intervention might aim to bring the item's cost in line with expectations.
- Finally, increases in material or other input costs might cause the item to exceed its original target cost and hence become a candidate for redesign.

The firm achieves kaizen cost savings by applying value analysis principles and can reduce costs in five ways: reduce parts count, use less expensive materials, increase supplier performance, shift production overseas, and reduce labor content.

---

13. A major function is a subassembly that supports a major part of the functionality of the end product. Examples include the gearbox and the engine cooling system of an automobile.

14. A group component is a subassembly that makes up a signify portion of a major function. Examples include the starter motor and radiator of an automobile.

(i) Reduce Parts Count. A firm can use several methods to reduce parts count. Two such ways include performing functions electronically, as opposed to mechanically, and creating more sophisticated molds to reduce the number of molded components. For example, the front lighting system of an automobile might originally have consisted of four molded components: two headlight panels and two side and indicator panels. A more sophisticated mold might allow a single panel to contain the headlight and side and indicator lights, thus reducing the number of parts from four to two.

(ii) Use Less Expensive Materials. Substituting high priced materials for lower priced ones has been a major source of cost-reduction opportunities for many firms since the 1970s and 1980s. For example, many firms now use plastic instead of glass or metal. Many firms, however, find it difficult to identify even cheaper materials.

(iii) Increase Supplier Performance. Given the high percentage of components that many firms source externally, they can reduce costs by educating suppliers (both independent and subsidiaries) in ways to reduce their costs.[15]

(iv) Shift Production Overseas. Firms can shift their manufacturing activities to lower cost production locations, such as some Asian countries.

(v) Reduce Labor Content. Firms can reduce the labor content of their products by increasing the level of automation or speeding up the production process. They can increase the level of automation by using more flexible machines such as robots. They can increase the speed of production by reducing the time it takes to perform a step in the production process for all product family members.

8.4 SUMMARY

Kaizen costing applies the philosophy of kaizen to specifically reduce the costs of products. Kaizen costing comprises two major programs: general and item specific. General kaizen costing programs reduce the costs of all products through focusing on either their direct or indirect costs. Kaizen costing for direct costs creates a steady cost-reduction pressure; the firm measures the program's objectives by time period. The firm might state the objective as "reduce overall production costs by N percent this year." Kaizen costing for indirect costs reduces indirect manufacturing costs by reducing overall complexity. Firms typically achieve this objective by significantly reducing parts complexity over a number of periods.

The item-specific programs operate at the individual product or component level. Events that indicate excessively expensive individual products or components trigger these programs. The programs reduce the costs of specific items by a preset amount. For new products, this amount typically equals the difference between their launch costs and target costs. The product-specific kaizen costing program takes over from the target costing program to ensure that the product quickly achieves its target cost. For mature products, the program focuses on maintaining its anticipated level of profitability so that the product achieves its life-cycle profitability objectives.

---

15. See Chapter 9.

A firm initiates component-specific kaizen costing when evidence suggests that an individual component is too expensive and that the firm needs to implement specific cost reduction. A firm can use several methods to identify the need for component-level kaizen costing. These include tear down of competitive products, overall low profitability of products that contain common components, and finally, a general belief that a particular component is too expensive.

CHAPTER 11

LOGISTICS AND MARKETING COSTS

JAMES M. REEVE, PHD, CPA
University of Tennessee

CONTENTS

11.1 INTRODUCTION 329

11.2 SUPPLY CHAIN ACTIVITIES 330

(a) Logistics Activities 330
(b) Marketing and Selling Activities 331

11.3 EXPENSE PLANNING AND CONTROL 332

11.4 TOTAL COST OF DELIVERY 336

(a) Total Cost of Ownership 339
(b) Relation Profitability Analysis 341

11.5 RELATION PROFITABILITY— EXAMPLE 345

(a) Direct Costs 345
(b) Activity Cost 346
(c) Post-Sale Activities 347
(d) Carrying Cost 347
(e) Margin Analysis 348

11.6 SUMMARY 349

11.1 INTRODUCTION

One day soon, you will sit down at a kiosk at an auto dealer and custom order your new car.[1] Within four days of order, the manufacturer will acquire and consume materials to assemble your car. In another three days, the car will arrive at the dealer's lot for you to drive away.

This illustration no longer confines the new automobile purchase to its product features, but also considers the underlying support systems for marketing and delivering the product. One-size-fits-all solutions no longer satisfy customers; this trend forces organizations to customize their marketing and distribution strategies into logical niches.[2] With this change, however, a fundamental question emerges. What tradeoffs exist between providing custom marketing and logistical solutions for increasingly narrow markets? What product and service functionality can a firm affordably provide to various segments? What asset commitments will allow a reasonable rate of return, and where can a firm maintain expense flexibility? This chapter will explore ways to answer these questions and examine case studies to illustrate the points.

The role of logistics is changing from one of warehousing and transportation to one of providing an integrated set of services that delivers the right product, in the right

---

1. See Ruderman, G., "The state of automotive make-to-order; Poor demand picture and legacy systems delay progress toward custom configurations" *MSI* Vol. 22, Issue 8, 2004.
2. Reeve, J. and Srinivasan, M., "How to Design Lean Supply Chains for Enhanced Flow," *Supply Chain Management Review*, forthcoming, 2005.

quantities, in the right quality, at the right time—all for the right cost. Consequently, organizations no longer consider logistics functions as only cost centers to squeeze for ever-increasing efficiency. Instead, logistics has a strategic role in the marketplace. Consider competing office furniture manufacturers. One offers furniture with a 30-day lead time and another with a seven-day lead time. Who wins? A seven-day lead time allows a building contractor to estimate the delivery and installation date better than does a 30-day lead time. Therefore, investments in short cycle logistical capabilities improve service functionality, resulting in enhanced revenue opportunities.[3]

Moreover, logistics integrate supplier and customer relations. As a result, we see increasing focus on managing logistical costs across organizational boundaries, rather than within a single organization.[4] When firms manage logistics across organizational boundaries, significant opportunities emerge to enhance the value of the total supply chain.[5] This creates, however, the new difficulty of apportioning the enhanced value to the individual value chain participants. This chapter shows how supply chain participants can establish the cost of supply chain activities in order to partition value among the participants.[6]

This chapter also addresses the cost management concerns associated with marketing expenditures. As with logistics costs, this discussion will show how to assess whether marketing expenditures return value to the firm. Such analyses often identify specific marketing costs with regions, customers, and channels. In addition, this chapter will show how to structure multidimensional contribution reports for evaluating several profit views simultaneously.

11.2   SUPPLY CHAIN ACTIVITIES

The supply chain consists of logistics and marketing activities that consume resources in the organization. This chapter will take an activity perspective in managing the costs and profit opportunities in the supply chain.

(a) LOGISTICS ACTIVITIES.   Logistics consists of "the process of planning, implementing, and controlling the efficient, cost-effective flow and storage of raw materials, in-process inventory, finished goods, and related information from point of origin to point of consumption for the purpose of conforming to customer requirements."[7] Theorists have recently expanded this definition to include activities in the service sector, such as managing the physical flow of customers (e.g., patients in a hospital) or segmented service provisioning (e.g., customizing bank services to customer segments).

Exhibit 11.1 shows the typical activities that this term encompasses for a manufacturing firm.[8] The complete physical and informational activities form a closed loop linking

---

3.   This is discussed in more detail in J. Reeve, "The Financial Advantages of the Lean Supply Chain," *Supply Chain Management Review* (March/April 2002):42-49.

4.   As discussed in Statements on Management Accounting Number 4-P, *Cost Management for Logistics* (Montvale, N.J.: IMA, 1992).

5.   For a discussion on the control mechanisms required to capture these values, see Dekker, H.C., "Control of inter-organizational relationships:evidence on appropriation concerns and coordination requirements," *Accounting, Organization, Society*, Vol. 29, 2004, pp. 27-49.

6.   See a brief discussion of how this is accomplished within the context of target costing in R. Cooper and R. Slagmulder, "Interorganizational Costing, Part 2," *Journal of Cost Management* (November 2003).

7.   Council of Logistics Management definition, 1986.

8.   An excellent reference identifying activities with logistics processes and various channel configurations is in *Performance Measurement: Applying Vlaue Chain Analysis to the Grocery Industry* (Joint Industry Project on Efficient Consumer Response), 1994.

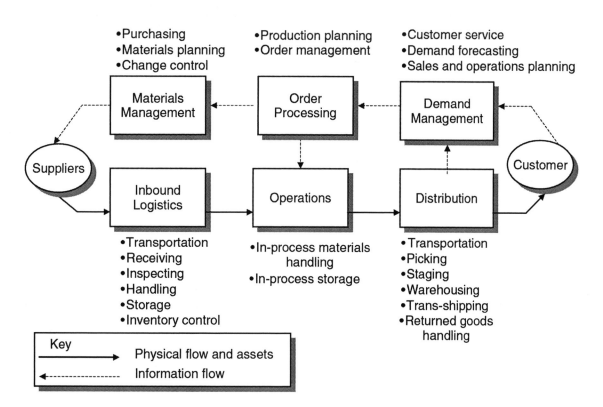

•Purchasing
•Materials planning
•Change control

•Production planning
•Order management

•Customer service
•Demand forecasting
•Sales and operations planning

•Transportation
•Receiving
•Inspecting
•Handling
•Storage
•Inventory control

•In-process materials
  handling
•In-process storage

•Transportation
•Picking
•Staging
•Warehousing
•Trans-shipping
•Returned goods
  handling

EXHIBIT 11.1 LOGISTICS ACTIVITIES

both upstream suppliers and downstream customers to the firm. The bottom of the exhibit identifies logistical activities required to physically move material from raw materials through distribution to the customer. These activities include the cost of people and assets required for moving and storing material through the various stages of transformation. The informational activities translate demand and inventory status information into production orders and materials requirements, as the top portion of the exhibit shows. These activities include the cost of transactions, planning, and change control typically considered a part of the support burden. Together, these activities form the backbone for managing logistics costs.

(b) MARKETING AND SELLING ACTIVITIES.   In addition to logistics costs, firms incur marketing and sales costs in downstream, customer-directed activities. These activities include the costs of selling, order taking, merchandising, advertising, promoting, and customer development. These activities may have product-related drivers (as with brand advertising), distribution channel-related drivers (as with channel promotions), or customer-related drivers (as in the case of managing a customer relation). Exhibit 11.2 includes examples of selling and marketing activities by product, channel, and customer.

Firms can manage supply chain costs with expense planning and control, or with total cost of delivery. Exhibit 11.3 compares these two methods. Expense planning and control supports cost center managers, such as warehouse or transportation managers. In this approach, the firm uses an expense simulation to simulate resource requirements according to planned activity requirements. Product line, customer, or other commercial managers use total cost of delivery measures to support alignment of logistics and marketing resources with strategic and profit objectives. These objectives reflect the nature of the supplier and customer relations. In addition, supply chain analysis can identify opportunities to make complex interfirm cost tradeoffs. In both instances, the firm can use activity-based information to inform the analysis.

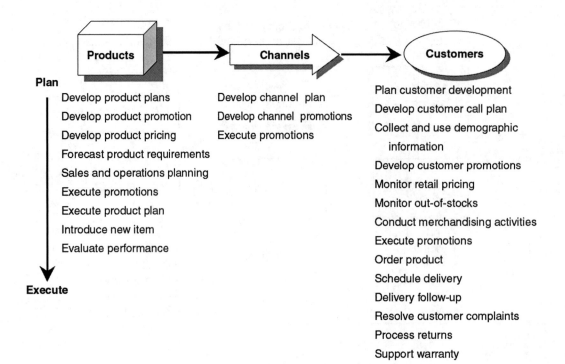

Plan

Develop product plans
Develop product promotion
Develop product pricing
Forecast product requirements
Sales and operations planning
Execute promotions
Execute product plan
Introduce new item
Evaluate performance

Execute

Develop channel plan
Develop channel promotions
Execute promotions

Plan customer development
Develop customer call plan
Collect and use demographic
  information
Develop customer promotions
Monitor retail pricing
Monitor out-of-stocks
Conduct merchandising activities
Execute promotions
Order product
Schedule delivery
Delivery follow-up
Resolve customer complaints
Process returns
Support warranty

EXHIBIT 11.2   SELLING AND MARKETING ACTIVITIES

	Cost Management Methods	
	Expense Planning and Control	Total Cost of Delivery
Targeted User	Cost center manager (e.g., warehouse manager)	Product or customer manager
Scope	Intra-firm	Inter-firm supply chain
Objective	Plan resources (e.g., warehouse staffing levels) and identify actual variance from plan.	Manage profits in value chain relationships and identify complex inter-firm tradeoff opportunities.
Method	Expense simulation	Activity tracing to upstream or downstream value chain partners

EXHIBIT 11.3   EXPENSE PLANNING AND CONTROL AND TOTAL COST OF DELIVERY

11.3   EXPENSE PLANNING AND CONTROL

Organizations can plan and control logistics costs by relating activities to their underlying resources.[9] To illustrate, the Volunteer Juice Co. has six warehouse activities, as Exhibit 11.4 shows. Employees unload pallets of 12 oz., 16 oz., and 32 oz. glass bottles

---

9.   Expense planning and control can be accomplished under a number of different design alternatives. My example is similar to an emerging design called the RCA (resource consumption accounting) model. See Anton Vand der Merwe, and David Keys, "The Case for RCA" (three part series) *Journal of Cost Management* (July/August-November/December) 2001 and Lynn Benjamin and Todd Simon, "A Planning and Control Model Based on RCA Principles," *Journal of Cost Management* (July/August 2003):. 20–27. See also T. Greenwood and J. Reeve, "Process Cost Management," *Journal of Cost Mangement* (Winter, 1994): 4–19.

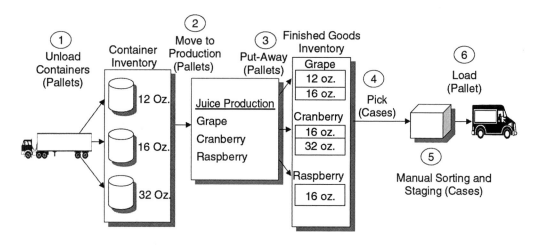

EXHIBIT 11.4 LOGISTICS ACTIVITIES: VOLUNTEER JUICE CO.

from trucks and put them into the container inventory (#1). Other employees then move the glass bottles to the production line to fill a production run of grape, or cranberry, or raspberry juice (#2). Workers place the completed production on pallets and put it into the finished goods inventory (#3). Customers purchase cases of juice product, which workers must select from the finished goods warehouse (#4).[10] Employees must sort, replace on pallets, and prepare these customized cases for delivery (#5). Workers then load the product on the truck (#6). Although an actual warehouse operation may have more products and activities, the basic concepts illustrated here will apply.

Expense planning begins by translating the anticipated demand into the six activities, which the firm then translates into resources. Exhibit 11.5 illustrates this relation. Reading from left to right, the firm plans and links the customer demand case volumes for the five juice SKUs (stock keeping units) to the six warehouse activities. The activity frequencies change in response to changes in the sales volume.[11] The process uses a physical measure of activity output, termed an activity base. For example, a *pallet move* measures the quantity effort, or service, associated with the *unload container* activity. Thus, in the first stage, the simulation must translate case volume from the demand information to activity bases, such as pallet moves.

Accountants must then link the physical activity base to their underlying resource requirements. Our example uses lift trucks and warehouse personnel as the two warehouse resources supporting the six activities. The cost simulation must model the unique cost behavior patterns of these resources. Resources may exhibit fully variable, fixed, stepped, or mixed cost behavior over a range of activity levels. In this example, the firm has a monthly cancelable lease for the lift trucks, so it incurs incremental step costs for the trucks. Thus, changes in lift truck demand results in incremental or avoidable costs. In contrast, the warehouse personnel have a union contract that prevents layoffs below 30 full-time equivalent (FTE) employees. Therefore, the firm faces fixed personnel cost

---

10. This simulation assumes that each order has multiple order lines, and that each order line is picked from the warehouse.

11. Sales volume is assumed equal to production volume. The simulation could be designed with unequal production and sales volumes and relating them separately to activities.

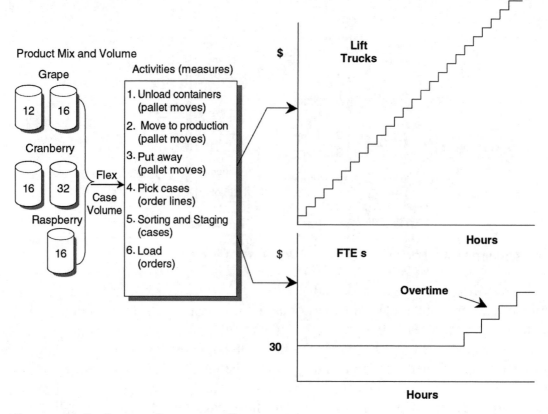

EXHIBIT 11.5   EXPENSE SIMULATION OVERVIEW

for all levels below 30 FTEs of effort. However, for requirements above 30 FTEs of effort, the firm must pay overtime.

The first stage of the simulation translates case demand information into activity base quantities. One can use a spreadsheet to model the necessary relations, as Exhibit 11.6 shows. Column two shows the monthly demand estimated for the five SKUs. Analysts need to develop a parameter that specifies the relation between demand and activity. This parameter translates the volume measure to a measure of activity base usage. For example, two activities in the spending simulation are "unload containers" and "pick cases." The

1	2	3	4	5	6
	Demand	Relation Parameters		Activity Base Frequency	
Products	Monthly Demand (cases)	Cases/ Full Pallet	Cases/ Order Line	Pallet Moves (Col.2 ÷ Col. 3)	Pick Moves, or Order Lines (Col.2 ÷ Col.4)
12 oz. Grape	12,000	32	10	375	1,200
16 oz. Grape	60,000	24	20	2,500	3,000
16 oz. Cranberry	24,000	24	12	1,000	2,000
32 oz. Cranberry	10,500	12	4	875	1,300
16 oz. Raspberry	46,800	24	18	1,950	2,600
Totals	153,300			6,700	10,100

EXHIBIT 11.6   DEMAND AND ACTIVITY

activity base measure for unload containers is *full pallet moves*, while for pick cases it is *pick moves*. Analysts can restate the demand information as full pallet moves by dividing the case demand by the number of cases per full pallet. Likewise, the pick moves, one for each order line, can be computed by dividing the demand by the cases per order line.

In the second stage, the simulation must translate the activity base into resource hours. The calculations in Exhibit 11.7 derive these relations. The first two columns of the table identify the six activities and their activity-base measures. The third column shows the total frequency for each activity base. This number comes from the first stage calculation. For example, the first three activities require 6,700 pallet moves to unload and put up the containers into the materials warehouse, move the containers to production, and put away the finished goods after filling. The number of pallet moves appears in Exhibit 6 as the fifth column sum. The first three activities have the same number of pallet moves because each activity moves full pallets. In addition, the empty containers have the same cubic size as full containers. Therefore, there is no difference in the activity frequency for moving empty or filled containers. This example also assumes that production runs result in output of exactly as many items as will fill an integer number of pallets, for any particular flavor, thus eliminating the need for any sorting during these activity phases.

Order lines drive the picking activity. An order line's size may not equal a full pallet size. Indeed, the average number of cases per order line is less than a full pallet for all five products (columns 3 and 4 in Exhibit 11.6). The total number of order lines shown in Exhibit 11.7 for the "pick case activity" is the sixth column total from Exhibit 11.6. Next, workers must sort the picked cases and stage them into full orders. The sorting and staging activity requires employees to handle individual cases, so the case volume drives this activity (sum of Exhibit 11.6 second column). Lastly, after staging, workers must load each order on an outbound truck. The average order has four order lines. Therefore, there are 2,525 orders (= 10,100 order lines for the month ÷ 4 average order lines per order) that drive the loading activity.

The analyst must then multiply the activity driver totals associated with each activity by a parameter. The parameter is the standard amount of time required to perform each

1	2	3	4	5	6	7
			Parameter	Resource	Resource Units	
Activities	Activity Unit of Measure	Activity Base Frequency	Hrs. per Activity Unit	Total Hours (Col. 3 × 4)	Number of FTEs (Col. 5 ÷ 160 hrs.)	Number of Trucks (Col. 5 ÷ 120 hrs.)
Unload containers	Pallet moves	6,700	0.07	469.00	2.93	3.91
Move to production	Pallet moves	6,700	0.05	335.00	2.09	2.79
Put away FG	Pallet moves	6,700	0.1	670.00	4.19	5.58
Pick cases	Order lines	10,100	0.1	1,010.00	6.31	8.42
Sorting and staging	Cases	153,300	0.02	3,066.00	19.16	
Load	Orders	2,525	0.08	202.00	1.26	1.68
Total					35.94	22.38

EXHIBIT 11.7 ACTIVITY AND RESOURCES

cycle of activity. This data input requires an engineering study. For example, it takes .10 hours (6.0 minutes), on average, to pick an order line from the finished goods warehouse and move it to the staging location. Multiplying the activity frequency by the standard cycle time yields the total amount of hours required to perform the work.

The last two columns of Exhibit 11.7 translate the total number of hours into the number of trucks and FTEs planned for the warehouse. One can calculate these numbers by dividing the total number of hours required to do the work by the monthly available hours per resource unit. We will assume that each employee has 160 hours available for productive work, while a truck has only 120 hours of available hours for productive work. The trucks have fewer available hours due to maintenance, congestion, and seasonal surge.

Calculations for resource units in columns 6 and 7 use the same total hours (column 5) calculation because every move activity requires both a driver and a truck. Therefore, the "hours per activity unit" parameter applies to both the truck and people resources simultaneously. More often, the resources will require unique parameters for the activities. Note the sorting and staging activity does not require a truck, and that the total hours do not include this resource.

Firms can plan resource requirements for alternative demand and operating scenarios. Inputting new demands in Exhibit 11.6 changes the scenario. A change in operations may require a change in activity or parameter relations. For example, if Volunteer Juice Co. improved their operations so that operations could load bottles from trucks directly to the line, then a new activity would replace two existing activities. One could then estimate the planned resource reduction from this change in operations.

Likewise, the simulation provides a tool for controlling of logistics operations. Assume the demand scenario in Exhibit 11.6 was the actual demand for the month. One could then compare the actual expenditures on people and capacities invested in trucks to the planned amount shown from the simulation in Exhibit 11.7. To illustrate, assume that Volunteer Juice Co. had 25 trucks for warehouse operations. The simulation suggests, however, that the warehouse needed only 23 to satisfy demand. The warehouse manager has spare capacity of two warehouse trucks. Depending on seasonal factors over the year, the company may have an opportunity to reduce the fleet. Assume further that the firm paid 30 employees straight time, and incurred another 1,200 hours of overtime. Was this overtime the right amount? The simulation indicates that the demand required 35.94 FTEs of work. Each FTE is worth 160 available hours. Therefore, the amount of overtime hours over 30 FTEs would equal 950 hours (= 5.94 FTEs × 160 hours per FTE), but the firm paid for 1,200 overtime hours. This difference would indicate inefficiencies in the warehouse operation. Furthermore, over time, the warehouse manager can estimate the tradeoff between hiring more employees and incurring overtime.

Although this illustration simplifies an actual scenario, it captures the essential elements of expense planning and control for logistics activities. The key element of this illustration lies in translating demand into activities, rather than translating demand directly into resources. This intermediate step provides greater precision in generating resource plans.

11.4   TOTAL COST OF DELIVERY

Exhibit 11.1 diagrammed supply chain activities. Exhibit 11.1 does not suggest that a single set of logistics activities will necessarily serve all customers for any single firm.

Rather than a single logistics system, organizations tailor their logistical systems to the unique requirements of the product, or channel, or customer.[12]

To illustrate, consider a firm that manufactures commercial aircraft components. The firm can manufacture components for the original equipment manufacturer (OEM), but must also make them available to airlines for after-market repairs. The components are the same, but each distribution channel has different logistics requirements, as shown in Exhibit 11.8.

The repair and overhaul distribution channel must respond quickly, especially if a damaged part grounds the aircraft (termed an *AOG*—aircraft on the ground). Consequently, the order is often unplanned, requiring a turnaround time within days. The firm must expedite the order and ship it by air to the point of need. In contrast, the firm can plan OEM orders and material requirements according to manufacturing lead-time offsets. The firm will process the orders in roughly first in, first out (FIFO) sequence; these orders represent demand for a period of time (a batch). The firm can plan for OEM requirements within the normal business systems of the organization, and must prepare for the unplanned high response events.

The firm must not only tailor the logistics systems to the various distribution channel/customer requirements, but also manage the cost and assets required to deliver unique customer values. This represents the *total cost of delivery*.

The total cost of delivery is the supply chain total cost, from supplier to end consumer. The firm can compare this cost to the customer's price preference to better align total delivery cost and service value. In the case of the aircraft component manufacturer, the customers of rapid response channel will be willing to pay a higher price than will the OEM customers. The airline customer values rapid response and will pay extra for this benefit, since an idled aircraft represents significant margin losses. Successful cost management in the supply chain provides such insight into the profit earned from alternative supply chain configurations. Armed with this type of information, managers can negotiate custom arrangements with suppliers and customers that reflect the total cost to deliver a product (or service).[13]

Characteristic	Logistics Channels	
	Rapid response channel	Planned response channel
Customer	Repair and overhaul (airlines)	OEM (aircraft manufacturer)
Span time	Inside manufacturing lead time	Outside manufacturing lead time
Transportation requirements	Immediate air freight	Over ground freight
Planning requirements	Unplanned	Planned
Handling	Expedite	FIFO
Storage	Strategic safety stock	Make to order (no inventory)
Volume	Singles	Batch

EXHIBIT 11.8 TAILORED LOGISTICS CHANNELS FOR AIRCRAFT COMPONENT MANUFACTURER

12. Joseph B. Fuller, James O. O'Conner, and R. Rawlinson, "Tailored Logistics: The Next Advantage," *Harvard Business Review* (May–June 1993): 87–98.

13. See Lisa M. Ellram and Ed Feitzinger, "Using Total Profit Analysis to Model Supply Chain Decisions," *Journal of Cost Management* (July/August 1997): 12–21.

Total cost of delivery shifts the customer/supplier relation away from negotiating only price. Using total delivered cost information, firms can negotiate price *and* behavior. For example, suppose a railroad provides transportation services for a company. A price based only on gross ton-miles does not distinguish between a customer providing predictable advance load requirements and one failing to do so. The customer providing load requirements in the morning of the train departure, for example, requires the railroad to incur significant additional costs. First, the railroad must maintain a sufficient railcar inventory on site to meet the customer's unknown and variable requirement, a significant investment by the railroad. In addition, the lack of prior notification makes it more difficult for the railroad to arrange back-haul opportunities (a full load for the return trip) on the rail cars, which again leads to poor use of assets. Lastly, the unknown load requirements can create system congestion and delays in blocking and classifying railcars.

How should the railroad respond to this situation? First, the railroad must identify the cost associated with the customer's behavior. With total cost of delivery, the railroad can identify the assets and expenses associated with non-notification. Then the railroad can begin to change its pricing to reflect the differences in customer requirements. The customer providing notification receives a low price, while the customer providing no notification must pay a higher price. This scenario resembles the airline industry's pricing of leisure versus business travel. Now the railroad customer has a price signal by which to evaluate the value of the service. The customer may discover that it can provide advance notification and prefer to take advantage of the price differential. Thus, these price signals can modify behavior and reduce total supply chain costs.

The tools to support supply chain profit analysis include *total cost of ownership* and *relation profitability analysis*.[14] Total cost of ownership focuses on upstream supplier relations, while relation profitability analysis focuses on downstream customer relations, as Exhibit 11.9 shows for the Towel and Tissue Paper Company.

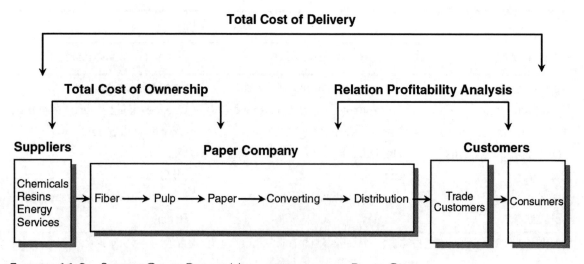

EXHIBIT 11.9   SUPPLY CHAIN PROFIT MANAGEMENT FOR A PAPER COMPANY

14.   See also B.J. LaLonde and T.L. Pohlen,"Issues in Supply Chain Costing," *The International Journal of Logistics Management* 7, 1 (1996): 1–12.

(a) TOTAL COST OF OWNERSHIP. In the most limited sense, the total cost of ownership (TCO) is a method of calculating the total cost of acquiring goods and services from a supplier.[15] The total cost includes not only the purchase price, but also the costs of any additional activities associated with the supplier relation. Exhibit 11.10 lists examples of these additional activity costs.

For example, assume the Towel and Tissue Paper Company from Exhibit 11.9 uses TCO to calculate the cost of supplier relations. First, the company must identify the approximate cost of the various activities, such as those noted in Exhibit 11.10. For example, assume that an engineering study develops the following activity costs:

Receiving inspection	$ 40 per shipment
Short shipment	220 per shipment
Returned shipment	600 per return
Late arrival	250 per shipment
Early arrival	140 per shipment

These activity costs reflect expenditure of resources (people, space, expenses) necessary to perform the activity. For example, the $140 for the early arrival includes the insurance and warehousing cost of holding the inventory for more days than required. Likewise, the returned shipment is the total cost of repackaging, loading, and administratively accounting for the return. In addition, the cost of the return should include an additional charge for the inventory held to accommodate the supplier's unreliability.

Assume two chemical suppliers each provide 4,000 gallons of the same chemical. The TCO performance of the two chemical suppliers appears in Exhibit 11.11.

Supplier A is not yet a qualified supplier; therefore, the firm must perform receiving inspections for all incoming shipments. In addition, of the 35 shipments, the firm rejected two and returned them to the supplier; another 18 shipments were either short or late. Supplier B is a qualified supplier: therefore, the firm need not perform any receiving inspection. Supplier B had only three shipments that deviated from plan. Therefore, although Supplier B's purchase cost per gallon exceeds that of Supplier A, Supplier B's total cost per gallon is less than Supplier A when considering TCO.

Purchasing Activity Costs	Receiving Activity Costs	Failure Activity Costs
Freight	Receiving inspection	Scrap disposition
Premium freight	Special handling	Rework
Purchase ordering	Receiving rejection and return	Lost yield
Problem resolutions	Short shipment	Warranty
Change due to nonavailability	Early arrival	
	Late arrival	

EXHIBIT 11.10 SUPPLIER-INDUCED TCO ACTIVITIES

15. See Lawrence P. Carr and Christopher, D. Ittner, "Measuring the Total Cost of Ownership: A Critical Linkage," *Journal of Cost Management* (Fall 1992): 42–51; and Lisa M. Ellram, "Activity-Based Costing and Total Cost of Ownership: A Critical Linkage," *Journal of Cost Management* (Winter 1985): 22–30; and Roodhooft, Filipt et al., "Optimized Sourcing Strategies Using Total Cost of Ownership," *Journal of Cost Management* (July/August 2003): 28–35.

	Supplier A		Supplier B	
	Frequency	TCO	Frequency	TCO
Purchase cost.............		$38,000		$42,000
Receiving inspections	35 × $ 40	1,400	None	-
Returned shipments.........	2 × $600	1,200	None	-
Short shipment	8 × $220	1,760	1 × $220	220
Late arrivals...............	10 × $250	2,500	2 × $250	500
Total.................		$44,860		$42,720

EXHIBIT 11.11   TCO COMPARISON OF CHEMICAL SUPPLIERS

Accountants can develop a TCO index used for evaluating supplier total cost performance. The index is the TCO per unit divided by the purchase price per unit. The index for Supplier A and B for 4,000 gallons would be:

$$\text{Supplier A: } \frac{\$11.215}{\$9.50} = 1.181 \qquad \text{Supplier B: } \frac{\$10.68}{\$10.50} = 1.017$$

Some firms use the index to adjust supplier price bids. Therefore, if Supplier A were to bid $10.00 per gallon, the firm would adjust the bid by a factor of 1.181, to $11.81 per gallon, for purposes of awarding the bid. A bid of $10.50 from Supplier B would be the low TCO bid ($10.50 × 1.017 = $10.68), even though the actual price bid exceeded that of Supplier A. TCO analysis rewards excellent supplier behavior and penalizes poor behaviors. This occurs when managing supply chain relations beyond price.

One must ask, however, if this emphasis on price and behavior reflects all criteria for selecting a supplier. If the firm views TCO as a method of managing supplier behaviors only, then it may neglect some important supplier integration issues. Given this concern, firms should expand TCO beyond its use as a tool for identifying supplier shortcomings. The supplier may add value to downstream elements (later functions) of the supply chain by providing additional service (earlier functions). For example, the chemical supplier could provide upstream engineering support to the downstream paper company, which reduces costs of manufacturing paper. The supplier may, for example, analyze the ways the chemical interacts with the paper-making process, and, thus, be able to improve yields, chemical input usage, or quality of the end product. The supplier provides a tangible benefit, at some cost. Without a method of valuing the costs and benefits, a rule for sharing the benefits will be difficult to establish.

Suppliers who adopt lean manufacturing principles can lead to significant downstream benefits. A lean supplier can respond faster to downstream requirements, while at the same time it can reduce inventory in the pipeline. These benefits can lead to significant savings to downstream customers. For example, the cost of markdowns represents the second largest cost of apparel retailing, after cost of goods. Markdowns occur when a retailer holds unsold goods that it purchased before the season began. Before the season begins, the firm must make the commitment. If the company orders too few goods, then it loses sales—if it orders too much, then markdowns result. What would happen if the apparel retailer could order and receive fashion goods weekly, rather than in quarterly programs? Would such a capability allow the retailer to catch most of the demand from a popular item and miss most of the markdowns from an unpopular item? Would the retailer be willing to pay more for such fast response capability? Transit time may require that domestic manufacturers (with higher labor costs) supply the goods, rather than more distant, perhaps Asian, operations that pay lower wages but have longer shipping times.[16] By evaluating the full total cost of ownership, one can answer these types of questions. Therefore, TCO should move beyond disciplining supplier shortcomings, but also reward behaviors that lead to tangible improvements.

(b) RELATION PROFITABILITY ANALYSIS. The flip side of TCO is the downstream, customer, side of the relation.[17] Unlike suppliers, the customer provides revenues, so one can expand the analysis to evaluate profitability of the distribution channel/customer relations. Partitioning profit among customer or channel participants, or both, provides insights regarding the following:

- The value provided by the firm to customers
- The maximizing sales effort for different customer/channels
- The drivers of underlying customer/channel costs
- The success or failure of customer strategies
- The pricing of various channel configurations
- The costs of horizontally linked functions

Relation profitability analysis combines logistics, marketing, and sales-related activities into a complete picture of the cost to serve the customer. A firm can examine the profitability of a relation for individual customers, region, distribution channel, and order size.

(i) Analysis by Individual Customers. One commonly sees the familiar Pareto principle in action: 20 percent of the customers yield 80 percent of the profitability. The other 80 percent are smaller customers whose business provides gross margins at break-even or below. One should also focus on the customer's potential in addition to its current profitability performance. A decision to invest in an unprofitable customer relation today may be justified upon its future potential. This suggests that a complete understanding of the profitability of a customer relation may require a longer, life-cycle, perspective. While few firms track this type of performance, a life-cycle perspective would provide insights about the financial returns on customer development activity.

Beyond analysis at the individual customer level, firms may classify individual customers along other attributes, such as region, distribution channel, and size. For example, Rigips, a German building supply company, stratifies its profit reporting as shown in Exhibit 11.12.

As Exhibit 11.12 shows, Rigips evaluates the profitability by individual retail outlets, by three different regional classifications of stores, by channel (e.g., local hardware, builder's wholesale, large retail), and by group (a chain of individual stores under a single corporate name).

(ii) Analysis by Region. Regional analysis groups customers within a geographical area under the responsibility of a manager. One can use regional profit information to evaluate regional managers and to support decisions such as the following:

- Changes in the intensity of sales coverage by adding or subtracting sales personnel.

---

16. T, Gilreath, J. Reeve, and C. Whalen, "Time Is Money," *Bobbin* (March 1995).
17. See also Foster, G., Gupta, M., and Sjoblom, L., "Customer Profitability Analysis: Challenges and New Directions," *Journal of Cost Management* (Spring 1996): 517.

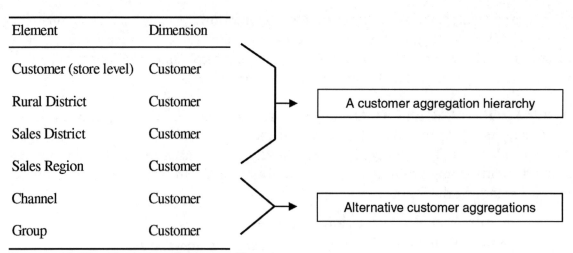

Element	Dimension
Customer (store level)	Customer
Rural District	Customer
Sales District	Customer
Sales Region	Customer
Channel	Customer
Group	Customer

A customer aggregation hierarchy

Alternative customer aggregations

EXHIBIT 11.12   DIFFERENT CUSTOMER CLASSIFICATIONS

- Changes in the intensity of advertising and promotional activity.
- Changes in the sales region boundaries. The influences of population changes, population density, types of industry, traffic conditions, and factors that affect the mobility of salespersons on operating costs affect the boundary decision.
- Changes in the methods of covering a territory, such as telephone, personal visit, mail, local advertising, or Internet. The costs of each approach, effectiveness, and customer density of a geographic area will affect the optimal method of covering a territory.

The costs of a region include the direct costs, such as the occupancy costs of the district office, district salaries, sales force salaries, promotional costs and sales force support costs. In addition to the direct costs, firms can allocate corporate support costs—such as customer billing, collection, or personnel recruiting costs—to a sales region. Firms can usually allocate centralized credit, billing, customer accounting, and related costs to regions by using units of functional service, such as number of customers, number of invoices, number of sales order lines, and number of bills of lading.

Firms often incur significant freight costs. They can record costs of delivery by a common carrier through the accounts payable system and code them to the region. However, the firm may need to allocate the costs of a corporate fleet to the region. Trips that cross multiple regional boundaries may require ton-miles, or some other measure of service, allocated to the region.

Exhibit 11.13 shows an example of a regional profit report for a specialty chemicals company. This profit report assigns the additional direct costs of the region—such as sales compensation, sales expenses, and promotional cost—to each region manager's profit statement. The report also assigns to the region manager indirect costs, such as centralized support and hiring, that represent the cost of services consumed by the division. The firm can use a service charge rate to allocate these latter costs to the region. For example, the turnover charge could represent a charge associated with hiring a new salesperson. The actual charge rate may be a function of whether the firm moves a current employee from another division into the division (a low rate), places a new employee into the division (a medium rate), or uses an employment agency to find a new employee to place in the division (a high rate).

The regional profit report provides the regional manager incentives to manage the profitability of the sales effort, rather than just sales volume. This aligns costs associated with acquiring and maintaining volume. Therefore, the division manager can begin to evaluate the tradeoffs and associations between resource expenditure and sales volume.

Sales		$12,456,000
Cost of goods sold		6,645,000
Gross profit		$ 5,811,000
Sales compensation		3,267,000
Sales expenses		
Business travel	$ 243,000	
Automobile	153,600	
Communications	92,800	
Supplies	32,500	521,900
Centralized support		
Sales order administration	245,000	
Collections	71,000	
Quotation	94,500	410,500
Hiring		
Turnover charge	194,500	
Relocation costs	32,400	226,900
Promotional		
Samples	31,700	
Literature	46,700	
Meetings and conventions	167,000	245,400
Net Margin		$ 1,862,300
Net Margin % of Sales		14.95%

EXHIBIT 11.13   REGIONAL PROFIT REPORT

(iii) Analysis by Distribution Channels.   Sellers often serve the same or different customers through different distribution channels. For example, the consumer of towel and tissue products may purchase the product from a club store, grocery store, or convenience store. All three of these represent different channels for selling the same product to the same customer. Alternatively, the seller may sell to some customers uniquely through different channels, such as wholesale, retail, consumer direct, or broker. The different channels have different costs for servicing and earn different margins. As a result, an organization can gain operational insight by evaluating channel profitability. For example, Exhibit 11.14 shows how a beverage company, such as Volunteer Juice Co., would evaluate the profitability of its major channels.

Exhibit 11.14 shows that the greatest net margins come from the airline distribution channel; however, this channel has small volume. Apparently, the airline channel has attractive pricing, and inexpensive distribution costs through the hub cities. At the other end of the spectrum, the university distribution channel has negative margins. The firm may decide to sacrifice margin to win exclusive distribution rights on campus, and, therefore, capture a new generation of consumers.

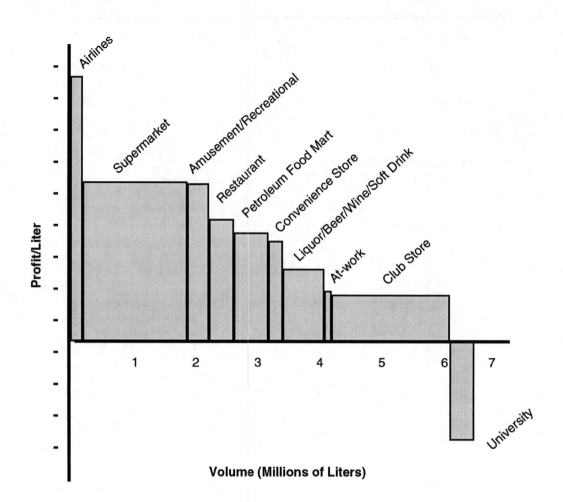

EXHIBIT 11.14   DISTRIBUTION CHANNEL PROFITABILITY ANALYSIS

(iv) Analysis by Order Size.   The order size of a particular customer or distribution channel influences marketing and logistics activities. For example, getting and filling a smaller order may cost the same as that of a larger order. This occurs because many of these activities, such as sales visit, order taking, paperwork, shipping, picking, invoicing, and collecting, vary with the number of orders, not the number of units sold with an order. As a result, smaller orders can become a financial burden to an organization. A cost study of this problem can help the firm do the following:

- Identify differential pricing points as a function of order size.
- Identify minimum-order-size requirements.
- Identify cost-reduction opportunities.
- Identify the order characteristics of unprofitable customers.

New supply chain practices move away from large infrequent orders to more frequent smaller orders, because customers do not wish to purchase goods before using them. Many customers require that suppliers ship goods so that they arrive when the customer consumes them. For example, Toyota's Georgetown, Kentucky assembly plant receives many of its purchased parts three times per day. This allows the assembly plant to maintain a minimum materials inventory, while still meeting the requirements of the assembly line. Given the small order problem identified above, what can a vendor do? The answer lies in changing the order-getting and filling process so that it becomes more economical to execute order transactions for smaller quantities of product.[18] Examples of such strategies are the use of vendor management inventories, blanket purchase orders, electronic data interchange, ordering, lean manufacturing, distribution center cross-docking, advance shipping notices, and consumption/replenishment (Kanban) materials control. These lean supply chain concepts (discussed in other chapters in this *Handbook*) allow companies to profitably sell, produce, and ship in small order quantities.

11.5 RELATION PROFITABILITY—EXAMPLE

Here, we illustrate analysis of relation profitability using the Towel and Tissue Company (TTC) data in Exhibit 11.9.[19] We will assume TTC sells home-use towel and tissue products to a number of trade customers and distribution channels as follows:

- Wal-Mart
- Target
- Kroger
- Sam's Warehouse
- Broker Distribution Channel
- Convenience Store Distribution Channel

These customers do not require the same logistics and marketing activities. TTC will use the activity information to identify the relation profitability for these customers. We begin by developing an activity worksheet for each relation. Exhibit 11.15 has a sample activity worksheet for the assumed Wal-Mart relation.

Note that the net revenue of the relation includes gross revenues, less discounts and incentives. After calculating gross profit, the firm should subtract activity costs associated with the relation to calculate the customer margin. Exhibit 11.16 lists the activities used by TTC in evaluating its customer relations. The costs associated with the relation include direct costs of the relationship, such as freight costs; activity costs, such as loading; and carrying costs associated with inventory and receivables.

(a) DIRECT COSTS.   The direct costs include the dollars spent on the customer relation for a particular activity. When possible, one should collect direct costs, rather than use allocated costs. For example, a firm can calculate the cost of advertising for the benefit of the customer (so-called *co-operative advertising*) by either tracking the direct costs of running ads from the accounts payable system or by assuming an activity rate for each ad. Under the latter approach, the firm must track the number of ads for each customer and multiply it by the advertising rate. While this tracks the frequency of advertising it does not capture differences in rates per ad. The analysis averages differences between a cooperative ad placed in a low circulation newspaper and a high circulation newspaper across all cooperative ads.

Our example tracks actual freight costs direct to each customer, thus avoiding averaging effects across all customers. The actual freight charge results from the interaction of the number of shipments, distance, size of shipment, weight, and cube. In this way, shipments of large quantities to close customers do not subsidize small quantities to distant ones. Moreover, this calculation captures additional movement and transshipment due to the customer's stock re-balancing demands.

---

18.   A good illustration is provided in Harvard Business School case, *Pillsbury: Customer Driven Reengineering* (HBS 9-195-144).

19.   This illustration is a stylized composite from a number of consulting experiences by the author.

Name	Units	Numbers
Revenue		
Gross Sales	dollars	75,400,000
Product returns	dollars	2,400,000
Volume Incentive	dollars	1,200,000
Net Sales	dollars	71,800,000
Product Costs		
Cost of goods	dollars	47,450,000
Plant Shipping and Handling Costs		
Freight Costs	dollars	940,000
Loading		
Bill of lading	shipments	450
Order loading	orders	700
Order sorting and consolidation	order lines	4.5
Material handling		
Number of warehouse moves	# of clamps	
Product Returns	# of returns	1,200
Inventory Carrying Costs		
Cycle inventory		
Order interval	months	1
Speculative inventory		
Cumulative forecast error	cases	30,000
Warranty costs	dollars	
Sales and Marketing Costs		
Customer planning and management	FTEs	1.5
Selling	orders	12
Collection administration		
Collection	invoices	
Adjustments	invoice adjustments	4
Cooperative advertising	dollars	
Order Entry Costs	order lines	
Receivable Carrying Costs		
Day's sales outstanding	Day's sales	58.1

EXHIBIT 11.15   RELATION ACTIVITY WORKSHEET: WAL-MART

(b) ACTIVITY COST. Often, the accounting system does not register activity costs directly from supporting payroll or accounts payable (AP) systems. Consequently, the firm must translate the resources into activities to facilitate assignment to the customer. For example, the loading activity is a function of three activity drivers, as follows:

Loading activity = [Order lines × Rate] + [Orders × Rate] + [Shipments × Rate]

Activity	Type
Freight costs	Direct cost
Loading activity	Activity cost
Material handling activity	Activity cost
Product return activity	Activity cost
Cycle inventory carrying costs	Carrying cost
Speculative inventory carrying costs	Carrying cost
Warranty costs	Direct cost
Customer planning and management	Activity cost
Selling	Activity cost
Collection administration	Activity cost
Cooperative advertising	Direct cost
Order entry costs	Activity cost
Receivable carrying costs	Carrying cost

EXHIBIT 11.16 ACTIVITIES RELATED TO CUSTOMER RELATIONS

The first term is the activity of sorting order lines into orders, the second term is the order loading activity, and the third term is the bill of lading paperwork. The analysis breaks down other activities in a similar manner. The rate represents the resource cost of performing an activity cycle, calculated by engineering analysis.

(c) POST-SALE ACTIVITIES. Beyond the current activities required to support a relation, additional relation activities occur after the point of sale. Obvious examples include longer-term servicing and warranty activities. These costs include the direct costs of the post-sale service, as captured by the accounting system, plus any additional administrative cost calculated by multiplying the activity rate by an activity driver, such as number of claims.

Post-sale activities also include costs that firms cannot easily estimate, such as environmental costs.[20] Under environmental costing, the firm must calculate the discounted present value of future environmental effects in order to estimate the profitability of a relation (or product). These future environmental effects include such events as *product take-back:* the disposition costs associated with a product at the end of its life. Accounting for the present value of product take-back can give companies incentive to design and sell products with end-of-life disposition in mind.

(d) CARRYING COST. In addition to the direct and activity costs of supporting a customer relation, one must also consider the imputed interest cost associated with assets invested in the relation. The analysis in Exhibit 11.15 includes both inventory and accounts receivable carrying costs. The accounting system registers accounts receivable directly to the customer in the accounting system, so its assignment is trivial. Inventory, however, will prove a more difficult asset to assign to the customer relation. One could address this by separating the inventory into the amount necessary to support the order

---

20. "Tools and Techniques of Environmental Accounting for Business Decisions" *Management Accounting Guideline #40*, IMA, 1996. See also work by Mark Epstein on this topic, e.g. M.J. Epstein, *Measuring Corporate Environmental Performance: Best Practices for Costing and Managing an Effective Environmental Strategy* (Montvale, N.J.: IMA, 1996).

cycle and the additional amount to support demand variation (or order uncertainty). The order cycle carrying cost is the imputed interest cost on the minimum inventory required to support the lead time. For example, if manufacturing lead time is one month from order, then to defend order fulfillment the firm must have an average safety stock of one month of inventory multiplied by the minimum daily demand rate. As lead time decreases, the amount of order cycle inventory required for the relation also decreases. Ultimately, a demand replenishment system may require only a few days of inventory in the system. Lead time reduction translates directly to inventory reduction and cost savings.

Firms may also need to hold speculative inventory in addition to order cycle inventory to cope with demand unpredictability. For example, if a customer has in the past ordered an average of 300 units per month with a standard deviation of 33 units, then the supplier must cope with this order variation by holding at least 400 units in inventory (a three-sigma defense—implying being able to satisfy demand 99 percent of the time; a two-sigma defense holds about 465 units, and guards against outages about 95 percent of the time.). The customer may also order fewer than 300 units, causing the supplier to hold inventory beyond that required by the demand. Firms can measure such variation over time and translate it into additional inventory that they must hold to cope with demand uncertainty. The sum of the mean absolute deviation from average provides an estimate of the amount of inventory required due to variation. A customer with variable demands places more extreme inventory pressures on the supplier than does one with lower variability. Likely, the noise in the estimates of statistical uncertainty (the standard deviation in the preceding example) will swamp the demand uncertainty, so that the results of the analysis are more likely guidelines than pinpoint control devices.

Some customers may require unique components for customer specific options. One can include these unique components in the customer specific inventory to calculate the carrying cost.

(e) MARGIN ANALYSIS.   Exhibit 11.17 summarizes the assumed relation profitabilities of all the customers from the worksheet details in Exhibit 11.15.

The gross profit number indicates that the convenience store distribution channel offers the greatest gross profitability, and Sam's Warehouse offers the lowest gross profitability. The gross profit number, however, does not completely describe the profitability of the relations. The net relation profit as a percent of sales provides a different interpretation. The convenience store channel has the lowest net relation profit at 9 percent of sales, while Sam's Warehouse has the greatest net relationship profit at 19 percent of sales, the opposite of the gross profit order. Why? The activity and carrying cost percentages explain the net results. The convenience store channel has intensive shipping, ordering, and handling activities because the convenience store channel requires many smaller orders to each store. Thus, for a given volume of towel and tissue products, the convenience store channel requires the most logistical support. In contrast, Sam's Warehouse requires the least support for a given volume of sales because Sam's requires full pallets of a single product.

In addition, Sam's asset carrying cost is also the lowest as a percent of sales because it employs a vendor managed inventory (VMI) strategy. Vendors under VMI will replenish inventory based on the previous period's demand. Naturally, the goal is to match production to demand by keeping the replenishment period small. Thus, a replenishment approach minimizes order cycle inventory, the largest source of carrying cost.

An organization that understands the components of profitability by customer relation has a basis for negotiating prices that are consistent with the services provided. If a distribution channel or customer requires intensive logistical support, then the pricing

Customer	Gross Profit as % of Sales	Activity Cost as % of Sales	Carrying Cost as % of Sales	Relation Profit as % of Sales
Wal-Mart	34%	20%	2%	12%
Target	30	15	4	11
Kroger	35	22	3	10
Sam's Warehouse	28	8	1	19
Broker channel	33	10	5	18
Convenience store channel	37	23	5	9

EXHIBIT 11.17 COMPARISON OF CUSTOMER RELATION PROFITABILITY

should reflect this bundle of additional services provided. Some companies unbundle and price the services separately from the product; this is termed *menu pricing*.

11.6 SUMMARY

This chapter explained how firms can manage logistics and marketing costs to support supply chain management. Firms can use total delivered cost to evaluate the supplier side of the supply chain, while they use relation profitability to support decisions for the customer side of the supply chain. In addition, they can use expense planning and control simulations to identify, plan, and control costs at any point in the supply chain.

CHAPTER 16

ALLOCATIONS OF COST AND REVENUE*

ROMAN L. WEIL, CPA, CMA, PHD, EDITOR
University of Chicago

CONTENTS

16.1 INTRODUCTION 465

16.2 PURPOSES OF COST ALLOCATION 466

16.3 DEFINITIONS 466

16.4 THE FUNDAMENTAL PROBLEMS 467

16.5 COMMON, OTHER THAN JOINT, COST ALLOCATION 468

    (a) Stand-Alone Method 468

    (b) Incremental-Cost Method 468

    (c) Shapley Value Method 468

    (d) Theory Provides No Right Answer 469

16.6 JOINT COST ALLOCATION 469

    (a) Relative Sales Value (at Splitoff) Method 470

    (b) Net Realizable Value (at Splitoff) Method 470

    (c) Constant Gross Margin Percentage Method 472

    (d) Physical Quantities Methods 472

    (e) Benefits Received Methods 472

    (f) Ability to Bear Method 473

    (g) Do Not Allocate Joint Costs without Compulsion 473

16.7 BYPRODUCTS 474

16.8 ALLOCATION OF REVENUE 475

    (a) Theory Provides No Right Answer 475

    (b) Bundled Lease Allocations 476

16.9 FURTHER READING 477

APPENDIX 16A STEP-DOWN AND RECIPROCAL METHODS FOR ALLOCATING SERVICE DEPARTMENT COSTS 478

BIBLIOGRAPHY 481

16.1 INTRODUCTION

Allocation issues arise in accounting to the extent historical costs provide the basis for valuation. If all balance sheet amounts reported fair values, few allocation issues would

---

*   Thanks to George Foster of Stanford University, some of whose unpublished writings I used in preparing this chapter. I have relied on Hugo Nurnberg's "Joint Products and By-Products," which appeared as Chapter 18 in the original *Handbook of Cost Accounting* and on M.W. Maher, C.P. Stickney, and R.L. Weil, *Managerial Accounting: An Introduction to Concepts, Methods, and Uses,* (Mason, Ohio: Thomson South-Western, 2006). The authors of the appendix to this chapter (Leslie Eldenburg and Naomi Soderstrom) originally wrote that material for Chapter 28. Because of its general applicability, the editors have moved it here.

arise.[1] This chapter discusses primarily cost allocations, but also discusses revenue allocations.

16.2   PURPOSES OF COST ALLOCATION

Accounting allocates costs to time periods (think amortization) and to products (think cost accounting). Why? Accountants allocate costs (and to a lesser degree, revenues) to do the following:

- Provide data to managers making decisions
- Aid in implementing decisions
- Evaluate how well implementations progress
- Motivate and evaluate employees
- Satisfy requirements of financial reporting
- Satisfy income tax regulations
- Provide the basis for reimbursement in cost-based contracts

Accountants tend to use the terms *cost assignment* and *cost allocation* interchangeably. Much of cost management focuses on the assignment of costs to cost objects, such as products, processes, and segments. Several other chapters in this book treat cost assignments. The easy issues in cost assignment involve direct costs and other costs where analysis can establish a cause-and-effect relation. If an activity or cost object causes a cost, the accountants assign that cost to the causing activity or cost object.

This chapter focuses on the more difficult issues where analysis cannot establish a cause and effect relation—situations involving joint products, joint costs, and common costs. The appendix to the chapter treats the allocation of service department costs to production departments. Although there is a cause-and-effect relation, no other chapter in this book addresses this issue, so the editors have put the material at the end of this chapter.

16.3   DEFINITIONS

Common costs. Common costs occur when a process produces multiple products. An automobile production line that produces sedans and SUVs incurs common costs. Costs can be common to periods of time, classes of customers, and sales territories.

Joint costs, joint-process costs, and *joint products. Joint costs* occur when a process inevitably produces multiple products (called joint products), not necessarily in fixed proportions, from a single process or resource. Here are some classic examples:

- A steer, whose total costs jointly enable production of the joint products meat and hides
- Petroleum lifted from underground, whose costs jointly enable production of the joint products gasoline and natural gas liquids

All joint costs are common costs, but not all common costs are joint. Management chooses to produce both sedans and SUVs on the same assembly line, causing the line's costs to be common. The commonality does not result from a fact of nature, but

---

1.   I'm tempted to write *no,* but we learn never to say *never* in accounting—well, almost never.

from conscious choice. Some writers use the term *joint-process costs* to refer to the joint costs of a manufacturing process, in contrast to the joint costs of the raw materials input to the process.

Byproducts. When a joint product has small value relative to other joint products, accountants call that joint product a *byproduct* and use simplified allocation methods for it. The example in Section 16.6 considers saw dust and wood chips produced as the inevitable output of converting logs into lumber.

Separable costs, the splitoff point, and *depth-of-processing decisions.* In producing joint products, the process typically reaches a stage, called the *splitoff point,* where further costs, called *separable costs,* are direct and caused by decisions to process further. The slaughter of a steer causes simultaneously production of meat and hides. The dressing of meat and the tanning of hides occur after the splitoff point. Management now has discretion as to cost incurrence: dispose of the entrails or process them further. We refer to the decision of whether to process further as a *depth-of-processing decision.* The decision to process further causes *separable costs.*

16.4   THE FUNDAMENTAL PROBLEMS

All methods of allocating joint costs are arbitrary. We require that the methods be systematic and rational, but nevertheless they are arbitrary.[2] No causal relation identifies a portion of the joint cost resulting from an individual joint product. To get one product inevitably requires getting the other and incurring the costs for both.

Allocating joint costs poses issues for accountants because the needs of allocated joint costs for financial reporting differ from those for decision making. Cost accounting systems serve multiple purposes, including product pricing, product emphasis, cost control, and reporting to internal and external constituents. The same set of computations rarely satisfies every purpose, as discussed in Chapter 3. Rather, analysts adjust the information contained in a cost accounting system to tailor the resulting cost figures and cost reports to the specific purpose at issue. The purpose at issue guides the set of costing methods.

Common costs, other than joint costs, result from management discretion. That discretion leads to methods for allocating common costs based on cause-and-effect relations. The difficulties arise because, typically, no unique answer results from these methods.

Consider the assembly line that produces both sedans and SUVs. Assume the total, common, cost of the line is $10 million. Assume further that an assembly line for sedans alone costs $6 million and that an assembly line for SUVs alone costs $9 million. If management says, "We started with sedans, the decision to add SUVs is incremental," then the accountant can say the decision to produce SUVs *causes* costs of $4 million (= $10 – $6). Cause-and-effect analysis allocates $6 million of common assembly line costs to sedans and $4 million to SUVs. If, however, management says, "We started with SUVs; the decision to add sedans is incremental," cause-and-effect analysis allocates $9 million of common costs to SUVs and $1 (= $10 – $9) million to sedans.

---

2. The word *arbitrary* in this context often causes difficulties in courtroom proceedings. Accountants use the word *arbitrary* to use terms in the *Oxford English Dictionary,* to imply discretion, that is, methods not based on the nature of things. Accountants do not mean whimsy nor random nor capricious, all of which to one degree or another associate with the word *arbitrary* in common usage.

In many situations, one cannot uniquely identify the base product and the incremental product, so these methods do not give unique answers. Because one can more easily understand the issues of allocating common—other than joint—costs, I address those first.

16.5 COMMON, OTHER THAN JOINT, COST ALLOCATION

Refer to the data in the previous example for the common $10 million cost of an assembly line for sedans and SUVs. Accountants have used the following methods to allocate these common costs.

(a) STAND-ALONE METHOD. Assume that if the manufacturer built separate, stand-alone assembly lines, one for sedans and one for SUVs, the total costs would equal $15 (= $6 + $9) million. The sedan line would cost 40 percent (6/15) of the total two-assembly line costs and the SUV line costs 60 percent (9/15). The stand-alone method uses these percentages to allocate the common costs: 40 percent, or $4 million, to sedans and 60 percent, or $6 million, to SUVs.

The stand-alone method allocates common costs in proportion to the costs the firm would incur if it undertook the common activities as separate activities. Some accountants think the stand-alone method is fair, but no one that I know of has an operational definition of *fair* to justify this label.

(b) INCREMENTAL-COST METHOD. The SUV and sedan example in Section 16.4 illustrates the incremental-cost method. This method assumes a base configuration of facilities and product, with a base cost. Then it hypothetically adds facilities and products, with incremental cost. The total of base cost and incremental cost equals the total common cost. The incremental-cost method allocates first to the base product all base costs and the incremental costs to the added product

The incremental-cost method generalizes to more than two common products. The assembly line could conceivably produce a third product, convertibles, a fourth, pick-up trucks, and so on. If one specifies the base product, and the order of incremental additions, a common cost allocation based on incremental costs results. If there are several, say n, products, each potentially incremental to the others, then there are $n \times (n - 1) \times (n - 2) \cdots 2 \times 1$ (often called "n factorial" and denoted $n!$) different allocations. For $n = 3$, there are potentially six different allocations ($3 \times 2 \times 1$).

In a negotiation context, whether allocating costs to cost objects within a company or in setting reimbursement rates in cost-plus contracts, every party wants to represent the incremental product or process, as incremental costs typically decline as the process adds products.

(c) SHAPLEY VALUE METHOD. Modern accounting theorists, following the lead of Joel Demski, have adopted the mathematical, game-theoretic construct of the Shapley Value to the incremental-cost method. (See Chapter 5 in this book, authored by Demski.) The Shapley Value method assigns to each of the common elements the average of the costs that the incremental-cost method would assign to each as primary and as incremental.

Consider Section 16.4's example: If sedans are the primary product, the allocation to them is $6 million; if they are the incremental product, their allocation is $1 million, an average of $3.5 [= (6 + 1)/2] million. If SUVs are the primary product, the allocation to them is $9 million; if they are the incremental product, their allocation is $4 million, an average of $6.5 [= (9 + 4)/2] million. The Shapley Value method assigns $3.5 million to sedans and $6.5 million to SUVs.

(d) THEORY PROVIDES NO RIGHT ANSWER.   Which of these methods—stand-alone, incremental, traditional, or Shapley—is right in theory? That question has no answer. No allocation will, better than the other, enable management to make wealth-enhancing decisions.

If management can show that one of the common costs was, indeed, incremental to the other, then cause-and-effect allocations emerge and a unique answer emerges. The facts of the case matter.

If management needs such an allocation, that need likely results from some contractual provision, such as the need to pay license fees to inventors of processes used on the assembly lines. If the license holders of the rights to the processes for the two sets of intellectual property have the same interests in both lines, then the allocation between the two lines does not matter, as amounts paid to each owner will be the same, no matter the allocation. If the owners have different interests, then the allocation matters to the owners. Still, theory provides no uniquely right answer. To get a uniquely right answer, one needs to look to the contract that the licensees have with the manufacturer. Most likely, the contract will not specify a method; in this case, economic theory does not provide an answer.

When the difference matters because the situation involves large dollar amounts, and when the contract does not address the allocation method, the issue likely ends up in litigation. We advise the court to do what seems equitable under the circumstances; neither economics nor accounting has one, correct, answer. A right answer might emerge from the specific facts.

16.6   JOINT COST ALLOCATION

Why should cost managers deal with allocating joint-process costs when joint-cost allocations are arbitrary? Organizations allocate joint costs to measure performance, to calculate rate-regulated prices, to estimate casualty losses (such as from fire or flood), to satisfy contractual obligations, and to resolve contractual disputes. Manufacturing companies must allocate joint costs to value inventories and cost of goods sold for financial and tax reporting. Although no cause-and-effect method can trace joint costs to joint products as ABC costing seeks to do in other production processes (see Chapter 6), the results of allocating joint costs in different ways in practice often affect managerial decisions in planning, performance evaluation, and decision making. Joint cost allocations should not affect managerial decisions aimed at maximizing net present value of cash flows, but in practice they often do.

This section discusses the following methods of joint cost allocation and ends with a suggestion to avoid them all.

- Relative sales value (at splitoff) method
- Net realizable value (at splitoff) method
- Constant gross margin method
- Physical quantities methods
- Benefits received method
- Ability to bear method

Many companies, particularly those in forest products, oil and gas, and chemicals and mining, produce multiple joint products from a joint process. For example, a forest products company can process timber (logs) into lumber of various grades and sizes. The company can convert resulting sawdust and wood chips into paper pulp. One input (timber) can yield several different products.

Exhibit 16.1 presents data for the costs that Humboldt Lumber Company incurs to process logs into lumber for a month.[3] Raw materials (rough logs) cost $250,000 and processing costs $110,000, resulting in total costs of $360,000. As Humboldt processes the logs, two joint products emerge at the splitoff point—standard lumber and specialty lumber.

(a) RELATIVE SALES VALUE (AT SPLITOFF) METHOD.   First, assume that a ready market for the two grades of lumber exists as they emerge from the splitoff point, enabling Humboldt to sell the two grades of lumber as is. Exhibit 16.1 shows these sales amounts as $504,000 for specialty lumber and $756,000 for standard lumber, $1,260,000 in total. Specialty lumber represents 40 percent (= $504,000/$1,260,000) of that total and standard lumber represents 60 percent. The relative sales value method allocates the joint costs in proportion to the relative sales values (see Panel A of Exhibit 16.1).

Some writers refer to this method as the Net Realizable Value Method, described next, because it represents a special case of that method, in that the firm need not incur additional processing costs necessary past splitoff to ready either joint product for immediate sale.

This method measures the value of the joint products immediately at the end of the joint process, and it is based on objectively measurable market prices. This method has no difficult calculations and requires no projections of management intent with respect to further processing and sales strategies. For these reasons, many accountants prefer this method when the company can sell the joint products immediately after splitoff.

(b) NET REALIZABLE VALUE (AT SPLITOFF) METHOD.   Now, assume that at least one of the joint products, in this example specialty lumber, requires further processing before the firm can sell it. Panel B of Exhibit 16.1 shows the additional processing costs as $97,000, so the net realizable value of specialty lumber at splitoff no longer equals $504,000, as before, but is $407,000 (= $504,000 − $97,000). This method, sometimes called the *NRV method,* allocates the joint costs in proportion to the net realizable values of the joint products.

The relative sales value method, discussed above, is a special case of the NRV method, because the two methods give the same results when the firm does not incur additional processing costs.

The basis underlying the NRV method is that revenue dollars from each joint product earns the same percentage contribution at the splitoff point as the revenue dollars from any other joint product. The net realizable value approach matches the input costs with revenues generated by the total of all joint products.

The NRV method does not give unique cost allocations, as it results in a different allocation for each combination of additional processing procedures and costs. For example, assume Humboldt has the option to make specialty lumber ready for immediate sale

3.   I have constructed this example from a simpler version of it in M.W. Maher, C.P. Stickney, and R.L. Weil, *Managerial Accounting: An Introduction to Concepts, Methods, and Uses,* (Mason, Ohio: Thomson South-Western, 2006), Chapter 15.

Joint Costs			Total
Raw materials (Logs)			$ 250,000
Conversion costs			110,000
Total Joint Costs Requiring Allocation			$ 360,000

Allocation of Joint Costs

A. Sales Value at Splitoffs
(No Additional Processing Costs)

	Specialty Lumber	Standard Lumber	Total
Sales value at splitoff....................	$ 504,000	$ 756,000	$1,260,000
Less: Additional processing costs	-	-	-
Net Realizable Value at Splitoff Point	$ 504,000	$ 756,000	$1,260,000
Proportionate Share			
$504,000/$1,260,000	40%		
$756,000/$1,260,000		60%	
Allocated Joint-Process Costs			
$360,000 x 40%	$ 144,000		
$360,000 x 60%		$ 216,000	

B. Net Realizable Value at Splitoff
(With Additional Processing Costs)

Final Sales Value	$ 504,000	$ 756,000	$126,000
Less: Additional processing costs	(97,000)	-	(97,000)
Net Realizable Value at Splitoff Point	$ 407,000	$ 756,000	$1,163,000
Proportionate Share			
$504,000/$1,260,000	35%		
$756,000/$1,260,000		65%	
Allocated Joint-Process Costs			
$360,000 x 35%	$ 126,000		
$360,000 x 65%		$ 234,000	

C. Constant Gross Margin Percentage Method

Final Sales Value	$ 504,000	$ 756,000	$1,260,000
Less: Additional processing costs	(97,000)	-	(97,000)
Net Realizable Value at Splitoff Point	$ 407,000	$ 756,000	$1,163,000
Less: Joint costs........................			(360,000)
Gross Margin on All Joint Products			$ 803,000
Gross Margin Percentage All Products			63.7%
(= $803,000/$1,260,000)			
Gross Margin on Individual Products			
= 63.7% x $504,000..................	$ 321,200		
= 63.7% x $756,000..................		$ 481,800	
Allocated Joint-Process Costs			
$407,000 – $321,200	$ 85,800		
$756,000 – $481,800		$ 274,200	

D. Physical Units Method

Board Feet of Lumber Produced	2,800	3,920	6,720
Proportionate Share			
2,800/6,720	42%		
3,920/6,720		58%	
Allocated Joint-Process Costs			
$360,000 x 42%	$ 150,000		
$360,000 x 68%		$ 210,000	

EXHIBIT 16.1   HUMBOLDT LUMBER COMPANY DATA FOR JOINT COST ALLOCATION EXAMPLES

using a different process, which takes more time and costs $100,000, but results in an immediate market price of $520,000. Exhibit 16.1 does not show this computation, but the allocations would change from 35:65 to 36:64. The supporters of the NRV method do not provide guidance on how to choose between alternative results.

(c) CONSTANT GROSS MARGIN PERCENTAGE METHOD. Whereas the NRV method assumes all joint products earn the same percentage gross margin at the splitoff point, the constant gross margin percentage method assumes all joint products earn the same percentage gross margin on final selling price, after additional processing costs. The NRV method does not use data on profits, as does the constant gross margin percentage method. In addition, in some circumstances, this constant gross margin percentage can result in negative allocations of joint costs to some products and allocations to other products larger than the total of joint costs. Exhibit 16.1, Panel C, demonstrates this method.

Although this chapter includes this method for the sake of completeness, no reason exists for preferring it to the NRV method.

(d) PHYSICAL QUANTITIES METHODS. The physical quantities method allocates joint-process costs based on a physical measure of volume, or weight, or other measure of physical characteristics. Consider the effect of this method on allocating the costs of a steer to bones and to steak based on weight. The resulting allocations bear no resemblance to economic amounts, so this method has little theoretical support.

Accountants sometimes use this method when volatile output product prices create uncertain market value after processing, or when significant additional processing of uncertain amounts must occur between the splitoff point and the first point of marketability. This approach may also be appropriate when the market does not set product prices—for example, regulated companies. In regulated industries, where market prices depend on allocated costs, allocating costs based on the regulated market prices would involve circularity.

Return to the Humboldt Company example. Assume that the company does not know market values at the splitoff point, but that it does know that for every $360,000 of joint costs in processing logs, it gets 2,800 board feet of specialty lumber and 3,920 board feet of standard lumber, a total of 6,720 board feet. This method allocates the joint costs, as in Panel D of Exhibit 16.1, in proportions 2,800/6,720 and 3,920/6,720.

(e) BENEFITS RECEIVED METHODS. Imagine an advertising campaign for a company with two products—one well known, with substantial sales, and one brand new in the market with few sales—for example, Starbucks coffee and Starbucks cola or Coca-Cola and Coca-Cola Coffee. Management wishes to allocate to the two products the common cost of the advertising program that promotes the general image of the company, rather than either specific product. Few companies can effectively accomplish this, but managements attempt it anyway.

Firms often use the benefits received criterion in situations that require a cost assignment, but no technically feasible way exists to relate specific causes and specific effects. Consider our advertising program example that promotes the corporation's general image. The firm can allocate the costs of such a program on the basis of product revenue. One could reason that products with higher revenues benefit more from the advertising than products with lower revenues and therefore ought to bear more of the advertising costs.

The benefits received method often arises in government contract accounting. Federal acquisitions regulations cite the benefits received criterion when discussing the costs allocable to a government contract:

A cost (is) allocable if it is assignable or chargeable to one or more cost objectives in accordance with the relative benefits received or other equitable relationship.

Subject to the foregoing a cost is allocable to a government contract if it:

- is incurred specifically for the contract;
- benefits both the contract and other work–and can be distributed to them in reasonable proportion to the benefits received; or it is necessary to the overall operation of the business, although a direct relationship to any particular cost objective cannot be shown.[4]

(f) ABILITY TO BEAR METHOD. The *ability to bear* method operates just as the benefits received method operates, but has a different rationale. Consider the allocation of central corporate overhead to divisions, one profitable and the other not. Some would allocate costs to the divisions in proportion to their profitability before the allocation, with profitability measured in any one of several ways. Allocations based on preallocation profitability are ability to bear methods.

If the only method that seems reasonable for allocating a joint cost is this ability to bear method, one should not allocate those costs at all. This method penalizes a profitable division with more allocated burden and subsidizes less-profitable divisions with fewer allocated costs. This can result in poor business decisions based on meaningless profitability numbers. Likely, nothing useful will result from such an allocation.

(g) DO NOT ALLOCATE JOINT COSTS WITHOUT COMPULSION. Accountants have long known that analysts will never make superior managerial decisions based on data resulting from joint cost allocations than when they base them solely on cause-and-effect or on incremental cost data. That is, if a cost does not result from some cause or incremental effort, then ignore it for decision making. Some managerial decisions require accounting data about joint processes and joint products but never do they require allocations of joint costs, unless regulations or contracts impose the requirement. Consider the following questions that require decisions about joint processes and joint products.

- Should management increase or decrease production of joint products?
- Given that management can change the mix of joint products (consider that the lumber mill might produce more standard lumber at the margin, by producing less specialty lumber), should it?
- Should we sell the joint product just after splitoff, or process it further (the depth-of-processing decision)?
- Has the purchasing department, which acquires raw materials for a variety of functions, been efficient?

None of these decisions requires joint cost allocations, nor will better decisions result from using allocated data.

Many managers believe they need joint cost allocations to derive prices. Economics teaches that markets determine selling prices based on industry-wide costs, not on specific

4. F. Alston, M. Worthington, and L. Goldsman, *Contracting With the Federal Government*, 3rd ed. (New York: Wiley), 1993, p. 136.

costs of specific firms. Some behavioral economists think a firm will generate more customer goodwill if customers believe sellers have based selling prices on costs. At that level, however, the difference in retail prices caused by differences in cost allocation methods likely has no impact on customer morale.

Legislative and administrative regulations of prices do, indeed, require cost allocations, but laws compel these. Net present value of cash flows does not increase from voluntarily allocated joint costs.

Some theorists advocate never giving decision makers data containing joint cost allocations. Others advocate *sterilized allocations,* by which they mean an allocation designed so as not to affect the decision.[5] Sterilized allocations pose problems because no one allocation sterilizes allocations for all decisions—each decision might need a different allocation. This means no single allocation method guarantees to sterilize for all decisions.

16.7   BYPRODUCTS

A byproduct results from a joint process but with small value relative to the joint products. The distinction is one of degree, not a bright line definition. The accountant can apply to byproducts the same accounting methods used for joint products, but because these methods were cumbersome before electronic data processing, accountants devised short-cut methods to deal with byproducts, by definition of low value.

The need to have separate accounting methods for byproducts has declined as electronic data processing has become widespread, so modern textbooks give little detail on methods specific to byproducts. Nurnberg provided the following summary:[6]

> There are two basic approaches to the accounting for by-products. In one, no accounting recognition is given to by-products at the time of production. Rather, accounting recognition is given at the time of sale, when either revenues or revenues less separable costs are recognized as a separate item in the income statement or as a reduction in the cost of the major products. In the other approach, accounting recognition is given to by-products at the time of production by assigning a portion of the joint costs to them at the splitoff point, thereby reducing the costs assigned to the major products.

Nurnberg illustrated eight methods of dealing with byproducts; these methods propose possible combinations of the following two revenue treatments and four reporting treatments. The two revenue treatments are

- Revenue from byproducts sold
- Revenue from products sold, less separable costs of processing and disposal

These revenue treatments can be reported in any of four ways:

- Additional revenue
- Other income
- A deduction from cost of the major products sold
- A deduction from cost of the major products produced

---

5.   This notion originated with Arthur L. Thomas; see his *The Allocation Problem: Part Two,* Studies in Accounting Research No. 9, American Accounting Association, 1974.

6.   Hugo Nurnberg, "Joint Products and By-Products," Chapter 18 in S. Davidson and R.L. Weil, *Handbook of Cost Accounting,* New York: McGraw-Hill, 1978, pp.18–18.

Nurnberg illustrated two additional methods that report either the net realizable value (or net realizable value reduced by a normal profit margin) as a deduction in the cost of the major products produced.

None of these has any theoretical superiority over any of the others, nor to treating byproducts as joint products. To repeat: All the methods produce arbitrary allocations and provide no aid to effective managerial decisions.

16.8 ALLOCATION OF REVENUE

Companies often bundle into a single sale items that they also sell separately. An example pertinent for this writer is the bundling of students' textbooks with accompanying study guides: the publisher sells each separately, or shrink-wraps the two together to sell at a discount. Because companies voluntarily bundle these items, the issues in dealing with the single revenue for a bundle of products resemble the issues of common cost, other than joint cost, allocation.

When all the components of the bundled product have separate selling prices, the allocation of revenue to the individual products can follow the stand-alone methods or the incremental product method.

In the textbook example, assume that the textbook sells for $100, the study guide sells for $40, and the joint, shrink-wrapped package for $112. How should the publisher allocate the $112 revenue to the two separate books? The publisher will need such allocations for royalty purposes, if the authors of the two books have different ownership percentages of the two books.

The stand-alone methods would allocate the $112 revenues in the proportions 100/140 to the text, resulting in $80 (= 100/140 × $112) and 40/140 to the study guide; $32 (= 40/140 × $112). The incremental methods would allocate $100 to the text and $12 (= $112 – $100) to the study guide if, as is likely, it viewed the textbook as the primary product and the study guide as incremental.

(a) THEORY PROVIDES NO RIGHT ANSWER. Which of these methods—stand-alone or incremental—enjoys the strongest theoretical support? That question has no answer. Neither allocation will, better than the other, enable management to make wealth-enhancing decisions. The logic here parallels that for choosing between common cost allocations. If the facts show that one product offers incremental value to the package, then the analysis will result in a unique, cause-and-effect allocation.

If management needs an allocation, and facts do not provide guidance, that need likely results from some contractual provision, such as the need to pay royalties to the authors of the two books. If the authors of the two books have the same interests in both books, then the allocation between the two books does not matter, as amounts paid to each author will be the same, no matter the allocation. If the authors have different interests, then the allocation matters to the authors. Still, theory provides no uniquely right answer. To get a uniquely right answer, one needs to look to the contract that the authors have with the publisher, which will likely not specify a method. In that case, economic theory also does not provide a unique answer.

When the difference matters because the situation involves large dollar amounts, and when the contract does not address the allocation method, the issue likely ends up in litigation. I advise the courts to do what seems equitable to them because neither economics nor accounting offers a single, correct, answer.

(b) BUNDLED LEASE ALLOCATIONS.   Difficulties arise when no readily identifiable, separate market exists for each of the products in the bundle. The Financial Accounting Standards Board (FASB) and the Securities and Exchange Commission (SEC) have required firms to allocate the total revenue to the components.[7]

Consider the modern lease, such as occurs when Xerox leases copying equipment to Motor Company (MC). Assume that Xerox enters into a seven-year lease with MC for a constellation of copying equipment. The lease requires MC to pay to Xerox $14,816.20 at the end of each of the seven years following the date of Xerox's delivering and installing the equipment on MC's premises. The copying equipment cost Xerox $23,000 to manufacture.

- The lease requires that Xerox will provide MC with on-site service and maintenance at no cost additional to the annual payment. Such service contracts ordinarily cost $2,000 per year.

- The lease requires that Xerox will provide MC with all toner and other supplies at no cost additional to the annual payment. Such supply contracts ordinary cost the user $1,200 per year.

- MC ordinarily must pay 15 percent per year, compounded annually to finance, over seven years, borrowings equivalent to that implicit in the lease.

Generally accepted accounting principles require Xerox to unbundle the monthly payment and allocate the amounts to four components: the machine, interest on the lease, supplies, and service/maintenance. Xerox transacts a substantial amount of its business through bundled leases, which because of the bundling, obscures the fair value of the equipment. Furthermore, Xerox's outright (i.e., unbundled) sales of equipment do not provide a practicable basis for making a direct estimate of fair value. Outright sales reflect many combinations of terms and prices, because of the variety of equipment configurations available. Furthermore, these outright sales take place within a wide range of possible prices negotiated between the salesperson and the customer. In addition, Xerox designs its outright sales prices to encourage customers to lease rather than buy, and therefore the prices for unbundled equipment sales do not directly relate to the fair value of the equipment as part of a bundled lease.

Thus, Xerox finds impracticable using outright sales of equipment as a basis for direct estimates of fair value. Because Xerox has difficulty making direct estimates of the equipment element of its bundled leases, the company instead makes direct estimates of the financing element. Xerox estimates the lessee's borrowing rate, then applies this rate to the known cash flow data for its leases for the period to measure the dollar amount of the leases' financing element and the equipment's implied selling price. Exhibit 16.2 illustrates this allocation.

Chapter 31 discusses how the SEC alleged that Xerox manipulated income by manipulating the interest rate, 15 percent in the example, used in the allocation.

---

7.   As this book goes to press, the FASB has this item on its agenda and the operative rules appear in EITF Consensus 00-21, *Revenue Arrangements with Multiple Deliverables,* issued January 2003. *EITF* means the Emerging Issues Task Force, a joint effort of the FASB, AICPA, and SEC. The FASB publishes these pronouncements.

Annual payment = $14,816.12; servicing and supplies total $3,200 per year

Amount allocated to equipment and financing = $14,816.12 - $3,200.00 = $11,616.12

Discount rate = Lessee's borrowing rate = 15 percent per year

Present value of seven annual payments discounted at 15 percent = $48,328

  (See Table 4 at end of the book, seven-period row; 15 percent column where

  factor is 4.16042; $11,616 x 4.16042 = $48,328)

End of Year	Gross Margin on Equipment		Revenue from Servicing	Revenue from Sales of Supplies	Interest Revenue[b]	Book Value of Lease Receivable
						$48,328
1	$25,328	[a]	$ 2,000	$1,200	$ 7,249	43,961
2			2,000	1,200	6,594	38,939
3			2,000	1,200	5,841	33,164
4			2,000	1,200	4,975	26,522
5			2,000	1,200	3,978	18,884
6			2,000	1,200	2,833	10,101
7			2,000	1,200	1,515	(0)
	$25,328 +		$14,000 +	$8,400 +	$32,985 =	$80,713 [c]

Annual
Payment = $14,816.12 $11,616.12   = for machine and interest

        $48,327.93 = Present value of payments for equipment

         23,000.00 = cost of equipment

[a] $25,327.93 = Gross margin on equipment

[b] Amount for year is .15 x book value of lease receivable from end of preceding year

[c] $ 80,713 = Gross margin, service and suppplies

        23,000 = Cost of machine

$ 103,713 = Total cash in

            = 7 x $14,816.12

EXHIBIT 16.2 ALLOCATION OF BUNDLED REVENUE TO FAIR VALUE OF EQUIPMENT AND FINANCING

16.9 FURTHER READING

This chapter has purposefully focused on the underpinnings of allocations and has given only a few examples, none of them detailed. For comprehensive illustrations of some of these methods, refer to cost accounting and managerial accounting textbooks. None, including those by the editors of this book, provides more thorough coverage than those by Horngren, Datar, and Foster.[8]

---

8.   Charles T. Horngren, Srikant M. Datar, and George Foster, *Cost Accounting: A Managerial Emphasis,* (Upper Saddle River, N.J.: Prentice-Hall, 2003), with new editions every three years. Any edition of this text will likely provide useful examples.

APPENDIX **16A**

STEP-DOWN AND RECIPROCAL METHODS FOR ALLOCATING SERVICE DEPARTMENT COSTS[9]

LESLIE ELDENBURG, PHD
University of Arizona

NAOMI SODERSTROM, PHD
University of Colorado, Boulder

Organizations have departments whose sole function is to service other departments within the organization, providing no products or services to customers. Examples include the employee cafeteria, the payroll department, the cleaning staff, and the information technology or computing services department. As part of their cost reporting requirements or preferences, organizations frequently allocate the costs of service departments to final products or processes. This allocation, which is a full cost allocation, ensures that all costs appear somewhere in the costs of goods and services provided to customers.[10] The preferred methods for allocating service department costs to producing departments are the step-down and reciprocal methods. Some regulators require that organizations use one of these.

STEP-DOWN METHOD

The step-down method parallels other cost allocation methods. All methods, one way or another, do the following:

1. Trace all costs as far as practicable.
2. Allocate to all departments (both service and revenue generating) any unallocated costs that apply to all departments—for example, building lease costs.
3. Allocate service department costs to revenue-producing departments.
4. Allocate revenue-producing department costs to products.

---

9.   The authors of this material originally included it in Chapter 28 of this book. The material generalizes to so many cost management contexts, that the editors have moved it from the original chapter and put it here, with other material on allocations.

10.   Other chapters in this book discuss the merits of full costing, and its alternatives. Here we show how to derive full costs, including service department costs; we do not argue that organizations should prefer full costing.

The following provides a simple example of calculations for each of the four steps. This example pertains to a health care setting, but the step-down method could apply to all organizations with service and production departments.

Step 1. Trace all costs as far as practicable.

COSTS BEFORE ALLOCATION (IN THOUSANDS)					
	Maint.	Admin.	Adult Clinic	Children's Clinic	Total
Building lease.....					$ 60
Salaries	$5	$10	$50	$45	$110
Supplies	$4	$ 6	$30	$35	$ 75
SOME POSSIBLE ALLOCATION BASES					
Square feet	400	100	4,500	5,000	10,000
Hours spent	350	650	1,000	3,000	5,000

The accounting system usually traces salary and supply information to each department. Most organizations have recordkeeping systems that gather this information internally. The system cannot trace some costs, such as the building lease, to particular departments but must allocate them to all departments.

Step 2. Allocate to departments any costs not already traced to departments. This step allocates the building lease costs based on each department's square footage.

ALLOCATION OF BUILDING LEASE COST					
	Maint.	Food Admin.	Adult Clinic	Children's Clinic	Total
Square feet......	400	100	4,500	5,000	10,000
	4%	1%	45%	50%	100%
Building lease	$ 2.4	$ .6	$ 27.0	$ 30.0	$ 60.0
Salaries	$ 5.0	$10.0	$ 50.0	$ 45.0	$110.0
Supplies.........	$ 4.0	$ 6.0	$ 30.0	$ 35.0	$ 75.0
Total...........	$11.4	$16.6	$107.0	$110.0	$245.0

After accountants have traced direct costs to each department and allocated common costs to all departments, they allocate service department costs (administration and maintenance in this example) to the revenue-generating departments, adult and children's clinics. A measure of service usage serves as the allocation base. This example uses the number of hours spent in each department to assign administration costs to the clinic, and uses the number of square feet per department to assign maintenance cost.

The step-down method reflects half of the interactions among service departments because each department drops out of the allocation scheme after the procedure has allocated its costs to other departments. The method allocates service department costs in a fixed sequence. Accountants allocate costs of the first service department to *all* other departments. They then allocate the costs of the second service department to all other departments (except the first service department). Once the analysis allocates a service department's costs to other departments, it does not allocate any further costs back to it. The process continues until accountants have allocated all service department costs to revenue-producing departments. Accountants often decide the order in which to allocate service departments by ranking the departments by their direct costs (largest to smallest) or by the amount of service provided to other departments. The analysis begins by allocating costs from the largest department (or the one that services the most other departments), followed by the next largest, and so on until all of the service departments' costs have been allocated.

Step 3. Allocate the service department costs to revenue-generating departments using the step-down method. In this example, administration is the largest department; accountants will allocate its costs first. Once the accountant has allocated the administration's costs, they omit the department from further allocation, so administration does not receive allocated costs from the maintenance department, even though maintenance provides service to the administration department.

	Maint.	Admin.	Adult Clinic	Children's Clinic	Total
Total............	$ 11.4	$ 16.6	$107.0	$110.0	$245.0
Hours spent......	400		4,500	5,000	9,900
	4%		45%	51%	
Admin...........	$ 0.7	$(16.6)	$ 7.4	$ 8.5	
Square feet......			4,500	5,000	9,500
			47%	53%	
Maint.	$(12.1)		$ 5.7	$ 6.4	
Full cost	$ 0.0	$ 0.0	$120.1	$124.9	$245.0

Step 4. To calculate a cost per service, or per patient, the accountant divides the fully allocated cost of each department by the number of services provided, or by the number of patients seen in the clinic over the time period that the organization incurred the costs. In this example, if the adult clinic recorded 5,000 patient visits, then the cost per patient for the adult clinic would equal $120,100/5,000—or $24.02 per patient.

RECIPROCAL METHOD

While the step-down method ignores interactions of the service departments, the *reciprocal* method of allocating costs takes them into consideration. For example, maintenance workers clean the administration area and administration personnel issue payroll checks and provide other services for maintenance workers. In our example, using the step-down method, we allocated administration costs to maintenance, but not vice versa. The reciprocal method recognizes the interactions through use of simultaneous linear equations of the sort taught in high school algebra.

The first two steps are identical to those in the step-down method. The analysis then takes the following steps.

Step 3. Set up simultaneous equations for the interactions among the service departments and solve them.

$$\text{Admin.} = (100/9,600)\text{Maint.} + \$16.6$$

$$\text{Maint.} = (350/4,350)\text{Admin.} + \$11.4$$

Solve these equations using the substitution method (and with rounding).

$$\text{Admin.} = .01(.08\text{Maint.} + \$11.4) + \$16.6$$

$$\text{Admin.} = .0008\text{Maint.} + \$.1 + \$16.6$$

$$.999\text{Admin.} = 16.7$$

$$\text{Admin.} = 16.7/.999 = 16.7$$

Substitute this into the Food Service equation.

$$\text{Maint.} = (.08)(16.7) + 11.4$$

$$\text{Maint.} = 12.7$$

Step 4. Allocate the costs from each service department to all other departments.

	Maint	Admin.	Adult Clinic	Children's Clinic	Total
Total	$ 11.4	$ 16.6	$107.0	$110.0	$245.0
Hours spent	350		1,000	3,000	4,350
	8%		23%	69%	
Admin.	$ 1.3	$(16.7)	$ 3.9	$ 11.5	
Square feet		100	4,500	5,000	9,600
		1%	47%	52%	
Maint.	$(12.7)	$ 0.1	$ 6.0	$ 6.6	
Full cost	$ 0.0	$ 0.0	$116.9	$128.1	$245.0

In this example, the reciprocal method's allocations are quite similar to the step-down method's allocation. As the number of service departments grows, allocated costs will vary more across the revenue-generating departments. The reciprocal method more accurately reflects cause-and-effect of service department costs because it reflects interactions of the service departments. Most spreadsheet programs have functions that will calculate solutions for simultaneous equations. Linear programming software will also perform these calculations.

BIBLIOGRAPHY

Alston, F., Worthington, M., and Goldsman, L. *Contracting With the Federal Government*, 3rd ed. (New York: Wiley), 1993, p. 136.

EITF Consensus 00-21. *Revenue Arrangements with Multiple Deliverables*. Issued January 2003.

Horngren, Charles T., Datar, Srikant M., and Foster, George. *Cost Accounting: A Managerial Emphasis* (Upper Saddle River, N.J.: Prentice-Hall, 2003).

Maher, M.W., Stickney, C.P., and Weil, R.L. *Managerial Accounting: An Introduction to Concepts, Methods, and Uses* (Mason, Ohio: Thomson South-Western, 2006), Chapter 15.

Nurnberg, Hugo. "Joint Products and By-Products." Chapter 18 in S. Davidson and R.L. Weil, *Handbook of Cost Accounting* (New York: McGraw-Hill Publishing Co., 1978), pp.18-18.

Thomas, L. *The Allocation Problem: Part Two*. Studies in Accounting Research No. 9, American Accounting Association, 1974.

FORECASTING PRO FORMA FINANCIAL STATEMENTS*

JAMES M. WAHLEN, PHD
Indiana University

CONTENTS

18.1 INTRODUCTION TO FORECASTING 504

18.2 PREPARING PRO FORMA FINANCIAL STATEMENTS 505

  (a) General Forecasting Principles 505

  (b) Six-Step Forecasting Plan 506

  (c) Practical Tips for Implementing the Six-Step Plan 509

  (d) Introduction to Starbucks: A Comprehensive Example 510

18.3 STEP 1: PROJECTING SALES AND OTHER REVENUES 514

  (a) Projecting Sales 514

  (b) Projecting Other Revenues 517

18.4 STEP 2: PROJECTING OPERATING EXPENSES 518

  (a) Projecting Cost of Sales 518

  (b) Projecting Store Operating Expenses 518

  (c) Projecting Other Operating Expenses 519

18.5 STEP 3: PROJECTING THE ASSETS ON THE BALANCE SHEET 519

  (a) Projecting Individual Assets 521

  (b) Projecting Assets that Vary as a Percent of Total Assets 526

18.6 STEP 4: PROJECTING LIABILITIES AND SHAREHOLDERS' EQUITY 527

  (a) Projecting Liabilities 527

  (b) Projecting Shareholders' Equity 528

18.7 STEP 5: PROJECTING INTEREST EXPENSE, INTEREST INCOME, INCOME TAX EXPENSE, AND THE CHANGE IN RETAINED EARNINGS 529

  (a) Interest Expense 529

  (b) Interest Income 530

  (c) Income Taxes 530

  (d) Net Income 530

  (e) Retained Earnings 530

18.8 BALANCING THE BALANCE SHEET 531

18.9 CLOSING THE LOOP: SOLVING FOR CO-DETERMINED VARIABLES 533

18.10 STEP 6: DERIVING THE STATEMENT OF CASH FLOWS 534

18.11 SHORTCUT APPROACHES TO FORECASTING 536

18.12 ANALYZING PRO FORMA FINANCIAL STATEMENTS 536

18.13 SENSITIVITY ANALYSIS AND STRATEGIC PLANNING 537

18.14 SUMMARY 537

---

* This chapter reflects many of the ideas developed in Chapter 10 of *Financial Reporting and Statement Analysis: A Strategic Perspective*, by Clyde Stickney, Paul Brown, and James Wahlen, Thomson International Southwestern Publishing, 5th edition. The interested reader should refer to that text for more complete discussion of pro forma financial statement forecasting in the context of financial statement analysis and equity valuation.

18.1   INTRODUCTION TO FORECASTING

This chapter discusses accounting for the future. Analysts use forecasting to develop a set of realistic expectations for the outcomes of future business activities. To capture these expectations, analysts use a set of forecasts referred to as *pro forma financial statements*.[1] Pro forma forecasts of financial statements–expected future income statements, balance sheets, and cash flow statements–present an integrated, articulated portrayal of the results of the firm's future operating, investing, and financing activities. These activities will determine the firm's future growth, profitability, cash flows, financial position, and risk. Using a forecasted set of financial statements, management aims to capture expectations for *all* of the factors that will determine the firm's future value-relevant payoffs to stakeholders.

Pro forma financial statements provide important analytic tools for managers and analysts because forecasts of future payoffs play a central role in valuation and other financial decision contexts. A firm's share value depends on its expected future payoffs to equity stakeholders, discounted for time and risk. Using a set of financial statement forecasts, the analyst can derive the future value-relevant payoffs to equity shareholders–earnings, cash flows, and dividends–which provide the fundamental bases for equity share value. Credit decisions require expectations for future cash flows available to make required future interest and principal payments. Managers' decisions about firm strategy, potential customer or supplier relations, potential mergers or acquisitions, potential carve-outs of divisions or subsidiaries, and even whether a firm presents a good employment opportunity, depend on their expected future payoffs and the risks of those payoffs.

Developing forecasts of future payoffs poses difficulties because one must estimate the effects of the activities that one expects to occur in the future, an analysis that involves uncertainty. Forecast errors can prove costly. Optimistic forecasts of future earnings and cash flows can lead the manager to overestimate a firm's value, and therefore make poor decisions based on an inflated value of the firm. On the other hand, conservative forecasts can lead the manager to understate a firm's future earnings and cash flows, missing valuable investment opportunities. Forecasters need to develop *realistic* (unbiased and objective–not optimistic nor conservative) expectations of future earnings and cash flows that lead to informed decisions.

To develop reliable forecasts that form the bases for sound decision-making, managers and analysts should draw upon all of their knowledge of the business to project the future. Developing forecasts draws upon the disciplines of accounting, finance, economics, and strategy. The analyst should base pro forma financial statements on expectations that reflect the economics of the industry, the competitive advantages and risks of the firm's strategy, the quality of the firm's accounting, and the drivers of the firm's profitability, growth, and risk. These elements provide the necessary foundations for forecasting, and they inform the analyst about the firm's critical risk and success factors. The same critical factors that serve as the focal points for the firm's strategy, growth, profitability, and risk become the focal points for forecasting pro forma financial statements.

This chapter first outlines a set of six steps for forecasting pro forma financial statements. The chapter then illustrates each of the steps by applying them to Starbucks, developing detailed pro forma financial statements for each of the three primary financial

---

1.   Throughout this chapter, we use the term *pro forma financial statements* to denote the expected future income statements, balance sheets, and statements of cash flows that capture the analyst's forecasts of the firm's future operating, investing, and financing activities.

statements. The chapter also describes a set of techniques to enhance the reliability of forecasts, including sensitivity analysis, iteration, and validity checks. The chapter also discusses some simplifying steps for shortcut forecasts based on time-series projections of sales, future earnings, and cash flows, and the conditions under which such shortcuts will not create forecast errors.

18.2 PREPARING PRO FORMA FINANCIAL STATEMENTS

Preparing a set of pro forma financial statements requires that an analyst consider numerous assumptions and relations. We suggest that one establish at the outset a flow, or a sequence of steps, to project the three principal financial statements (cash flow statement, balance sheet and income statement). One should implement these steps while following several general but important principles. This section offers a set of such principles, describes a six-step forecasting plan, and then concludes with several practical coaching tips on implementing the six-step sequence.

(a) GENERAL FORECASTING PRINCIPLES. Several key principles of forecasting deserve mention.

First, the objective of forecasting is to produce objective and realistic expectations of the future business activities. To maximize forecast reliability and minimize costly forecast errors, pro forma financial statements should provide unbiased predictions of the firm's future operating, investing, and financing activities, and should be neither conservative nor optimistic.

Second, pro forma financial statements should be comprehensive. The pro forma financial statements should include *all* expected future operating, investing, and financing activities to ensure complete forecasts. For example, suppose an analyst forecasts expected future sales growth and then simply projects expected future earnings assuming a constant profit margin on sales. This approach fails to consider all of the elements that determine profitability from sales, and leads to incomplete earnings forecasts. By assuming a constant profit margin on sales, one would ignore whether selling, general, and administrative (SG&A) expenses will increase more slowly than sales growth because of economies of scale or scope.

Third, pro forma financial statements must have internally consistent assumptions and relations. Pro forma financial statements should rely on the *additivity* within financial statements and the *articulation* across financial statements to avoid internal inconsistencies in forecasts. The analyst can rely on the internal discipline of accounting across the three primary financial statements to reduce the possibility of errors from internally inconsistent assumptions. For example, sales growth forecasts will likely drive forecasts of growth in related elements of the financial statements, including future costs of sales, inventory, accounts receivable, and property, plant, and equipment. In turn, forecasts of future growth in inventory, receivables, and property, plant, and equipment will likely affect growth in related elements, including accounts payable, depreciation, short-term and long-term borrowing, interest expense, and owners' equity issues. Each of these elements will, in turn, have implications for the firm's cash flows. To capture the complex relations among operating, investing, and financing activities, pro forma financial statements should add up and should articulate with each other. The balance sheet should reflect all of the elements of financial position and should balance; the income statement should reflect all of the revenues, expenses, gains, and losses each period; the statement of cash flows should reflect all of the cash inflows and outflows implied by the income statement and the changes in the firm's balance sheet.

Fourth, pro forma financial statements must have externally valid assumptions. Forecast assumptions should pass the tests of common sense and reality checks. For example, do the sales growth forecast assumptions reflect the competitive conditions in the industry, including market demand and price elasticity for the firm's products? Analysts should ensure that the assumptions in the pro forma financial statements reflect the past as well as plans and capabilities for the future. In addition, analysts should avoid building forecasts based on wishful thinking. That is, analysts should not create forecasts based on what they hope the firm will do, nor on what they think the firm should do, but instead the forecasts should capture what the analyst believes the firm actually can and will do in the future.

(b) SIX-STEP FORECASTING PLAN.   To prepare a set of pro forma financial statements, analysts should organize the numerous assumptions and relations that they will use into operating, investing, and financing activities. This *activity-based forecasting* perspective enables analysts to identify the necessary sequence of steps to project the three principal financial statements. The particular sequence of steps may vary, depending on the reason for preparing the pro forma financial statements. For most forecasts, this six-step sequence works well:

Step 1. Project revenues from sales and other revenue-generating activities.

Step 2. Project operating expenses (for example, cost of goods sold and SG&A expenses) and derive projected operating income (income before interest expense, interest income, and income taxes).

Step 3. Project the operating assets and liabilities (for example, cash, inventory, receivables, property, plant, and equipment, accounts payable, accrued expenses) necessary to support the level of operations projected in steps 1 and 2.

Step 4. Project the funding structure (for example, short-term and long-term borrowing, short-term and long-term investments in financial assets, and shareholders' equity except for retained earnings) necessary to support the level of operations projected in step 3.

Step 5. Calculate the cost of financing the funding structure projected in step 4.

   a. From projected operating income from step 2, subtract interest expense on short-term and long-term borrowing and add interest income on short-term and long-term financial asset investments to derive projected income before tax.

   b. Subtract projected income tax to derive projected net income.

   c. Subtract expected dividends from net income to obtain the projected change in retained earnings.

   d. At this point, check to ensure that the projected balance sheets are in balance. If they do not balance, the projected financial structure may need adjustments (for example, the firm may need additional financing), and analysts will need to repeat steps 4 and 5 until the balance sheet balances.

Step 6. Derive the statement of cash flows from the projected income statements and balance sheets.

Exhibit 18.1 summarizes this six-step procedure.

Statement of Income and Retained Earnings | | **Balance Sheet** |
		Assets	**Liabilities and Shareholder's Equity**
Revenues ⇦ **STEP 1: Project Operating Revenues**		Cash	Accounts Payable
+ Sales Revenue		Accounts Receivable	Accrued Expenses
+ Other Operating Revenues		Inventories	
		Other Current Assets	
		Property, Plant and Equipment	
Operating Expenses: ⇦ **STEP 2: Project Operating Expenses**			
− Cost of Goods Sold			
− Selling, General and Administrative Expenses	**STEP 3: Project Operating Assets and Liabilities** ⇧		
Operating Income			
	STEP 4: Project Financial Capital Structure ⇧	Short-term and Long-term Investment Securities	Short-term and Long-term Borrowing
− Interest Expense			Contributed Equity Capital
+ Interest Income			Retained Earnings
− Income Taxes	**STEP 5: Project Interest Expense, Interest Income, Income Taxes, Net Income, Dividends, and the Change in Retained Earnings** ⇧		
Net Income			
− Dividends			
Change in Retained Earnings			
		Total Assets =	**Total Liabilities and Shareholders' Equity**

EXHIBIT **18.1** PREPARING PRO FORMA FINANCIAL STATEMENTS

STEP 6: Project Cash Flows from Operating, Investing and Financing Activities		
Statement of Cash Flows		
Operations	Investing Activities	Financing Activities
Net Income	Net Capital Expenditures on Property, Plant and Equipment	Change in Short-term and Long-term Borrowing
Depreciation Expense		Issue or Repurchase of Common Equity
Other Adjustments	Purchase or Sale of Short-term and Long-term Investment Securities	Dividends
Change in Receivables		Other Financing Transactions
Change in Inventories	Other Investing Transactions	CASH FLOW FROM FINANCING
Change in Other Current Assets	CASH FLOW FROM INVESTING	
Change in Accounts Payable		
Change in Accrued Expenses		
CASH FLOW FROM OPERATIONS		

EXHIBIT 18.1 PREPARING PRO FORMA FINANCIAL STATEMENTS (CONTINUED)

(c) PRACTICAL TIPS FOR IMPLEMENTING THE SIX-STEP PLAN. We suggest several practical tips on implementing the six-step sequence. *Analysts should consider these six steps as integrated and interdependent tasks, not necessarily sequential or linear.* The order in which an analyst implements these six steps and the amount of emphasis placed on each step will depend on the integration of the firm's operating, investing, and financing activities. For example, forecasts of revenues for a retail chain or restaurant chain may first require forecasts of the number of new stores that will open. The sales forecasts for a manufacturer may depend on building a new productive plant, which may depend on obtaining additional long-term debt financing.

The amounts on the three pro forma financial statements must articulate. For example, the change in retained earnings should include net income minus dividends. The change in accumulated depreciation on the balance sheet should reflect depreciation expense on the income statement. The change in the property, plant, and equipment amounts on the balance sheet should incorporate the effects of any capital expenditures, and the statement of cash flows should add the amount of depreciation expense (a non-cash expense) back to net income, and subtract capital expenditures. The net cash flow on the statement of cash flows must agree with the change in the cash balance on the balance sheet.

Preparing pro forma statements requires at least one flexible financial account, and an iterative and circular process. Firms rely on flexible accounts–usually financial assets and liabilities–to expand and contract with the firm's need for capital. For example, a firm that needs to finance growth in assets may need to increase short-term or long-term borrowing, or reduce investments in short-term or long-term financial assets, or issue equity shares. A firm that generates excess cash may deploy that cash by paying down debt, or investing in financial assets, or paying dividends, or repurchasing its own shares. Therefore, the analyst should adjust flexible financial accounts as necessary to appropriately match the firm's future financial structure with the firm's future operations. Thus, the process of producing a set of pro forma financial statements will require several iterations and a degree of circularity. For example, the first pass through a set of pro forma financial statements may reveal to the analyst a need to increase borrowing to finance future expenditures and to make the balance sheet balance. Increased borrowing, however, will require the analyst to increase interest expense to reflect the cost of the additional debt capital, which in turn means that income taxes will fall and net income will fall. As a consequence, retained earnings will fall, which means the analyst may have to increase borrowing a bit more. The analyst will repeat the process until the balance sheet balances and it articulates with the income statement and the statement of cash flows.[2]

The quality of the pro forma financial statements, and therefore the quality of the decisions based on those statements, will not exceed the quality of the forecast assumptions. Less technically: garbage-in, garbage-out. The analyst should justify each assumption, especially the most important assumptions that reflect the critical risk and success factors of the firm's strategy. In addition, the analyst can impose reality checks on the assumptions by analyzing ratios and common-size financial statements (which express income statement amounts as a percent of revenues and balance sheet amounts as a percent of total assets) using the pro forma financial statements. These analytical tools may identify certain assumptions as unrealistic or inconsistent with one another.

---

2. Most computer spreadsheet software packages facilitate iterative and circular processes. For example, in *Excel*, under the Tools/Options/Calculation menu, one can check the Iteration box to set the spreadsheet to automatically compute iteratively (for example, 100 times) until the iterated computations converge to a specified maximum change.

Analysts should conduct sensitivity analyses on the pro forma financial statements. The analyst should assess, for example, the extent to which earnings will vary across different sales growth scenarios (for example, comparing across different growth rate assumptions that reflect most likely, optimistic, and pessimistic forecasts). Some of the assumptions will have bigger consequences than others, and sensitivity analyses will help the analyst assess the extent to which pro forma forecast results depend on key assumptions.

(d) INTRODUCTION TO STARBUCKS: A COMPREHENSIVE EXAMPLE. The subsequent sections of this chapter illustrate the six-step procedure described above by using the analysis of Starbucks' financial statements through 2003, referred to in the exhibits as "Year 13." Starbucks is the leading U.S. retail chain of premium coffee shops. Starbucks successfully developed and expanded a European idea–enjoying a coffee-based beverage, and sharing that experience with others in a comfortable, friendly environment. The Starbucks 2003 Annual Report refers to this as the *Starbucks Experience.*

Starbucks has grown from just a single store near Pike's Place Market in Seattle to a global company with 7,225 locations worldwide at the end of 2003. In 2003 alone, Starbucks opened 1,201 new retail locations; Starbucks owns and operates 602 of these locations, and licenses the remaining 599 to others.[3] Most of Starbucks' retail stores (5,201 stores) at the end of 2003 are in the United States, amounting to one Starbucks retail location for approximately every 50,000 U.S. residents.[4] Starbucks does not want to focus only on the U.S. market, however, and has plans to expand globally, with already more than 2,000 stores outside of the United States.

To further expand the business model, Starbucks also has a licensing agreement with Kraft Foods to market and distribute Starbucks' whole bean and ground coffee throughout the United States in approximately 19,500 grocery and warehouse club stores. Furthermore, Starbucks sells whole bean and ground coffee through institutional foodservice companies (such as SYSCO Corporation) that service business, education, office, hotel, restaurant, airline and other foodservice accounts.

Exhibit 18.2 presents the financial statements for Starbucks for Years 11 to 13. Exhibit 18.2 also presents Starbucks' financial statement data in common-size format and in rate of change format.[5] This chapter analyzes these financial statement data to develop forecast assumptions and to compute pro forma financial statements for Starbucks for Year 14 to Year 18, which we label Year +1 to Year +5 to denote that they are forecasts, rather than actual statements.[6]

---

3.   In addition, in 2003 Starbucks acquired 64 company-owned stores and 74 licensed stores in an acquisition of Seattle's Best Coffee Co.

4.   By comparison, in year 13 there is one Subway sandwich shop for approximately every 19,000 U.S. residents, and one McDonalds restaurant for approximately every 21,000 U.S. residents.

5.   Common size income statements present all income statement items scaled as a percent of sales, while common size balance sheets present all balance sheet items scaled as a percent of total assets. Rate of change financial statements present all items on the financial statements expressed as a percent of growth relative to the prior year. The compound rate of change is the compound growth rate in each financial statement item over the relevant period.

6.   A spreadsheet program (like Microsoft *Excel*) is a useful computational tool for preparing pro forma financial statements. The proper design and the preparation of a spreadsheet for pro forma financial statements provide an excellent learning process to enhance and solidify understanding of the relationships between various financial statement items. Once you become comfortable with pro forma financial statements and spreadsheets, then using the forecast spreadsheets will save considerable time when preparing forecasts in the future.

STARBUCKS: CONSOLIDATED STATEMENTS OF INCOME:
FISCAL YEARS 11–13

	Amounts in Millions			Common-Sized			Rates of Change		
	11	12	13	11	12	13	12	13	Compound
Retail	$2,229.6	$2,792.9	$3,449.6	84.2%	84.9%	84.6%	25.3%	23.5%	24.4%
Specialty	419.4	496.0	625.9	15.8	15.1	15.4	18.3	26.2	22.2
Net Revenues	$2,649.0	$3,288.9	$4,075.5	100.0%	100.0%	100.0%	24.2%	23.9%	24.0%
Cost of Sales (including occupancy)	1,112.8	1,350.0	1,685.9	42.0	41.0	41.4	21.3	24.9	23.1
Gross Profit	$1,536.2	$1,938.9	$2,389.6	58.0%	59.0%	58.6%	26.2%	23.2%	24.7%
Store Operating Expenses	868.0	1,109.8	1,379.6	32.8	33.7	33.9	27.9	24.3	26.1
Other Operating Expenses	72.4	106.1	141.3	2.7	3.2	3.5	46.5	33.2	39.7
Depreciation and Amortization	163.5	205.6	237.8	6.2	6.3	5.8	25.7	15.7	20.6
General and Administrative Expenses	179.9	234.6	244.6	6.8	7.1	6.0	30.4	4.2	16.6
Income from Equity Investees	27.7	33.4	38.4	1.0	1.0	0.9	20.6	14.8	17.6
Operating Income	$ 280.2	$ 316.3	$ 424.7	10.6%	9.6%	10.4%	12.9%	34.3%	23.1%
Interest and Other Income, Net	10.8	9.3	11.6	0.4	0.3	0.3	-13.6	25.0	3.9
Other Gains (Losses)	(2.9)	13.4	—	(0.1)	0.4	0.0	(554.5)	na	(100.0)
Income Before Income Taxes	288.0	339.0	436.3	10.9	10.3	10.7	17.7	28.7	23.1
Provision for Income Taxes	107.7	126.3	168.0	4.1	3.8	4.1	17.3	33.0	24.9
Net Income	$ 180.3	$ 212.7	$ 268.3	6.8%	6.5%	6.6%	17.9%	26.2%	22.0%

EXHIBIT **18.2** STARBUCKS FINANCIAL STATEMENTS FROM YEAR 11 TO 13

STARBUCKS: CONSOLIDATED BALANCE SHEETS:
FISCAL YEARS 11–13

	Amounts in Millions			Common-Sized			Rates of Change		
	11	12	13	11	12	13	12	13	Compound
Current Assets									
Cash and Equivalents	$ 113.2	$ 99.7	$ 200.9	6.1%	4.5%	7.4%	(12.0)%	101.6%	33.2%
Short-Term Investments	107.3	227.7	149.1	5.8	10.3	5.5	112.1	(34.5)	17.9
Receivables	90.4	97.6	114.4	4.9	4.4	4.2	7.9	17.3	12.5
Inventories	221.3	263.2	342.9	12.0	11.9	12.6	18.9	30.3	24.5
Prepaid Expenses and Other Assets	29.8	42.4	55.2	1.6	1.9	2.0	42.0	30.3	36.0
Deferred Income Taxes, net	31.9	42.2	61.5	1.7	1.9	2.3	32.4	45.6	38.9
Total Current Assets	$ 593.9	772.6	924.0	32.2%	34.9%	33.9%	30.1%	19.6%	11.7%
Long-term Investments	–	–	$ 136.2	0.0%	0.0%	5.0%	na	na	na
Equity and Other Investments	$ 63.1	$ 102.5	144.3	3.4	4.6%	5.3%	62.5%	40.7%	51.2%
Property and Equipment, Gross	1,741.0	2,080.2	2,434.7	94.3	93.9	89.2	19.5	17.0	18.3
Accumulated Depreciation	(605.2)	(814.4)	(1,049.8)	(32.8)	(36.8)	(38.5)	34.6	28.9	31.7
Property and Equipment, Net	$1,135.8	$1,265.8	$1,384.9	61.5%	57.2%	50.7%	11.4%	9.4%	10.4%
Other Assets and Goodwill	53.7	73.5	140.4	2.9	3.3	5.1	36.8	91.1	61.7
Total Assets	$1,846.5	$2,214.4	$2,729.7	100.0%	100.0%	100.0%	19.9%	23.3%	21.6%

EXHIBIT 18.2 STARBUCKS FINANCIAL STATEMENTS FROM YEAR 11 TO 13 (CONTINUED)

STARBUCKS: CONSOLIDATED BALANCE SHEETS:
FISCAL YEARS 11–13

	Amounts in Millions			Common-Sized			Rates of Change		
	11	12	13	11	12	13	12	13	Compound
Current Liabilities									
Accounts Payable	$ 127.9	$ 136.0	$ 169.0	6.9%	6.1%	6.2%	6.3%	24.3%	14.9%
Accrued Expenses	157.4	229.4	310.6	8.5	10.4	11.4	45.7	35.4	40.5
Accrued Taxes	70.3	54.2	54.9	3.8	2.4	2.0	(22.9)	1.3	(11.6)
Deferred Revenue	26.9	42.3	73.5	1.5	1.9	2.7	57.0	73.9	65.2
Current Portion of Long-Term Debt	62.7	0.7	0.7	3.4	0.0	0.0	(98.9)	1.7	(89.3)
Total Current Liabilities	$ 445.3	$ 462.6	608.7	24.1%	20.9%	22.3%	3.9%	31.6%	16.9%
Deferred Income Taxes, net	19.5	23.5	34.2	1.1	1.1	1.3	20.4	45.6	32.4
Long-Term Debt	5.8	5.1	4.4	0.3	0.2	0.2	(12.3)	(14.2)	(13.3)
Total Liabilities	$ 470.6	$ 491.2	647.3	25.5%	22.2%	23.7%	4.4%	31.8%	17.3%
Shareholders' Equity									
Common Stock	791.6	930.4	998.5	42.9%	42.0%	36.6%	17.5%	7.3%	12.3%
Retained Earnings	589.7	801.3	1,069.7	31.9	36.2	39.2	35.9	33.5	34.7
Accumulated Other Comp. Income/(Loss)	(5.4)	(8.6)	14.2	(0.3)	(0.4)	0.5	58.7	(266.0)	na
Total Shareholders' Equity	$1,375.9	1,723.2	2,082.4	74.5%	77.8%	76.3%	25.2%	20.8%	23.0%
Total Liabilities and Shareholders' Equity	$1,846.5	2,214.4	2,729.7	100.0%	100.0%	100.0%	19.9%	23.3%	21.6%

EXHIBIT 18.2 STARBUCKS FINANCIAL STATEMENTS FROM YEAR 11 TO 13 (CONTINUED)

All financial statement amounts throughout this chapter appear in millions. The spreadsheets make all computations to multiple decimal places. Because we report all dollar amounts in this chapter in millions, some minor rounding differences will occasionally arise and make it appear that various subtotals and totals disagree with the sum of the individual items that comprise the subtotal or total.

18.3   STEP 1: PROJECTING SALES AND OTHER REVENUES

(a) PROJECTING SALES.   One must first project revenues from the principal business activities of the firm, which often involve sales of products or services. The expected level of revenues can serve as a basis for deriving many of the other amounts in the pro forma financial statements.

Sales volumes and prices determine sales numbers. In the case of sales *volume*, some firms (e.g., automobile manufacturing and beverages firms) report sales volume figures, enabling the analyst to assess separately volume and price as drivers of historical sales growth, and to use them as a framework for predicting future sales. Other firms report volume-related measures of operating activities that the analyst can use to forecast sales, such as new stores for retailers and restaurant chains, and passengers and passenger-seat-miles for airlines. A firm in a mature industry (for example, consumer foods) with little expected change in its market share might anticipate volume increases equal to the growth rate in the population within its geographic markets. A firm that has increased its operating capacity consistent with the high growth rate anticipated in a particular industry (for example, biotechnology or computer software) might use this expected growth rate when projecting volume increases.

When projecting *prices,* one must consider the expected rate of general price inflation in the economy, and the effects of changes in foreign currency exchange rates on sales denominated in foreign currencies. One must also consider factors specific to the firm and its industry that might affect demand and price elasticity, such as excess capacity, shortages of raw materials, substitute products, technological changes in products or production methods, and similar factors. Capital-intensive firms, such as paper manufacturers, may require several years to add new capacity. If a firm competes in a capital-intensive industry that analysts expect to operate near capacity for the next few years, then price increases will likely occur. On the other hand, if a firm competes in an industry in which excess capacity already exists or new capacity will become available soon, then price increases seem less likely. A firm in transition from the high growth to the maturity phase of its life cycle, or a firm that plans technological improvements in its production processes (e.g., some portions of the computer industry) might expect increases in sales volume but decreases in sales prices per unit. If a firm has established a competitive position for its brand name in its markets, or has successfully differentiated unique characteristics for its products, then that firm may have a greater potential to increase prices, or to avoid price declines, than another firm with generic products.

If sales have grown at a reasonably steady rate in prior periods and nothing indicates that economic, industry, or firm-specific factors will change significantly, then the analyst can project this growth rate into the future. If a major acquisition or divestiture affected the historical growth rate, then the analyst should remove the effect of this event when making projections (unless the firm's strategy includes additional future acquisitions). Projecting sales for firms with cyclical sales patterns (for example, heavy machinery, property-casualty insurance, investment banking) can prove difficult. Their historical growth rates for sales might reflect wide variations in both direction and amount from year to year. The analyst can project a varying growth rate that maintains this cyclical sales pattern in these cases.

(i) Starbucks Sales Growth. Starbucks competes in the fast food chain industry through its chain of coffee shops, and in the consumer foods industry through its sales of coffee beans and ground coffee in grocery stores and foodservice accounts. One would characterize both of these industries in the United States as mature and competitive. In consumer foods, for example, industry sales have grown recently at the growth rate for the general population, approximately 2 percent per year.

Starbucks has defied the characteristics of firms in mature industries, generating an average compounded sales growth rate of 24.0 percent between 1999 and 2003 (Year 9 and Year 13 in the exhibits). Total sales and sales growth rates for Starbucks appear in Exhibit 18.3.

Starbucks discloses information about sales and operating profits for its two major operating segments, Retail and Specialty. The Retail segment includes retail sales of coffee beverages and related products through Starbucks' U.S. and international company owned and operated stores. The Specialty segment includes revenues from licenses of Starbucks stores and related sales of product to store licensees, as well as revenues from product sales through its distributorship arrangements, such as with Kraft (grocery stores and warehouse clubs) and SYSCO (foodservice accounts). Starbucks discloses information about new store openings and comparable store sales, two key drivers of their sales growth in both the Retail and Specialty segments. Net sales amounts, growth rates, new store openings, and growth rates by segment for Starbucks appear in Exhibit 18.4. By analyzing these sales growth data, an analyst can develop more detailed and accurate sales forecasts for each segment.

(ii) Retail Sales Forecasts. The Retail segment, Starbucks' largest segment generating roughly 85 percent of total sales, experienced a compound sales growth rate of 24.2 percent between Years 11 and 13, driven largely by increases in new company-operated stores each year (roughly 600 new stores per year) coupled with modest increases in sales per average store-year (averaging roughly 4.0 percent). The modest increase in average sales per store-year likely reflects the relatively mature price-competitive coffee market, and the fact that Starbucks already charges premium prices for its coffee beverages. An analyst might expect that sales growth per average store-year will continue at 4.0 percent per year into the future, and that Starbucks will continue to open roughly 600 company-operated stores per year. If these projections hold, then Exhibit 18.5 shows the Retail segment sales forecasts for Years +1 to +5 (in millions).

(iii) Specialty Sales Forecast. Starbucks' Specialty segment accounted for roughly 15 percent of total sales, and experienced a compound sales growth rate of 22.2 percent

	Year 11	Year 12	Year 13
Total Sales.	$2,649.0	$3,288.9	$4,075.5
Growth rates		+24.2%	+23.9%
Compound growth rate			+24.0%

EXHIBIT 18.3 TOTAL SALES AND GROWTH RATES (IN MILLIONS)

	Year 11	Year 12	Year 13
Retail Segment Sales (millions)..................	$2,229.6	$2,792.9	$3,449.6
Percent of total sales.............................	84.2%	84.9%	84.6%
Growth rates.....................................		+25.3%	+23.5%
Compound growth rate...........................			+24.4%
Total company-operated stores....................	3,266	3,880	4,546
Net new stores opened during year.................	647	614	666
Growth rate in company-operated stores	+24.7%	+18.8%	+17.2%
Sales per average store-year (in thousands)	$ 757.8	781.7	818.8
Sales growth rates per average store-year...........		+3.2%	+4.7%
Specialty Segment	$ 419.4	$ 496.0	$ 625.9
Percent of total sales.............................	15.8%	15.1%	15.4%
Growth rates.....................................		+18.3%	+26.2%
Compound growth rate...........................			+22.2%
Specialty revenue components:			
Other revenue...................................	$ 272.6	$ 313.8	$ 369.1
Growth rate in other revenues......................		+15.1%	+17.6%
License revenue.................................	$ 146.8	$ 182.2	$ 256.8
Growth rate in license revenues		+24.1%	+40.9%
Total licensed stores	1,443	2,006	2,679
Net new licensed stores opened during year..........	561	563	599
Growth rate in licensed stores.....................	+63.6%	+39.0%	+33.5%
Revenue per average store-year (in thousands)........	$ 126.3	$ 105.7	$ 109.6
Revenue growth rates per average licensed store-year ...		−16.5%	+3.7%

EXHIBIT 18.4   STARBUCKS SALES GROWTH ANALYSIS BY SEGMENT (IN MILLIONS)

Year	New Stores	Total Stores at Year End	Average Store-Years (a)	Sales per Average Store-Year (b)	Total Retail Sales (c = a × b)	Expected Growth Rate
13 (actual)		4,546	4,213	$0.8188	$3,449.6	
+1 (forecast) ..	+600	5,146	4,846	0.8516	4,126.9	+19.6%
+2 (forecast) ..	+600	5,746	5,446	0.8856	4,823.0	+16.9%
+3 (forecast) ..	+600	6,346	6,046	0.9210	5,568.4	+15.5%
+4 (forecast) ..	+600	6,946	6,646	0.9579	6,366.2	+14.3%
+5 (forecast) ..	+600	7,546	7,246	0.9962	7,218.5	+13.4%

EXHIBIT 18.5   RETAIL SALES FORECASTS (IN MILLIONS)

between Years 11 and 13. Starbucks discloses that the largest share of Specialty sales arises from sales of Starbucks products through distributorships. These sales have grown at a compounded rate of roughly 16 percent per year over Years 11 to 13. An analyst might expect that these sales will continue to grow at double-digit rates (assume 12 percent growth on average) for the next five years. The other main contributor to

Starbucks' Specialty sales comes from license revenues. License revenues grow, in part, with Starbucks licensing new stores in the United States and around the world. Over Years 11 to 13, Starbucks licensed between 560 and 600 new stores a year. An analyst might expect Starbucks' to license roughly 600 new stores a year over the next five years, and that average revenues from license stores will grow at 3.0 percent per year, based on worldwide inflation and population growth. Exhibit 18.6 shows sales forecasts for the Specialty segment over the next five years (in millions).

(iv) Combined Sales Growth. Combining both sets of sales forecasts for these segments, we assume that Starbucks will generate sales growth of 19.7 percent in Year +1, and continue to generate double-digit sales growth through Year +5 (see Exhibit 18.7).

(b) PROJECTING OTHER REVENUES. Other revenues for Starbucks primarily include earnings from unconsolidated equity-method affiliates (reported as Income from Equity Investees on Starbucks' 2003 [Year 13] income statement). This source of income has grown steadily for Starbucks in recent year:14.8 percent growth in year 13. For simplicity, we project Income from Equity Investees will continue to grow at 14.0 percent per year in the future. To be consistent, when we forecast the balance sheet we will forecast that Starbucks' investments in equity affiliates will also grow at a 14.0 percent annual rate. Together, these assumptions imply Starbucks will earn a constant average rate of return from its unconsolidated equity method subsidiaries.

	Other Revenues			License Revenues					
Year	Growth Rates	Amount (a)	New Stores	Stores at Year End	Avg. Store-Years (b)	Revenue per Avg. Store-Year (c)	Amount (d = b × c)	Total Specialty Revenue (e = a + d)	Growth Rate
13 actual		$369.1		2,679	2,343	$0.1096	$256.8	$625.9	
+1 forecast	+12%	413.4	+600	3,279	2,979	0.1129	336.3	749.7	+19.8%
+2 forecast	+12%	463.0	+600	3,879	3,579	0.1163	416.3	879.3	+17.3%
+3 forecast	+12%	518.6	+600	4,479	4,179	0.1198	500.7	1,019.3	+15.9%
+4 forecast	+12%	580.9	+600	5,079	4,779	0.1234	589.7	1,170.6	+14.8%
+5 forecast	+12%	650.5	+600	5,679	5,379	0.1271	683.7	1,334.2	+14.0%

EXHIBIT 18.6 SPECIALTY SALES FORECASTS (IN MILLIONS)

Year	Total Retail Sales	Total Specialty Revenues	Total Revenues	Expected Growth Rate
13 (actual)......	$3,449.6	$ 625.9	$4,075.5	
+1 (forecast)....	4,126.9	749.7	4,876.6	+19.7%
+2 (forecast)....	4,823.0	879.3	5,702.3	+16.9%
+3 (forecast)....	5,568.4	1,019.3	6,587.7	+15.5%
+4 (forecast)....	6,366.2	1,170.6	7,536.8	+14.4%
+5 (forecast)....	7,218.5	1,334.2	8,552.7	+13.5%

EXHIBIT 18.7 COMBINED SALES GROWTH (IN MILLIONS)

18.4   STEP 2: PROJECTING OPERATING EXPENSES

The procedure for projecting operating expenses depends on the degree to which the various operating expense items have fixed or variable components. If certain operating expenses behave as variable costs and the analyst anticipates no changes in their behavior relative to sales, then the analyst can project those future operating expenses by multiplying the sales forecast by the appropriate common-size income statement percentages, as from Exhibit 18.2. Equivalently, we can project those operating expenses to grow at the same rate as sales.

Alternatively, if the cost structure contains certain expenses with fixed-cost components that will not change (or will change relatively slowly) as sales increase (that is, the firm experiences economies of scale), then using the common size income statement approach described above can result in excessive expense projections. In this case, the analyst should estimate the firm's variable and fixed cost structure. Capital-intensive firms often have high proportions of fixed costs in their cost structures. When the percentage change in cost of goods sold or selling and administrative expenses in prior years is significantly less than the percentage change in sales, one can assume the presence of fixed costs. Using the historical growth rates for individual cost items presents one way of reflecting the effects of different mixes of variable and fixed costs.

When projecting operating expenses using projections as a percent of sales, the analyst should remember that an expense as a percent of sales can change over time as: (a) expenses change, holding sales constant, or (b) sales change, holding expenses constant, or (c) both types of changes occur simultaneously. As an example of case (a), the analyst may expect an expense to become a smaller fraction of sales over time if the firm will reduce the expense per dollar of sales through economies of scale or operating efficiencies. As an example of case (b), the analyst may expect the firm will hold expenses constant, but will face increased competition for sales and therefore may have to lower sales prices, causing the expected expense-to-sales ratio to increase. In scenario (c), if the analyst expects both effects will occur simultaneously, the net result on the projected expense-to-sales percentage will depend on which of the two the analyst expects to have a proportionally greater effect.

(a) PROJECTING COST OF SALES. Starbucks' cost of sales amounts include costs of coffee beverages and other products sold, as well as expenses for store rent. The cost of sales percentage declined from 42.0 percent of sales in Year 11 to 41.4 percent in Year 13. This pattern suggests that Starbucks has some proportion of the cost of sales that behaves like a fixed cost; a likely candidate is the rent component, because store rent remains relatively fixed as sales grow. Based on this pattern and a proportion of fixed costs, an analyst might assume that Starbucks will achieve additional reductions in the cost of sales percentage over time, gradually reducing this cost to roughly 40.0 percent of sales by Year +5. Our costs of sales forecasts through Year +5 appear in Exhibit 18.8.

(b) PROJECTING STORE OPERATING EXPENSES. Starbucks' store operating expenses include labor and payroll related expenses. This expense item increased from 32.8 percent to 33.9 percent of sales during Years 11 through 13. In part, these increases reflect rising salary and benefits costs for Starbucks employees. Given that Starbucks' strategy includes providing high quality service as part of the *Starbucks Experience*, one might project store operating costs to continue to rise slowly as a percent of sales in the future. Assuming marginal increases in store operating costs as a percent of sales in future years, Exhibit 18.9 shows our forecasts for store operating costs.

Year	Total Revenues	Percentage of Revenues	Costs of Sales
13 actual	$4,075.5	41.4%	$1,685.9
+1 forecast . . .	4,876.6	41.0%	1,999.4
+2 forecast . . .	5,702.3	40.8%	2,326.5
+3 forecast . . .	6,587.7	40.5%	2,668.0
+4 forecast . . .	7,536.8	40.2%	3,029.8
+5 forecast . . .	8,552.7	40.0%	3,421.1

EXHIBIT 18.8 COSTS OF SALES FORECASTS (IN MILLIONS)

Year	Total Revenues	Percentage of Revenues	Costs of Sales
13 actual	$4,075.5	33.9%	$1,379.6
+1 forecast. . . .	4,876.6	34.1%	1,662.9
+2 forecast. . . .	5,702.3	34.3%	1,955.9
+3 forecast. . . .	6,587.7	34.5%	2,272.7
+4 forecast. . . .	7,536.8	34.7%	2,615.3
+5 forecast. . . .	8,552.7	34.9%	2,984.9

EXHIBIT 18.9 FORECASTS FOR STORE OPERATING COSTS (IN MILLIONS)

(c) PROJECTING OTHER OPERATING EXPENSES. Starbucks recognized various recurring operating expenses, labeled on the income statement as other operating expenses (3.5 percent of total revenues in year 13), and general and administrative expenses (6.0 percent of total revenues in year 13). For simplicity, we assume that these expenses will remain the same proportions of total revenues in the future. Depreciation expense (5.8 percent of total revenues in year 13) will grow with capital expenditures on property, plant, and equipment. Section 18.5(a)(vi) describes the forecasts of depreciation expense together with property, plant, and equipment.

Exhibit 18.10 presents pro forma statements of income and retained earnings for Years +1 through +5. We discuss the projections of interest income, interest expense, income tax expense, net income, and the change in retained earnings after projecting Starbucks' balance sheet.

18.5 STEP 3: PROJECTING THE ASSETS ON THE BALANCE SHEET

We prepare the asset side of the pro forma balance sheet next. We project individual assets and then sum individual asset amounts to obtain total assets. We take this approach first to illustrate how to develop forecasts that capture different drivers of growth in different types of assets, allowing the mix of the firm's assets to change over time. Section 18.11 briefly describes short-cut approaches for projecting total assets, such as using sales and total asset turnover rates to forecast total assets and then using the common-size balance sheet percentages, as from Exhibit 18.2, to allocate this total among individual asset items.

STARBUCKS: FORECASTS OF PRO FORMA CONSOLIDATED INCOME STATEMENTS

(Amounts in millions)	Actual			Forecasts				
	11	12	13	Year +1	Year +2	Year +3	Year +4	Year +5
Retail	$2,229.6	$2,792.9	$3,449.6	$4,126.9	$4,823.0	$5,568.4	$6,366.2	$7,218.5
Specialty	419.4	496.0	625.9	749.7	879.3	1,019.3	1,170.6	1,334.2
Net Revenues	$2,649.0	$3,288.9	$4,075.5	$4,876.6	$5,702.3	$6,587.6	$7,536.8	$8,552.7
Cost of Sales (including occupancy)	1,112.8	1,350.0	1,685.9	1,999.4	2,326.5	2,668.0	3,029.8	3,421.1
Gross Profit	$1,536.2	$1,938.9	$2,389.6	$2,877.2	$3,375.7	$3,919.6	$4,507.0	$5,131.6
Store Operating Expenses	868.0	1,109.8	1,379.6	1,662.9	1,955.9	2,272.2	2,615.3	2,984.9
Other Operating Expenses	72.4	106.1	141.3	170.7	199.6	230.6	263.8	299.3
Depreciation and Amortization	163.5	205.6	237.8	289.5	335.5	381.5	427.5	473.5
General and Administrative Expenses	179.9	234.6	244.6	292.6	342.1	395.3	452.2	513.2
Income from Equity Investees	27.7	33.4	38.4	43.8	49.9	56.9	64.8	73.9
Operating Income	$ 280.2	$ 316.3	$ 424.7	$ 505.3	$ 592.6	$ 696.5	$ 813.1	$ 934.7
Interest and Other Income, Net	10.8	9.3	11.6	14.4	15.7	17.6	19.4	21.2
Other Gains (Losses)	(2.9)	13.4	—	—	—	—	—	—
Income Before Income Taxes	$ 288.0	$ 339.0	$ 436.3	$ 519.7	$ 608.2	$ 714.1	$ 832.5	$ 955.9
Provision for Income Taxes	107.7	126.3	168.0	197.5	231.1	271.3	316.4	363.2
Net Income	$ 180.3	$ 212.7	$ 268.3	$ 322.2	$ 377.1	$ 442.7	$ 516.2	$ 592.6

EXHIBIT 18.10   FORECASTS OF STARBUCKS' PRO FORMA FINANCIAL STATEMENTS FROM YEAR +1 TO +5

(a) **PROJECTING INDIVIDUAL ASSETS.** To develop forecasts of individual assets, the analyst must first link historical growth rates for individual assets to historical growth rates in sales or other activity-based drivers of assets. The analyst can then use those links to develop forecasts of individual assets based on sales growth forecasts, particularly for assets integrally related to sales (accounts receivable, inventories, and fixed assets). By using turnover rates to develop forecasts for individual assets, the analyst can capture the projected level of operating activity and permit changes in the expected relation between individual assets and operating activities such as sales. Our projections of individual assets for Starbucks illustrate the use of a combination of drivers, including common-size percentages, growth rates, and asset turnovers. Exhibit 18.11 presents the projected balance sheets through Year +5. The following discussion explains the projections of individual assets.

(i) **Cash and Investment Securities.** Starbucks' cash holdings varied between Years 11 to 13, while it has increased its holdings of short-term and long-term investment securities. At the end of Year 13, Starbucks had an unusually large cash balance roughly equivalent to 18 days of sales (computed as 365 days divided by the ratio of total revenues to ending cash, or 365 / [$26,935 /$683]), but its average cash balances were closer to 14 days' sales in Years 11 and 12. Starbucks needs a certain amount of cash on hand to maintain sufficient liquidity for day-to-day operations. We assume Starbucks will maintain year-end cash balances equivalent to roughly 14 days of sales, leading to the projections in Exhibit 18.12.

To make the three primary pro forma financial statements articulate, the change in cash balance on the balance sheet each year should agree with the net change in cash on the projected statement of cash flows. Section 18.8 of this chapter shows how to compute the implied statement of cash flows.

Short-term and long-term investments on Starbucks' Year 13 balance sheet have grown to represent 5.5 percent and 5.0 percent of total assets, respectively. We assume that these investment securities balances will continue to grow but remain in the same proportion to total assets. We therefore project the dollar amount of short-term and long-term investment securities each year as a function of all of the other asset amounts. We also include on the pro forma income statements any interest income that we expect the cash and investment securities to earn.

(ii) **Accounts Receivable.** Starbucks' retail sales are primarily cash-based sales of coffee beverages to retail consumers, but the Specialty revenues are primarily sales to commercial enterprises that will involve credit terms and accounts receivable. Starbucks' accounts receivable collection period has declined steadily from an average of 79 days in Year 11 to an average of 67 days in Year 13 (computed as 365 days divided by the ratio of specialty revenues to ending accounts receivable, or 365/[$625.9/$114.4]). We project accounts receivable by assuming Starbucks will maintain an average 67-day collection period in the future. The projected amounts appear in Exhibit 18.13.

Because we rely on ending accounts receivable balances to compute turnover rates and collection periods, the above approach produces estimates of the *ending* accounts receivable balance for the year. Forecasts based on asset turnover rates using year-end account balances assume a degree of stationarity in the relation between sales and ending balances. This approach can, however, introduce artificial volatility in ending balances. For example, if Starbucks experienced an unusually small increase in receivables relative to sales in Year 13 (just prior to our forecast period), then the Year +1 projected increase in receivables could become quite large. The large increase in Year +1 then triggers

	Actual			Forecasts				
	11	12	13	Year+1	Year +2	Year +3	Year +4	Year +5
Current Assets								
Cash and Equivalents	$ 113.2	$ 99.7	$ 200.9	$ 187.0	$ 218.7	$ 262.7	$ 289.1	$ 328.0
Short-Term Investments	107.3	227.7	149.1	167.4	185.8	201.8	215.4	227.0
Receivables	90.4	97.6	114.4	137.6	161.4	187.1	214.9	244.9
Inventories	221.3	263.2	342.9	405.4	471.7	540.9	614.3	693.6
Prepaid Expenses and Other Assets	29.8	42.4	55.2	60.9	67.6	73.4	78.3	82.5
Deferred Income Taxes, net	31.9	42.2	61.5	60.9	67.6	73.4	78.3	82.5
Total Current Assets	$ 593.9	$ 772.6	$ 924.0	$1,019.1	$1,172.7	$1,329.2	$1,490.3	$1,658.6
Long-Term Investments	–	–	136.2	152.2	168.9	183.4	195.8	206.3
Equity and Other Investments	63.1	102.5	144.3	164.5	187.5	213.7	243.6	277.8
Property and Equipment, Gross	1,741.0	2,080.2	2,434.7	2,894.7	3,354.7	3,814.7	4,274.7	4,734.7
Accumulated Depreciation	(605.2)	(814.4)	(1,049.8)	(1,339.3)	(1,674.8)	(2,056.2)	(2,483.7)	(2,957.2)
Property and Equipment, Net	1,135.8	1,265.8	1,384.9	1,555.4	1,680.0	1,758.5	1,791.0	1,777.5
Other Assets and Goodwill	53.7	73.5	140.4	152.2	168.9	183.4	195.8	206.3
Total Assets	$1,846.5	$2,214.4	$2,729.7	$3,043.4	$3,377.9	$3,668.2	$3,916.6	$4,126.5

EXHIBIT 18.11 STARBUCKS: FORECASTS OF PRO FORMA CONSOLIDATED BALANCE SHEETS (IN MILLIONS)

	Actual			Forecasts				
	11	12	13	Year+1	Year +2	Year +3	Year +4	Year +5
Current Liabilities								
Accounts Payable	127.9	136.0	169.0	180.9	209.9	240.1	272.2	307.1
Accrued Expenses	157.4	229.4	310.6	371.6	434.6	502.0	574.4	651.8
Accrued Taxes	70.3	54.2	54.9	65.7	76.9	88.8	101.6	115.3
Deferred Revenue	26.9	42.3	73.5	87.9	102.8	118.8	135.9	154.2
Current Portion of Long-Term Debt	62.7	0.7	0.7	0.7	0.7	0.7	0.7	0.7
Total Current Liabilities	$ 445.3	$ 462.6	$ 608.7	$ 706.8	$ 824.8	$ 950.4	$1,084.7	$1,229.0
Deferred Income Taxes, net	19.5	23.5	34.2	40.9	47.9	55.3	63.3	71.8
Long-Term Debt	5.8	5.1	4.4	3.7	3.0	2.3	1.6	0.9
Total Liabilities	$ 470.6	$ 491.2	$ 647.3	$ 751.4	$ 875.6	$1,008.0	$1,149.6	$1,301.7
Shareholders' Equity								
Common Stock	791.6	930.4	998.5	1,113.2	1,235.6	1,341.8	1,432.6	1,509.4
Retained Earnings	589.7	801.3	1,069.7	1,164.5	1,252.4	1,304.2	1,320.2	1,301.2
Accumulated Other Comp. Income/(Loss)	(5.4)	(8.6)	14.2	14.2	14.2	14.2	14.2	14.2
Total Shareholders' Equity	$1,375.9	$1,723.2	$2,082.4	$2,291.9	$2,502.3	$2,660.2	$2,767.0	$2,824.8
Total Liabilities and Shareholders' Equity	$1,846.5	$2,214.4	$2,729.7	$3,043.4	$3,377.9	$3,668.2	$3,916.6	$4,126.5

EXHIBIT 18.11 STARBUCKS: FORECASTS OF PRO FORMA CONSOLIDATED BALANCE SHEETS (IN MILLIONS) (CONTINUED)

	Annual Sales	Average Sales per Day	Days Sales in Cash	Year-End Cash Balances
Year +1 Projected.....	13.4	$ 4,876.6	14 days	$187
Year +2 Projected.....	15.6	5,702.3	14 days	219
Year +3 Projected.....	18.0	6,587.7	14 days	253
Year +4 Projected.....	20.6	7,536.8	14 days	289
Year +5 Projected.....	23.4	8,552.7	14 days	328

EXHIBIT 18.12   PROJECTED YEAR-END CASH BALANCES

	Specialty Revenues	Accounts Receivable Collection	Ending Accounts Receivable
Year +1 Projected	$ 749.7	67 days	$138
Year +2 Projected	879.3	67 days	161
Year +3 Projected	1,019.3	67 days	187
Year +4 Projected	1,170.6	67 days	215
Year +5 Projected	1,334.2	67 days	245

EXHIBIT 18.13   PROJECTION OF ENDING ACCOUNTS RECEIVABLE

an unusually small increase in Year +2 to compensate, and so on, creating an artificial volatility in ending receivables. The analyst can mitigate the variability in this pattern by estimating the average rate of growth in receivables expected over several periods and use this growth rate. One could also use average asset turnover rates to forecast average balances and then compute the ending balance implied by the beginning balance and the average (that is, the implied ending balance should equal two times the average balance minus the beginning balance). For our purposes, we will rely on turnover rates based on year-end balances because it introduces only slight measurement error in the case of Starbucks.

(iii) Inventories.   Based on the ending balance in inventory in Year 13, Starbucks took an average of roughly 74 days to sell inventory (computed as 365 days divided by cost of sales divided by ending inventory). We project inventories using an average inventory turnover period of 74 days, or equivalently, an average turnover rate of roughly 4.9 times per year. The projected amounts appear in Exhibit 18.14.

	Cost of Sales	Inventory Turnover	Ending Inventories
Year +1 Projected......	$1,999.4	4.9	$405
Year +2 Projected......	2,326.5	4.9	472
Year +3 Projected......	2,668.0	4.9	541
Year +4 Projected......	3,029.8	4.9	614
Year +5 Projected......	3,421.1	4.9	694

EXHIBIT 18.14   PROJECTED ENDING INVENTORIES (IN MILLIONS)

(iv) Other Current Assets.   Starbucks' balance sheet includes other current assets, such as prepaid expenses and deferred income taxes, net. These two other current asset accounts have remained at roughly 2.0 percent of total assets over Years 11 through 13, so we assume that they will each remain at 2.0 percent of total assets in the future.

(v) Equity and Other Investments.   Starbucks' equity and other investments primarily represent its equity interests in unconsolidated affiliates. As mentioned in the discussion of Income from Equity Investees in Section 18.3(b), we assume that these investments will grow at an annual rate of 14.0 percent during the next five years.

(vi) Property, Plant, and Equipment (PP&E).   Starbucks' capital expenditures involve acquiring fixed assets for new stores, refurbishing old stores, and expanding infrastructure such as roasting plants, information systems, and administrative offices. Starbucks' recent past capital expenditures data (from the statement of cash flows) implies that each new store requires an average of roughly $600,000 in new PP&E. Assuming they will add 600 new company-owned stores a year amounts to $360 million in store-based capital spending. In addition, we assume that Starbucks will spend roughly $100 million per year on other capital expenditures, totaling $460 million per year in capital expenditures.[7] Each year of additional capital spending will trigger additional depreciation. In Year 13, Starbucks recognized $238 million in depreciation expense. Depreciation expense forecasts assume a ten-year useful life, straight-line depreciation, and zero salvage value. Growth in net property, plant, and equipment will therefore reflect the gross capital expenditures minus depreciation expense each year. The projected amounts appear in Exhibit 18.15.

When forecasting fixed assets for capital-intensive firms or firms for which fixed asset growth is a critical driver of future sales growth and earnings, analysts should invest time and effort in developing detailed forecasts of capital expenditures and depreciation expense schedules. For such firms, these capital expenditures can comprise a large part of the balance sheet and can have a material effect on the analysts' forecasts of earnings, cash flows, and firm value.

	Property, Plant, and Equipment				
Year	Capital Expenditures	Ending Balance at Cost	Depreciation Expense	Accumulated Depreciation	Ending Balance Net
13 actual		$2,435		$(1,050)	$1,385
+1 Forecast	$460	2,895	$(289)	(1,339)	1,555
+2 Forecast	460	3,355	(335)	(1,675)	1,680
+3 Forecast	460	3,815	(381)	(2,056)	1,759
+4 Forecast	460	4,275	(427)	(2,484)	1,791
+5 Forecast	460	4,735	(473)	(2,957)	1,778

EXHIBIT 18.15   PROJECTED PROPERTY, PLANT AND EQUIPMENT (IN MILLIONS)

7.   In the management and discussion section of Starbucks' Year 13 annual report, management noted it expected capital expenditures of $450 to $475 million in our forecast Year +1, so our estimate is in the ballpark.

Cash	$ 187
Accounts Receivable.	138
Inventories	405
Property, Plant and Equipment (net).	1,555
Equity and Other Investments.	165
Subtotal of assets	$2,450

EXHIBIT 18.16   PROJECTION OF ASSETS FOR YEAR +1

(vii) Other Assets and Goodwill.   Other assets for Starbucks include goodwill and other identifiable intangible assets from acquisitions. U.S. GAAP no longer requires amortization of goodwill or other intangible assets with indefinite lives. These assets, however, will undergo periodic impairment tests, which could trigger significant write-downs of goodwill if the test results deem them impaired. These intangible assets can increase dramatically in a given year as a result of an acquisition of another firm with significant intangible assets (as Starbucks did in Year 13).

In the case of Starbucks, Other Assets and Goodwill amount to 5.1 percent of assets in Year 13. Analysts find it difficult to project with confidence substantial increases or decreases in other intangible assets from corporate events such as acquisitions, sales of subsidiaries, or impairment test write-downs. We can project, however, that Starbucks will likely continue to invest in other intangible assets as it acquires companies with new products and brands in order to drive future sales growth. Therefore, we forecast that other assets and goodwill grow in proportion to total assets, remaining roughly 5.0 percent of total assets in the future.

(b) PROJECTING ASSETS THAT VARY AS A PERCENT OF TOTAL ASSETS.   We can now project asset amounts that we expect will vary as a percentage of total assets, including short-term investment securities (5.5 percent), long-term investment securities (5.0 percent), prepaid expenses (2.0 percent), deferred tax assets (2.0 percent), and other assets and goodwill (5.0 percent), for a total of 19.5 percent. Exhibit 18.16 shows the projected amounts for Year +1 for all of the individual assets other than these assets.

The $2,450 subtotal represents 80.5 percent (= 100 percent – 19.5 percent) of total assets. Projected total assets therefore equal $3,043 (= $2,450/0.805). Short-term investment securities equal $167 million (= 0.055 × $3,043), long-term investment securities equal $152 million (= 0.050 × $3,043), prepaid expenses equal $61 million (= 0.020 ×$3,043), deferred tax assets equal $61 million (= 0.020 × $3,043), and other assets and goodwill equal $152 million (= 0.050 × $3,043). Exhibit 18.17 shows the

Year	Total Assets	Short-Term Investments (5.5%)	Long-Term Investments (5.0%)	Prepaid Expenses (2.0%)	Deferred Tax Assets (2.0%)	Other Assets and Goodwill (5.0%)
+1. . . .	$ 3,043	$ 167	$ 152	$ 61	$ 61	$ 152
+2. . . .	3,378	186	169	68	68	169
+3. . . .	3,668	202	183	73	73	183
+4. . . .	3,917	215	196	78	78	196
+5. . . .	4,127	227	206	83	83	206

EXHIBIT 18.17   PROJECTED TOTAL ASSETS FOR YEARS +1 TO +5

projected amounts for total assets, short-term investment securities, long-term investment securities, prepaid expenses, deferred tax assets, and other assets and goodwill in Years +1 to +5.

18.6   STEP 4: PROJECTING LIABILITIES AND SHAREHOLDERS' EQUITY

Once analysts forecast the asset side of the pro forma balance sheet, they must next project liabilities and shareholders' equity. For firms that target and maintain a particular capital structure over time, the analyst can use the common-size balance sheet percentages to project amounts of individual liabilities and shareholders' equities. The common-size balance sheet for Starbucks in Exhibit 18.2 shows that the balance sheet percentages for total liabilities fluctuated from 25.5 percent of total assets in Year 11, down to 23.7 percent in Year 13. Complementarily, shareholders' equity fluctuated from 74.5 percent of total assets in Year 11, up to 76.3 percent in Year 13. If the analyst believes that Starbucks' funding will consist of roughly 25.0 percent liabilities and 75.0 percent equities in the future, then one could use these common-size percentages to project individual liabilities and equities. Alternatively, the analyst can project individual liabilities and shareholders' equity accounts using historical growth rates or turnover ratios. This section illustrates how to forecast Starbucks' individual liabilities and equities using a combination of common-size percentages, growth rates, and turnover ratios, in order to develop forecasts that incorporate the projected levels of operating activities and permit changes in the expected behavior of individual liability and equity amounts over time. We consider each account next.

(a) PROJECTING LIABILITIES

(i) **Accounts Payable.** Future credit purchases of inventory and Starbucks' payment policy to its suppliers will likely drive accounts payable. During the last three years, the average payables period has averaged roughly 32 days. We assume Starbucks will maintain an accounts payable period of 32 days in the future. To forecast future accounts payable balances, we begin by calculating forecasts of purchases on account, and then divide an accounts payable turnover ratio of 11.4 [= 365 days/32 days] to compute the ending balance in accounts payable, as Exhibit 18.18 shows.

(ii) **Accrued Expenses, Accrued Taxes, Deferred Revenues, and Deferred Income Taxes, net.** Starbucks' accrued expenses liability amounts to $311 million at the end of Year 13 and it reflects expenses related to store operating activities (payroll, utilities, etc.), other operating activities, general and administrative activities. In addition, Starbucks

	Year +1	Year +2	Year +3	Year +4	Year +5
Cost of Sales	$1,999	$2,327	$2,668	$3,030	$3,421
Plus Ending Inventory	405	472	541	614	694
Less Beginning Inventory	(343)	(405)	(472)	(541)	(614)
Purchases	$2,061	$2,394	$2,737	$3,103	$3,501
Payables Turnover Ratio	11.4	11.4	11.4	11.4	11.4
Accounts Payable	$ 181	$ 210	$ 240	$ 272	$ 307

EXHIBIT 18.18   PROJECTING ACCOUNTS PAYABLE

also recognizes a current accrued liability for income taxes payable amounting to $55 million at the end of Year 13. Also, Starbucks recognizes a current liability for deferred revenue in the amount of $74 million, which comprises advances that Starbucks' customers have made for gift and debit cards, redeemable for Starbucks' beverages and products. Starbucks also recognizes a small liability for deferred income taxes, which amounts to $34 million at the end of Year 13. Because these accrued liability amounts vary with sales and taxable income, we forecast that they will grow proportionately with total revenues, as Exhibit 18.19 shows. The analyst interested in greater forecast precision could forecast the amounts more specifically based on underlying drivers directly related to each liability (such as growth in store openings for accrued expenses, growth in taxable income for accrued taxes and deferred taxes, etc.)

(iii) Short-term Borrowing, Long-term Debt and Current Portion of Long-term Debt. Starbucks does not rely on a significant amount of short-term or long-term debt to finance its operations, but it uses 5- to 10-year operating leases for their stores, which, under U.S. GAAP in Year 13, do not appear on the balance sheet. Long-term debt on the balance sheet at the end of Year 13 amounts to only $4.4 million, with an additional $0.7 million recognized as a current portion of long-term debt. Starbucks' annual report footnotes provide a schedule for when the remaining payments to retire long-term debt come due. Each year over the 5-year forecast horizon, an incremental $0.7 million payment is due, and the outstanding balance in long-term debt falls accordingly. We use these amounts for the forecasts of future long-term debt and current portions of long-term debt. Note that if the analyst expects Starbucks will find it necessary or desirable to borrow substantial amounts in the future to finance growth, then the forecasts of long-term debt should reflect these future borrowings. Given that Starbucks has not had significant amounts of long-term debt in the past, and given that our forecasts of future cash flows will ultimately show a healthy cash flow from operations to finance future growth, it does not appear Starbucks will need (or will likely choose) to begin long-term borrowing.

(b) PROJECTING SHAREHOLDERS' EQUITY

(i) Common Stock. This equity capital account increases as the firm raises capital by selling shares to investors. Common stock has steadily grown for Starbucks from $792 million at the end of Year 11 to $999 million at the end of Year 13, in part due to Starbucks using stock for acquisitions of other companies and in part due to issues of stock to employees for compensation and bonuses. We assume that common stock issues will

Year	Total Revenue Growth Rates	Accrued Expenses	Accrued Taxes	Deferred Revenues	Deferred Taxes
13....		$ 311	$ 55	$ 74	$ 34
+1....	+19.7%	372	66	88	41
+2....	+16.9%	435	77	103	48
+3....	+15.5%	502	89	119	55
+4....	+14.4%	574	102	136	63
+5....	+13.5%	652	115	154	72

EXHIBIT 18.19   PROJECTION OF ACCRUED LIABILITIES THAT VARY WITH REVENUE (IN MILLIONS)

Year	Total Assets Growth Rates	Common Stock
13..........		$ 999
+1..........	+11.5%	1,113
+2..........	+11.0%	1,236
+3..........	+8.6%	1,342
+4..........	+6.8%	1,433
+5..........	+5.4%	1,509

EXHIBIT 18.20   FORECAST OF COMMON STOCK (IN MILLIONS)

occur in the future, and that common stock will grow in proportion to total assets. Exhibit 18.20 shows our forecasts of Starbucks common stock.

(ii) Accumulated Other Comprehensive Loss.   According the Starbucks' Statement of Common Shareholders' Equity at the end of Year 13, Accumulated Other Comprehensive Loss primarily includes the cumulative effects of gains and losses from foreign currency translation adjustments, and to a lesser extent some unrealized fair value gains and losses on investments securities deemed available for sale. The foreign currency translation adjustments relate to Starbucks' international operations in countries whose currencies have changed in value relative to the U.S. dollar. We assume Starbucks will continue to hold and possibly expand these international operations. It is difficult to forecast, however, whether the U.S. dollar will increase or decrease in value relative to the foreign currencies of Starbucks' international operations, or whether Starbucks will either hedge or limit their exposure to foreign currency movements. Thus, we project that Starbucks will experience gains/losses on foreign currency translation adjustments (and fair value gains and losses) that are on average zero (equally likely to be positive or negative in any given year), and so Accumulated Other Comprehensive Loss will remain at its current level.

(iii) Treasury Stock.   If a firm repurchases some of its outstanding shares, then the firm recognizes the cost of the repurchases in a treasury stock account (a contra-equity account). The treasury stock account decreases (that is, becomes more negative) when the firm repurchases some of its shares. The treasury stock account increases (becomes less negative) when the firm's treasury shares are reissued on the open market, are used to meet stock option exercises, are exchanged in merger or acquisition transactions, or are retired. Starbucks does not have a treasury stock account in Year 13, so we forecast that this will remain the case in future years.

18.7   STEP 5: PROJECTING INTEREST EXPENSE, INTEREST INCOME, INCOME TAX EXPENSE, AND THE CHANGE IN RETAINED EARNINGS

(a) INTEREST EXPENSE.   We can now project our first-iteration estimate of interest expense, based on our projected balances in interest-bearing capital, including Short-term Borrowing, Current Maturities of Long-term Debt, and Long-term Debt, and the

| Year | Cash, Short-Term, and Long-Term Investments | | | Rate of Return | Interest Income |
	Beginning	Ending	Average		
+1	$ 486.2	$ 506.6	$ 496.4	2.9%	$ 14.4
+2	506.6	573.4	540.0	2.9%	15.7
+3	573.4	637.8	605.6	2.9%	17.6
+4	637.8	700.3	669.1	2.9%	19.4
+5	700.3	761.3	730.8	2.9%	21.2

EXHIBIT 18.21 PROJECTING INTEREST INCOME (IN MILLIONS)

interest applicable to each of those types of debt. The terms, interest rates and maturity dates of outstanding debt usually appear in a firm's long-term debt footnote to the financial statements. As discussed above, Starbucks has an immaterial amount of interest-bearing debt and therefore an immaterial amount of interest expense. We did project that Starbucks will not borrow additional interest-bearing debt in the future, so it is safe to forecast that interest expense will be immaterial.

(b) INTEREST INCOME.   We can also project our first-iteration estimates of Starbucks' interest income on financial assets, such as cash and cash equivalents as well as short-term and long-term investments in securities. In Year 13, Starbucks recognized $11.6 million in income on an average balances in cash, short-term, and long-term investments of $406.8 (= [$99.7+$200.9+$227.7+$149.1+$0+$136.2]/2) million during Year 13, for an average return of 2.9 percent. This rate of return is probably reasonable because it reflects the low interest rate environment in the economy in Year 13, and it is likely that Starbucks holds cash, short-term, and long-term investments in low-risk but liquid instruments. Assuming interest rates remain at low levels, the projected amounts for Interest Income appear in Exhibit 18.21.

(c) INCOME TAXES.   Starbucks' income tax note shows the reconciliation between the statutory tax rate and the average, or effective, tax rate. Starbucks experienced an effective tax rate of 38.5 percent during Year 13. Starbucks discloses that it expects to face an effective tax rate of approximately 38.0 percent in the future. Following this disclosure, we assume that the effective tax rate for Year +1 and beyond will be 38 percent.

(d) NET INCOME.   We have now projected all of the elements of the income statement, including first-iteration assumptions about interest expense and interest income. Recall that Exhibit 18.10 contains the complete pro forma income statement forecasts. Exhibit 18.22 shows our projected net income amounts and the implied growth rates in net income.

(e) RETAINED EARNINGS.   The Retained Earnings account typically increases by the amount of net income (or decreases for net loss) and decreases for dividends. Starbucks' dividend payout policy for common shareholders has been zero (no dividends paid) during Years 11 to 13. For our first pass assumptions, we project that Starbucks will maintain a zero dividend payout policy in the future, as Exhibit 18.23 shows.

	Net Income	Percentage Increase
Year 13 Actual.......	$268	
Year +1 Projected	322	20.1%
Year +2 Projected	377	17.0
Year +3 Projected	443	17.4
Year +4 Projected	516	16.6
Year +5 Projected	593	14.8

EXHIBIT 18.22   PROJECTING NET INCOME AND GROWTH RATES (IN MILLIONS)

	Year +1	Year +2	Year +3	Year +4	Year +5
Beginning of Year	$ 1,070	$ 1,392	$ 1,769	$ 2,212	$ 2,728
Plus Net Income..............	322	377	443	516	593
Less Dividends to............					
Common Shareholders	(0)	(0)	(0)	(0)	(0)
End of Year	$ 1,392	$ 1,769	$ 2,212	$ 2,728	$ 3,321

EXHIBIT 18.23   PROJECTING RETAINED EARNINGS (IN MILLIONS)

18.8   BALANCING THE BALANCE SHEET

Even though we have completed first-iteration forecasts of all of the amounts on the income statement and balance sheet, our balance sheet will not balance, because we have forecast individual asset and liability accounts to capture their individual operating activities, which do not vary together perfectly. Currently, our projections of total assets minus our projections of liabilities and common shareholders' equity (other than retained earnings), and retained earnings indicate the amounts by which our balance sheets do not balance. (See Exhibit 18.24).

The difference between the projected totals of assets and the projected totals of liabilities and shareholders' equity each year represents the amounts by which we must adjust a flexible financial account to balance the balance sheet. The change in the difference

Projections:	Year +1	Year +2	Year +3	Year +4	Year +5
Total Assets.........................	$3,043	$3,378	$3,668	$ 3,917	$ 4,127
Liabilities............................	751	876	1,008	1,150	1,302
Shareholders' Equity (other than Retained Earnings	1,127	1,250	1,356	1,447	1,524
Retained Earnings	1,392	1,769	2,212	2,728	3,321
Total Liabilities and Shareholders' Equity ..	3,270	3,895	4,576	5,325	6,147
Difference	(227)	(517)	(908)	(1,408)	(2,020)
Change in the difference	(227)	(290)	(391)	(500)	(612)

EXHIBIT 18.24   OUT-OF-BALANCE BALANCE SHEET

	Year +1	Year +2	Year +3	Year +4	Year +5
Beginning of Year	$ 1,070	$ 1,165	$ 1,252	$ 1,304	$ 1,320
Plus Net Income.	322	377	443	516	593
Less Dividends to					
Common Shareholders	(227)	(290)	(391)	(500)	(612)
End of Year	$ 1,165	$ 1,252	$ 1,304	$ 1,320	$ 1,301

EXHIBIT 18.25 RECALCULATION OF RETAINED EARNINGS (IN MILLIONS)

represents the new increment by which we must adjust the flexible financial account each year. Thus, in Year +1, our first-iteration forecasts project that liabilities and equities will exceed assets by $227 million. We need to adjust a flexible financial account by $227 million (either increase a financial asset account or decrease a financial liability or shareholders' equity account) to balance the balance sheet. In Year +2, our first-iteration projections indicate liabilities and equities will exceed assets by $517 million, so we will need an additional adjustment of $290 million in Year +2, and so on.

We could use a number of Starbucks' flexible financial accounts for this adjustment, depending on Starbucks' strategy for investments and capital structure. We could consider the following options:

- Increase cash or short-term securities if we expect Starbucks will reinvest this capital in liquid securities;
- Increase long-term investment securities if we expect Starbucks will reinvest this capital in long-term investments;
- Initiate dividends or treasury stock repurchases if we expect Starbucks will distribute this capital to shareholders.

Our forecasts imply that Starbucks will continue to generate substantial amounts of positive cash flow, so we assume that Starbucks will initiate dividend payments in the future. We therefore adjust upwards our dividends forecasts each year by the amount of the necessary adjustment to balance the balance sheet. We refer to this amount as an *implied dividend*. Note that we could have assumed that Starbucks will distribute the excess capital to shareholders through treasury stock repurchases rather than dividends *per se*. In either case, the assumption that Starbucks will return the cash to shareholders through increased dividends or treasury stock repurchases will have equivalent effects on total assets, total liabilities, total shareholders' equity, and net income. After adjusting our dividends projections to include the implied dividends necessary to balance the balance sheet, we recalculate retained earnings as shown in Exhibit 18.26.

Projections:	Year +1	Year +2	Year +3	Year +4	Year +5
Total Assets	$3,043	$3,378	$3,668	$3,917	$4,127
Liabilities.	751	876	1,008	1,150	1,302
Shareholders' Equity other than					
Retained Earnings	1,127	1,250	1,356	1,447	1,524
Retained Earnings	1,165	1,253	1,304	1,320	1,301
Total Liabilities and Shareholders' Equity. . .	$3,043	$3,378	$3,668	$3,917	$4,127
Difference	$ 0	$ 0	$ 0	$ 0	$ 0

EXHIBIT 18.26 SUMMARY OF PRO FORMA BALANCE SHEET (IN MILLIONS)

Implied Cash Flows:	Forecasts Year +1	Year +2	Year +3	Year +4	Year +5
Operating Activities:					
1. Net income	$ 322.2	$ 377.1	$ 442.7	$ 516.2	$ 592.6
2. Depreciation and amortization	289.5	335.5	381.5	427.5	473.5
3. Deferred income taxes, net	7.3	0.2	1.6	3.0	4.3
4. Accounts receivable	(23.2)	(23.8)	(25.7)	(27.8)	(30.0)
5. Inventories	(62.4)	(66.3)	(69.2)	(73.4)	(79.3)
6. Prepaid expenses	(5.7)	(6.7)	(5.8)	(5.0)	(4.2)
7. Accounts payable	11.9	29.0	30.2	32.1	34.8
8. Accrued compensation	61.0	62.9	67.5	72.3	77.4
9. Accrued taxes	10.8	11.1	11.9	12.8	13.7
10. Deferred revenue	14.4	14.9	16.0	17.1	18.3
Cash flows from operations	$ 625.9	$ 734.0	$ 850.7	$ 974.9	$1,101.2
Investing Activities:					
11. Short-term investments	(18.3)	(18.4)	(16.0)	(13.7)	(11.5)
12. Long-term investments	(16.0)	(16.7)	(14.5)	(12.4)	(10.5)
13. Equity and other investments	(20.2)	(23.0)	(26.2)	(29.9)	(34.1)
14. Changes in PP&E	(460.0)	(460.0)	(460.0)	(460.0)	(460.0)
15. Changes in other assets and goodwill	(11.8)	(16.7)	(14.5)	(12.4)	(10.5)
Cash flows from investing activities . .	$(526.3)	$(534.9)	$(531.2)	$(528.4)	$ (526.6)
Financing Activities:					
16. Changes in long-term debt	(0.7)	(0.7)	(0.7)	(0.7)	(0.7)
17. Changes in common stock	114.7	122.4	106.2	90.9	76.8
18. Implied dividends paid	(227.4)	(289.1)	(390.9)	(500.2)	(611.6)
Cash flows from financing activities	$(113.4)	$ (167.5)	$(285.5)	$(410.0)	$ (535.5)
19. *Net cash flow*	$ (13.8)	$31.7	$34.0	$36.4	$39.0
Beginning balance	200.9	187.0	218.7	252.7	289.1
Ending balance	$ 187.0	$ 218.7	$ 252.7	$ 289.1	$ 328.0

EXHIBIT 18.27   FORECASTS OF STARBUCKS' PRO FORMA STATEMENTS OF CASH FLOWS FOR YEAR +1 TO +5 (IN MILLIONS)

Exhibit 18.27 summarizes the final pro forma balance sheet amounts (shown in detail in Exhibit 18.11).

18.9   CLOSING THE LOOP: SOLVING FOR CO-DETERMINED VARIABLES

Instead of balancing the balance sheet by adjusting implied dividends, we can plug the excess funds to interest-earning accounts (for example, investment securities). For firms with significant amounts of debt, we can assume the firm uses the excess funds to pay down interest-bearing debt. In either case, we would need to adjust accordingly the projected amounts for interest income or interest expense on the income statement. This would create an additional set of co-determined variables within our pro forma financial statements forecasts. For example, assume we use Long-term Investments as our flexible financial account and adjust it upward by the amount Starbucks will require to balance assets with liabilities and shareholders' equity. To calculate the necessary plug to Long-term Investments, we need to know all of the other asset, liability, and shareholders' equity amounts, including retained earnings. To forecast retained earnings, we must know net income, which depends on interest income on Long-term Investments. To calculate Retained Earnings, we also need to know dividends, which might vary with Net Income. Thus, we need to solve for at least five unknown variables simultaneously.

This problem is not as intractable as it might seem, thanks to computational capabilities of computer spreadsheet programs such as *Excel*. To solve for variables simultaneously in *Excel*, for example, first click on the Tools menu, and then click on the Calculations menu, and then click on the Iterations box, so that *Excel* will solve and resolve circular references 100 times until all the calculations fall within the specified tolerance for precision. Then we can program each cell to calculate the variables we need, even if they are simultaneously computed.

18.10 STEP 6: DERIVING THE STATEMENT OF CASH FLOWS

The final step involves deriving projected statements of cash flows directly from the projected income statements (Exhibit 18.10) and balance sheets (Exhibit 18.11). We capture all of the changes in the pro forma balance sheets each year and express these changes in terms of their implied effects on cash. Increases in assets imply uses of cash; decreases in assets imply sources of cash. Increases in liabilities and shareholders' equity imply sources of cash; decreases in liabilities and shareholders' equity imply uses of cash. Exhibit 18.27 presents the pro forma statement of cash flows for Starbucks for Years +1 through +5. The derivation of each line item appears below.

> *Line 1, Net Income*: We use the amounts in the pro forma income statement.
>
> *Line 2, Depreciation and Amortization Expense*: We assume that the addback for depreciation expense equals the change in accumulated depreciation on the pro forma balance sheets. The addback for amortization expense is zero because we forecast that under U.S. GAAP in Year +1, Starbucks will not amortize goodwill or other intangible assets with indefinite lives on the pro forma balance sheets. If Starbucks recognizes certain types of intangible assets with definite lives that it amortizes, then adding back zero amortization expense is an error but the error is not material. This error primarily understates cash flow from operations (by the amount of the omitted amortization addback) and overstates cash flow from investing (where the change in Other Assets appears), but does not affect net cash flows.
>
> *Lines 3–10, Changes in Operating Asset and Liability Accounts*: Changes in current and noncurrent accounts that reflect operating activities (other than cash), including inventories, receivables, accounts payable, accrued expenses, and deferred revenue, appearing on the pro forma balance sheets.
>
> *Lines 11–13, Short- and Long-Term Investment Securities and Equity Investments (net)*: The statement of cash flows classifies purchases and sales of investment securities as investing transactions. We use the changes in these accounts on the pro forma balance sheet to derive the amounts for these items on the statement of cash flows.

There is likely to be some error in the implied cash flow amount from investment securities. This change should be increased (become less negative) for the excess (if any) of equity earnings over dividends received from unconsolidated affiliates (which is a non-cash increase in this asset amount). Similarly, the excess of equity earnings over dividends received should also be subtracted from net income in the operating section of the statement of cash flows. Rather than making assumptions about this relatively immaterial item (the effects of which completely offset each other), we chose to simply treat the changes in investments fully as investing transaction. This choice will slightly overstate cash flows from operating activities, and slightly understate cash flows from investing activities by an equivalent amount, but it will not affect the net change in cash each year.

Line 14, Property, Plant and Equipment: The amount on this line equals the projected capital expenditures included in the change in property, plant, and equipment on the pro forma balance sheet in Exhibit 18.11. We assume that Starbucks did not sell or retire depreciable assets each year. As a check, the analyst should be sure that the statement of cash flows captures the net cash flow implications of property, plant, and equipment (for example, the addback for depreciation expense minus capital expenditures, net of any asset sales is equal to the change in net property, plant, and equipment on the pro forma balance sheet).

Line 15, Other Assets: We enter the change in Other Assets and Goodwill on this line. The change in Other Assets on the pro forma balance sheet is the net of acquisitions. As discussed above, we assume that the amount of amortization of goodwill is zero, and the amortization of other intangible assets is sufficiently immaterial that we treat the change in Other Assets fully as an investing transaction.

Line 16, Debt Capital: Changes in debt capital (current portions of long-term debt and long-term debt) on the pro forma balance sheet are financing activities.

Line 17, Changes in Common Stock: The amounts represent the changes in the Common Stock account on the pro forma balance sheet.

Line 18, Dividends: The amount for common dividends equals the projected amount each year (discussed in Section 18.7(e)).

Line 19, Net Change in Cash: The aggregate of the amounts on lines (1) to (18), which should equal the change in cash on the pro forma balance sheet.

The analyst should note that the statement of cash flows will not reconcile with the pro forma income statement and balance sheets if the balance sheets do not balance and if the income statement does not articulate with the balance sheets (that is, the change in retained earnings should include net income).

Unlike historical balance sheets and income statements, historical statements of cash flows commonly do not provide good bases for projecting the future because many of the line items on the statement are difficult to reconcile with historical changes in balance sheets. This occurs because the statement of cash flows can aggregate numerous cash flows on each line item and the analyst may not be able to identify what amounts have been aggregated. For example, the statement may report separately the aggregate cost of a business acquisition on one line, but the business acquisition could cause changes in many asset and liability accounts, recognizing the acquisition of various assets and liabilities. In addition, the analyst may not be able to verify the details of the reported cash flows. For example, the statement might disclose separately the amount of marketable securities purchased and sold, and the analyst cannot verify those amounts because the analyst can observe only the net change in the marketable securities balance during the year. Thus, we recommend simply computing the implied statement of cash flows from the pro forma income statements and balance sheets, which the analyst can observe and verify.

18.11 SHORTCUT APPROACHES TO FORECASTING

Thus far, the chapter has emphasized a methodical, detailed approach to forecasting individual accounts on the pro forma income statement and balance sheet, allowing the analyst to incorporate expected changes in operating activities related to each account. In some circumstances, however, it may be necessary to forecast income statement and balance sheet totals directly without carefully considering each account. Shortcuts have the potential to introduce forecasting error if the shortcut assumptions do not fit each account very well. On the other hand, if the firm is stable and mature in an industry in steady-state equilibrium, then it may be efficient and reliable to use shortcut forecasting techniques that project current steady-state conditions to the future.

One shortcut approach projects total sales and net income using the firm's recent sales growth rates to project sales, and common size income statement percentages to project individual expenses and net income. This shortcut approach assumes existing relations between sales and expenses will persist into the future.

In a similar vein, we can take a shortcut approach to forecast the balance sheet by projecting total assets using the recent historical growth rate in total assets. An alternate shortcut approach to projecting total assets uses the total asset turnover ratio, which explicitly links sales growth and asset growth. Once the analyst projects total assets, common-size balance sheet percentages provide the basis for allocating this total to individual assets, as well as to liabilities and shareholders' equity. In using these common-size percentages, the analyst assumes that the firm maintains a constant mix of assets, liabilities, and equities, regardless of the level of total assets. Equivalently, the analyst assumes that each asset, liability, and equity account grows at the same growth rate as that of total assets. Using common-size balance sheet percentages to project individual assets, liabilities and shareholders' equity encounters (at least) two potential shortcomings. First, the common-size percentages for individual assets, liabilities, and shareholders' equity are not independent of each other. Second, using the common-size percentages does not permit the analyst to easily change the assumptions about the future behavior of an individual asset.

18.12 ANALYZING PRO FORMA FINANCIAL STATEMENTS

As a reality check on the reasonableness of our forecast assumptions and their internal consistency with one another, one can analyze the pro forma financial statements using financial statement analysis ratios and other analytical tools. For example, the analyst can compare projected growth rates in sales with projected growth rates in net income, to assess whether the income statement assumptions imply reasonable profit margins in light of sales growth projections.

The analyst can also check the implications of forecast assumptions on the projected rate of return on assets and the projected rate of return on common equity (and its components—profit margin, asset turnover, and capital structure leverage). If the results show increases in the rates of return on common equity, for example, the analyst can assess whether the profitability, efficiency, and leverage assumptions driving the increase are reasonable.

The analyst can also assess whether the forecast assumptions imply changes in liquidity ratios, solvency ratios, and interest coverage ratios over time. Analyzing such ratios can help the analyst assess whether the projections are likely to alter the firm's credit risk.

Financial statement ratios can confirm whether our forecast assumptions are reasonable and whether we have implemented them correctly (that is, we have done the computations correctly). Unfortunately, such ratios cannot confirm whether our assumptions are correct. These ratios do not tell us whether we have accurately and realistically captured Starbucks' sales growth and profitability in the future. For this confirmation, only time will tell.

18.13 SENSITIVITY ANALYSIS AND STRATEGIC PLANNING

Pro forma financial statement forecasts can serve as the base case from which the analyst assesses the impact of various critical forecast assumptions for the firm, and from which the analyst can test strategic planning ideas for the firm. For example, with these pro forma financial statements, the analyst can assess the sensitivity of projected net income and cash flows to key assumptions about the firm's sales growth rates, gross profit margins, selling, general and administrative expenses, and other assumptions. For example, using the pro forma financial statements as the base case, the analyst can assess the impact on Starbucks' profitability from a one-point increase or decrease in sales growth, or from a one-point increase or decrease in the gross profit margin.

The analyst can also use the pro forma financial statements to assess the sensitivity of the firm's liquidity and leverage to changes in key balance sheet assumptions. For example, the analyst can assess the impact on Starbucks' liquidity and solvency ratios from varying the long-term debt to assets ratios and the interest expense assumptions. Lenders and credit analysts can use the pro forma financial statements to assess the conditions under which the firm's debt covenants may become binding. For example, suppose Starbucks' long-term debt and revolving line of credit agreements require that Starbucks maintain certain minimum liquidity and interest coverage ratios. The pro forma financial statements provide the analyst a structured approach to assess how far net income and cash flows would need to decrease, and how much long-term debt and interest expense would need to increase before the minimum interest coverage ratio becomes binding.

Pro forma financial statements also enable the analyst to test the potential impact of strategic planning ideas. Suppose Starbucks is considering at the beginning of Year +1 a new contract with a distribution channel that should enable Starbucks to increase revenues by $1 billion by Year +3, and that it should be able to sustain this new level of sales into the future. The analyst can adapt the pro forma financial statements to incorporate the projected effects of these potential future sales, as well as related incremental expenses, receivables, inventory, property, plant and equipment, and capital relatively efficiently into expectations for Starbucks' future earnings, balance sheets, and cash flows.

18.14 SUMMARY

The preparation of pro forma financial statements requires numerous assumptions about the growth rate in sales, cost behavior of various expenses, levels of investment in working capital and fixed assets, mix of debt and equity financing, and others. The analyst should develop realistic expectations for these activities, and capture those expectations in pro forma financial statements that provide an objective and realistic portrait of the firm in the future. The analyst should study the sensitivity of the pro forma financial statements to the assumptions made and to the impact of different assumptions. After developing realistic expectations for future earnings, cash flows, and dividends using pro forma financial statement projections, the analyst can then begin to make decisions with these data, including decisions about the firm as a potential equity investment, or a potential credit risk, or a strategic plan.

CHAPTER 20

THEORY OF CONSTRAINTS*

Eric Noreen, PhD, CPA, CMA
University of Washington

CONTENTS

20.1 INTRODUCTION 573

20.2 CONSTRAINTS IN A JOB SHOP 574

20.3 THE GOAL 574

20.4 THROUGHPUT ACCOUNTING 575

20.5 CREATING WEALTH AS MEASURED BY PRESENT VALUE OF CASH FLOW 575

20.6 THE PROCESS OF ONGOING IMPROVEMENT 576

   (a) Step 1: Identify the System's Constraint(s) 576

   (b) Step 2: Exploit the System's Constraint(s) 576

   (c) Step 3: Subordinate All Else to Exploiting the System's Constraint(s) 577

   (d) Step 4: Relax the Constraint(s) 578

   (e) Step 5: If the Constraint Has Been Broken, Go Back to Step 1 578

20.7 IMPLICATIONS OF TOC FOR COST AND MANAGEMENT ACCOUNTANTS 579

   (a) Total Quality Management (TQM) and Business Process Reengineering 579

   (b) Efficient Production Scheduling 580

   (c) Implications for Efficiency Measures 580

   (d) Controlling Fixed Costs in TOC 582

   (e) Measuring the Profitability of Products 582

   (f) Constraint Pricing 583

   (g) Strategic Pricing in TOC 584

20.8 SUMMARY 585

BIBLIOGRAPHY 585

20.1 INTRODUCTION

The Theory of Constraints (TOC) can affect all aspects of management—decision making, planning, day-to-day operations, and performance evaluation. Any organization can use it. Most organizations will find TOC revolutionary because it fundamentally changes the way an organization functions. Similarities exist among portions of TOC and popular management movements such as just in time (JIT, discussed in other chapters of this *Handbook*), time quality management (TQM), and the balanced scorecard (discussed in Chapter 25).

---

* Some of the material in this chapter has been taken, with permission, from *The Theory of Constraints and Its Implications for Management Accounting*, by Eric Noreen, Debra Smith, and James T. Mackey (Great Barrington, Mass.: The North River Press, 1995). The book was the result of a project sponsored by the Institute of Management Accountants' Foundation for Applied Research and Price Waterhouse-Europe.

One chapter cannot examine the full breadth and range of TOC. This chapter will discuss TOC solutions to the problem of managing a job shop. Note, however, that TOC focuses on *deriving* solutions to problems; it does not offer a collection of solutions to specific problems. This chapter provides only an example of the kinds of solutions that one can derive using TOC techniques. Nevertheless, the solutions to the problem of managing a job shop prove interesting and important in their own right and have direct and obvious implications for cost and management accountants.

20.2   CONSTRAINTS IN A JOB SHOP

A job shop consists of multiple work centers, each performing various tasks. The work centers typically work at various rates. Different products (or services) can take different routes through these work centers and can place different demands on the work centers. Also, different products (or services) have different due dates and the job shop produces them in different volumes. This diversity presents a challenge to anyone managing a job shop.

Every job shop is in one of two situations: Either capacity equals or exceeds demand for the company's products, or demand exceeds capacity. If demand exceeds capacity, the company has a production constraint. We will discuss this situation first.

Managing a job shop becomes much more difficult when demand exceeds capacity than when capacity exceeds demand. If capacity exceeds demand, management can exploit slack to take on more work and to expedite jobs that are behind schedule. If demand exceeds capacity, any changes or disruptions in the schedule can have ripple effects that negatively affect many jobs.

What determines the capacity of a job shop? To keep the discussion simple, assume all products and services go through the same work centers in the same sequence, and they all require roughly the same amount of processing at each work center. Further assume that the rate of output does not vary at any work center. In this simple case, the work center with the lowest rate of output will determine the entire system's capacity. This work center is the *bottleneck* in the system.

The TOC literature makes a useful analogy between a system and a chain. Just as the weakest link determines the strength of a chain, the rate of output of the slowest work center determines the system's output (i.e., capacity).

If different products go through different routing sequences and place different demands on work centers and if the rate of output of each work center varies, then the bottleneck may not be the work center with the lowest *average* rate of output. Any one system, however, will still have only one bottleneck. (A system consists of all the steps required to make one product or service.) A system with more than one bottleneck will prove inherently unstable, and a single bottleneck will shortly emerge.

In summary, each system has only one bottleneck, and the average rate of output of the bottleneck determines the entire system's capacity. This insight has several implications for managing job shops. Before discussing those details, we need to establish what management should try to accomplish.

20.3   THE GOAL

An organization can specify any goals it desires, but in most cases, a company's primary goal is to increase owners' wealth—to earn income. This requires a focus on the net present value of cash flows. Consequently, management should evaluate every decision based on its effect on cash flows, both now and in the future. This line of reasoning places the Theory of Constraints solidly in the relevant costs school of thinking pioneered by Ronald Coase in Britain in the 1930s and adopted by all mainstream management accounting textbooks since the 1950s.

Note that if a company focuses on maximizing its cash flows, both now and in the future, we cannot speak of *attaining the goal*. The desire for more is insatiable.

20.4 THROUGHPUT ACCOUNTING

The distinction between fixed and variable costs becomes important when decisions involve choices between different levels of activity. For small changes in activity, only the variable costs are relevant because, by definition, changes in activity (up to some quantity) do not affect fixed costs. Accounting theorists have advocated variable costing for decades as a way to structure accounting reports to highlight the difference between variable and fixed costs. Variable costing includes only variable production costs in inventory valuations and treats fixed production costs as period expenses. The income statement deducts the variable costs from sales to arrive at the total contribution margin. Net profit equals the contribution margin less fixed cost.

The Theory of Constraints uses a version of variable costing called *throughput accounting*. In throughput accounting, the contribution margin is called *throughput* and fixed costs are called *operating expenses*. To avoid confusion, this chapter uses the more conventional terms *contribution margin* and *fixed costs*. Also, this chapter uses the term *throughput* to mean the rate at which the company produces output. In the Theory of Constraints, the unit contribution margin equals the selling price minus the costs of direct materials and other totally variable costs. Labor is not a totally variable cost.

Throughput accounting takes a more conservative approach than conventional financial accounting to revenue recognition. Throughput accounting delays revenue recognition until a consumer makes an irrevocable purchase. For example, sales to wholesalers or retailers who can return the product do not count as revenue in throughput accounting.

When placed in the context of the history of management accounting thought, TOC updates variable costing to recognize the fixed nature of much of direct labor and to delay revenue recognition. TOC recognizes that management can use variable costing statements to estimate relevant costs and benefits much more easily than absorption costing statements. TOC, like variable costing, contains no incentives to boost income by building inventories.

20.5 CREATING WEALTH AS MEASURED BY PRESENT VALUE OF CASH FLOW

Companies have only two ways to increase the net present value (NPV) of cash flows: either reduce spending on fixed cost items or increase the company's total contribution margin. A company will realize limited savings from reduced spending on fixed items. Reduced spending will, at some point, cut into productive capacity. Moreover, if reduced spending involves involuntary changes in personnel, morale will likely suffer. If morale suffers, the quality and quantity of goods and services produced for sale will likely drop. Even if management could reduce spending on fixed items to zero without any loss of productive capacity and without any effect on the company's total contribution margin, the goal of increasing NPV of cash flows requires increasing the total contribution margin. Sooner or later, managers must focus on increasing the total contribution margin.

A company can increase the total contribution margin in four different ways: (1) changing selling prices (discussed in Section 20.7(g)), (2) changing the product mix (discussed in Section 20.7(e)), (3) reducing variable costs, and (4) increasing the quantity of goods that it produces and sells. The third method, reducing variable costs, may not be feasible. But even if the company can reduce variable costs, it can increase the NPV of cash flows only a limited amount by taking this approach. A production constraint would seem to rule out the fourth method—that of increasing the quantity of goods produced and sold. By effectively managing the constraint, however, the company can uncover additional hidden capacity. Moreover, this can usually be done without incurring any significant additional fixed costs. The next section provides an overview of how an organization can accomplish this.

20.6   THE PROCESS OF ONGOING IMPROVEMENT

Exhibit 20.1 summarizes the process of managing constraints to obtain more throughput. TOC refers to this as the *process of ongoing improvement* because a company that follows these five steps can continually increase its throughput and hence its profits.

(a) STEP 1: IDENTIFY THE SYSTEM'S CONSTRAINT(S).   If you want to increase the system's throughput (i.e., the rate of output) and the average rate of output of the system's bottleneck determines the system's throughput, then clearly the company has to increase the average rate of output of the bottleneck. The first step is to identify the system's bottleneck (i.e., constraint). For now, suppose management has identified the constraint as a specific work center.

(b) STEP 2: EXPLOIT THE SYSTEM'S CONSTRAINT(S).   If demand exceeds capacity, the company can't satisfy all of its potential customers. Management has to decide what to do and *what not to do*. It must prioritize. How should management prioritize jobs? The answer to this question lies in nearly every introductory management accounting textbook. The company should prioritize the use of a constrained resource using the contribution margin per unit of the constrained resource. The following example illustrates this principle.

A workshop in Indonesia makes brass gongs and brass bells using a simple process. Workers pour molten brass into a mold, allow it to cool, and then file and polish the brass. The workshop produces molten brass from brass ingots that it heats in a kiln. With a capacity of 10 kilograms of molten brass per hour, the kiln is the constraint in the system. Data concerning the gongs and bells appear in Exhibit 20.2. (The currency in Indonesia is the rupiah, denoted here by Rup.)

Step 1.   Identify the system's constraint(s).

Step 2.   Exploit the system's constraint(s).

Step 3.   Subordinate everything else to exploiting the constraint(s).

Step 4.   Elevate the constraint(s).

Step 5.   If a constraint has been broken, go back to Step 1.

EXHIBIT 20.1   THE PROCESS OF ONGOING IMPROVEMENT

The constraint is the amount of molten brass that the kiln can produce. The capacity of the kiln is 10 kilograms of brass per hour.

	Gongs	Bells
Selling price per unit	Rup 10,000	Rup 5,000
Variable cost per unit	6,000	2,000
Contribution margin per unit (a).	Rup 4,000	Rup 3,000
Molten brass per unit (b)	0.50 kg	0.25 kg
Contribution margin per kg of molten brass (a) ÷ (b).	Rup 8,000 per kg	Rup 10,000 per kg

Contribution margin per unit of the constrained resource

EXHIBIT 20.2 AN EXAMPLE OF PRIORITIZING THE USE OF A CONSTRAINED RESOURCE

If demand exceeds capacity, which of the two products—gongs or bells—should receive higher priority? We can see from Exhibit 20.2 that the gongs have a higher contribution margin per unit than the bells. A gong, however, requires twice as much molten brass (0.50 kg) as does a bell (0.25 kg). To maximize the amount of money the company makes, it should maximize the contribution margin generated from the limited supply of molten brass. (Any fixed costs are irrelevant because the company will be operating at capacity and incurring the same fixed costs whether it produces gongs or bells.) If one kilogram of molten brass is available, the workshop can use it to make two gongs or four bells. The contribution margin from two gongs is Rup 8,000 (= 2 gongs × Rup 4,000 per gong) and from four bells is Rup 12,000 (= 4 bells × Rup 3,000 per bell). Therefore, even though the bells have a lower contribution margin per unit than the gongs, they make more efficient use of the constrained resource and should have higher priority. Note that one can obtain the same answers—Rup 8,000 for gongs and Rup 12,000 for bells—by dividing the contribution margin per unit by the amount of the constrained resource each unit requires as in Exhibit 20.2.

To summarize, if a bottleneck exists, an organization cannot fully satisfy demand. To decide which work to do and which to omit, management should compute the contribution margin per unit of the constrained resource for each job or product. In the absence of overriding factors—such as maintaining good relations with a key customer—the company should first drop the job or product with the lowest contribution margin per unit of the constrained resource.

(c) STEP 3: SUBORDINATE ALL ELSE TO EXPLOITING THE SYSTEM'S CONSTRAINT(S).
Recall the chain analogy in Section 20.2. If management wants to increase the chain's strength, it doesn't make sense to waste time increasing the strength of links that are already stronger than the weakest link. Instead, improvement efforts should focus on strengthening the weakest link.

In a job shop, management should focus on increasing the bottleneck's rate of output and ensuring that the bottleneck never has downtime waiting for work. The bottleneck sets the pace for the entire system.

(d) STEP 4: RELAX THE CONSTRAINT(S).   Relaxing the constraint means increasing the constraint's effective capacity. Management can do this in various ways, including the following:

- *Don't waste any of the constrained resource.* For example, inspect units before they go through the constraint, not after. A defective unit rejected after it passes through the constraint reduces the total output and sales of the company by one unit. A defective unit rejected before it passes through the constraint has no effect on total output and total sales.
- *Keep the bottleneck operating all of the time.* Arrange for relief workers when bottleneck workers take breaks. Schedule maintenance during holidays, weekends, and after normal working hours.
- *Reduce setup time on the bottleneck.* Setups that take a work center off-line reduce total output and total sales. Assign otherwise idle workers to the bottleneck to help with setups or to do setups off-line.
- *Focus reengineering efforts on the bottleneck.* Eliminate unnecessary steps. Use the creative energies of workers to find new ways of doing things better and faster. Reengineer products so that they require less of the bottleneck resource.
- *Add capacity to the bottleneck.* Add another machine or another worker to the bottleneck. Subcontract bottleneck work.

Some of these examples of relaxing the constraint cost little, while others involve some expenditures. How does a manager know when the cost of relaxing the constraint exceeds the benefit? How does one measure the benefit of relaxing the constraint? The benefit of relaxing the constraint equals the additional contribution margin that the company would realize. Returning to the example of the Indonesian company that makes gongs and bells, suppose that the workshop could fabricate additional molten brass by paying overtime wages to the foundryman at the rate of Rup 7,000 per hour. Does the benefit of paying overtime wages exceed this cost? To answer this question, we need to know what the company would do with the additional molten brass if it were available. From the earlier discussion, the company would probably have shifted production from gongs to bells because of the bells' higher contribution margin per kg of molten brass. (Recall that the gongs' contribution margin per kg of molten brass was Rup 8,000, whereas the bells' was Rup 12,000.) Assuming that the workshop already satisfies all of the existing demand for bells without working overtime, the company would use the additional molten brass from working overtime to produce gongs. The benefit to the company from producing more gongs would equal Rup 8,000 per kg of molten brass. Since the kiln generates 10 kg of molten brass per hour, the value of adding another hour of capacity in the foundry equals Rep 80,000 (= 10 kg × Rup 8,000 per kg). Since this exceeds the cost of Rup 7,000 per hour for the foundry worker, the benefit of overtime exceeds the cost.

In general, the value of relaxing the constraint (i.e., increasing its capacity) is the contribution margin per unit of the constrained resource for the marginal job, the one management would next add to the schedule if the workshop had additional capacity.

(e) STEP 5: IF THE CONSTRAINT HAS BEEN BROKEN, GO BACK TO STEP 1.   A company may increase the constraint's capacity so much that it is no longer the bottleneck. If that happens, the whole cycle begins again. Management identifies the new constraint, exploits it, relaxes it, and, perhaps, eliminates it. Through this process, the organization continues to increase the NPV of cash flows.

Note that this process never ends. If the goal is to increase cash flow, which has no limit, the organization will always face at least one constraint.

This concludes the brief overview of the five steps for ongoing improvement. This overview provides the basis for the next section, which examines some implications of TOC for cost and management accountants.

20.7 IMPLICATIONS OF TOC FOR COST AND MANAGEMENT ACCOUNTANTS

(a) TOTAL QUALITY MANAGEMENT (TQM) AND BUSINESS PROCESS REENGINEERING.
Interest in TQM and business process reengineering has waned, partly because companies have tried to embrace too many business movements (including TOC) in rapid succession. Perhaps even more important, operating improvements that resulted from TQM and business process reengineering frequently failed to increase profits. When viewed through a TOC lens, this failure seems almost inevitable unless companies can focus TQM and business process reengineering on constraints.

Suppose that a company uses TQM, or business process reengineering, or some other technique to improve a process that is not a bottleneck. Improvement usually means redesigning the process to increase its rate of output while consuming fewer resources—perhaps by omitting non-value-added steps. How can such an improvement at a *non-bottleneck* increase profits? If the process is not a bottleneck, speeding it up just creates more excess capacity. Excess capacity has some value, since it provides additional protection from random disruptions, but the benefits may be small and seldom realized.

Business process improvements can also lead to more profits by eliminating spending on no-longer-needed resources or redeploying them to better uses. Note that reducing the use of a resource or even eliminating the resource entirely doesn't increase profits unless the company also reduces spending. For example, writing off obsolete machines does nothing to improve future cash flows or current profits. To benefit from the reduction in the use of a resource, the company must reduce spending or redeploy the resource to a better use. When people are the excess resource, reducing spending can become a delicate problem. If a TQM or reengineering exercise identifies positions that the company no longer needs, future improvement efforts will face resistance and will likely fail. The alternative to laying off people is to reassign them. But where should the company reassign the excess people? On the one hand, reassigning them to a nonbottleneck work center will simply increase the excess capacity in that work center. Transferring excess personnel to the bottleneck, on the other hand, can have an immediate and dramatic effect on profits by increasing the amount of finished output that the company can produce and sell.

Note what happens if the business improvement program focuses on the bottleneck constraint. Speeding up the bottleneck yields immediate and substantial improvements in the bottom line. If the company can process one more unit per hour at the bottleneck, the contribution margin from that unit will drop directly to the bottom line.

In sum, to significantly affect profits, *business process improvement efforts should focus on the bottleneck constraint.* Moreover, if improvements in a work center that is not a bottleneck create excess resources, the company should ordinarily redeploy excess resources to the bottleneck.

(b) EFFICIENT PRODUCTION SCHEDULING. The problem of scheduling a job shop to ensure that diverse jobs are completed on time has bedeviled managers for decades. TOC solves this problem by focusing on the bottleneck.

Ordinarily, the work centers that lie downstream from the bottleneck, where work follows the bottleneck in time, are not critical. These downstream work centers can process units at a faster pace than the bottleneck, so anything that the bottleneck finishes will pass through the remaining work centers with only minimal delays.

However, work centers that lie upstream from the bottleneck in the production process should be closely monitored. The upstream work centers must ensure that the bottleneck is not idle. Any time lost on the bottleneck is lost forever and results in lower profits. The upstream work centers should also be monitored to ensure that work in process inventories do not pile up in front of the bottleneck. As we will discuss below, some inventories are necessary in front of the bottleneck. However, without sufficient monitoring, these inventories can pile up and become a real problem. The bottleneck should dictate the pace of all other upstream work centers. In particular, managers must resist the temptation to increase the rate of output of the upstream work centers beyond the bottleneck's capacity. If the bottleneck can process only 10 units per hour, but the upstream work centers process 12 units per hour, work-in-process inventory will grow at the rate of two units per hour. As long as the upstream work centers continue producing at a faster pace than the bottleneck can process units, the work-in-process inventory will increase.

The just-in-time (JIT) movement has taught us that excessive work in process inventories create operating problems, such as long cycle times, high defect rates, obsolescence, poor on-time delivery performance, and high holding and storage costs. Indeed, JIT strives to eliminate work in process inventories entirely.

TOC takes a slightly less radical approach than does JIT, striving to eliminate work in process inventories everywhere except at one location—just before the bottleneck. This strategically located buffer inventory protects the bottleneck from upstream disruptions. If the work centers upstream of the bottleneck experience problems that disrupt the flow of throughput, the buffer inventory should allow the bottleneck to continue processing units until the disruption ends. In the absence of this buffer inventory, any upstream disruption shuts down the bottleneck. This wastes productive capacity and results in the permanent loss of contribution margin and of profit.

TOC refers to this efficient production scheduling as *drum-buffer-rope*. The *drum* is the bottleneck. The *buffer* is the inventory maintained in front of the bottleneck to ensure that it is not idle. The *rope* pulls jobs through the manufacturing system.

(c) IMPLICATIONS FOR EFFICIENCY MEASURES. Almost all job shops rely on some measure of work center efficiency to help control operations and to evaluate the performance of direct labor workers and their supervisors. TOC shows that this reliance is misplaced.

Labor efficiency measures take several forms, but almost all compare hours earned (or charged to product) to hours actually worked or hours actually paid. Hours earned is the standard hours allowed for the actual output of the period. For example, if center Z has processed 100 units of Product X this month, and if the standard for Product X is 0.2 hour per unit in work center Z, then work center Z would earn 20 hours (= 0.2 hour per unit × 100 units). In some organizations, the efficiency measure equals the ratio of hours earned to actual hours. In other organizations, the efficiency measure is a standard cost variance that equals the difference between the actual hours and the hours earned multiplied by the standard hourly wage rate. If the actual hours exceed the actual hours earned, the variance is unfavorable. If the actual hours earned exceed the actual hours, the variance is favorable.

The actual hours in the efficiency measure may be the actual hours worked during the month or it may be the actual hours paid during the month, the difference between the two consisting of idle time, training time, break time, and so on. Suppose the actual hours in the efficiency measure refer to the actual hours paid. In many companies, direct labor workers are permanent employees who work at least a specified number of hours a week—in the United States, commonly 40 hours a week. Employees receive payment for the entire 40 hours, even if the organization does not have enough work to keep them fully occupied.

How can work center supervisors avoid unfavorable labor efficiency variances if the company guarantees direct-labor workers payment for a 40-hour week? Supervisors can accomplish this by ensuring that everyone in the work center produces a rate of output at least as high as the standard specifies for every hour they receive payment. If the workers receive payment for 40 hours a week and the standard equals five units per hour, then the work center must process 200 units (= 40 hours/week × 5 units per hour) per week per worker to avoid an unfavorable variance.

Companies vary in how they set standards, but let us suppose that a company bases its standard on how much time a reasonably competent worker should require to complete a task when working efficiently, with some allowances for required personal breaks. By setting the standard in this way, the work center will avoid an unfavorable variance only if it operates at capacity all of the time.

What happens if every work center attempts to operate at capacity so as to avoid unfavorable efficiency variances? If work centers upstream of the bottleneck process units at a faster pace than the bottleneck can handle, work in process inventories will pile up in front of the bottleneck, with no increase in completed units. This will increase costs and create operational problems, with no increase in revenues.

Furthermore, if the organization holds work center supervisors responsible for direct labor efficiency variances, supervisors will tend to run large batches of the products with the most generous standards rather than produce small batches of products that customers may prefer. This will lead to large inventories of products that the work center can easily make (but the customers may not want) and insufficient production of items that customers demand.

Nonbottleneck work centers *should* be idle part of the time. If they are not, the result is excessive work-in-process inventories with no increase in revenue. Therefore, assuming that the standards have been set to encourage operating each work center at capacity, *the nonbottleneck work centers ordinarily should have unfavorable labor efficiency variances.*

Should the labor efficiency variance at the *bottleneck* be favorable or unfavorable? At least initially, the bottleneck should have an unfavorable labor efficiency variance. After management has initially identified a constraint, supervisors should temporarily assign to the bottleneck people who would otherwise be idle. By doing mundane housekeeping chores, they can free the time of more experienced workers and thereby increase the total amount that the workshop produces at the bottleneck. The output per worker (including the temporarily assigned workers) at the bottleneck work center may decline, but the total output will increase. When business process improvement efforts focus on the bottleneck, the output per worker should increase and the labor efficiency variance should improve.

In summary, all of the work centers—except for the bottleneck—should have *unfavorable* labor efficiency variances. Moreover, it is not clear whether the bottleneck should have a favorable or unfavorable labor efficiency variance. This suggests that management should abandon the use of labor efficiency measures to evaluate performance.

Management could fix the labor efficiency variance reporting system by recalibrating the labor standards to indicate a favorable variance if a nonbottleneck work center meets the plan and an unfavorable variance otherwise. This would require recalibrating the labor standard each period because the amount of work that a nonbottleneck work center should do depends on the precise product mix. Companies can use other, simpler, and more direct ways to monitor how well the nonbottleneck work centers follow the plan. For example, managers can generally spot problems quickly by checking the buffer inventory that immediately precedes the bottleneck. A decreasing buffer inventory signals that the company may have problems upstream from the bottleneck that it should immediately address.

TOC requires many managers to change their basic approach—particularly those who manage nonbottlenecks. Those managers should *not* focus on whether everyone works hard and maximizes efficiency. Instead, their basic task is to feed the bottleneck on schedule.

This section has discussed labor efficiency. The same issues occur with measures of machine efficiency and with overhead efficiency variances. If the company holds work center supervisors responsible for these variances, excess work in process inventories will almost inevitably result.

(d) CONTROLLING FIXED COSTS IN TOC.   TOC pays little attention to fixed costs, but leads to insights for controlling fixed costs. Fixed costs are the costs of providing capacity. Ordinarily, additional resources should be provided only at the bottleneck. Additional resources to expand capacity in nonbottleneck work centers should be questioned. Of course, resources may expand capabilities as well as capacity, and additional capacity may be required even in a nonbottleneck work center if it occasionally becomes the bottleneck. Nevertheless, managers in TOC tend to take a hard line on increases in fixed costs, ignoring pleas for additional resources in nonbottleneck work centers. This approach contrasts with the presumption in some non-TOC organizations that entitles every department to last year's budget plus some percentage. To a large extent, TOC organizations control fixed costs by just saying no to increases.

(e) MEASURING THE PROFITABILITY OF PRODUCTS.   Managers often want to know the relative profitability of segments of the business. The segments could be products, customers, regional sales offices, or any other way of looking at a part of the overall organization. For discussion purposes, we will focus on products, but the analysis would apply to any other segment.

Relative profitability differs from absolute profitability. A product is absolutely profitable if the company makes higher profits with the product than without the product. Managers need to know absolute profitability, but they also should rank the profitability of all the absolutely profitable products. Why? If a situation forces the company to choose between producing and selling product A or product B, for example, management will want a measure of relative profitability.

What would force a company to choose among products? A constraint of some sort must exist. If no constraint exists, management need not make a tradeoff. If a constraint exists, the company cannot satisfy the demand for all products and must rank the products.

(*Note:* The constraint does not necessarily have to be a production constraint. It could be a policy constraint. This extremely important issue is discussed in the TOC literature.)

How should one measure the relative profitability of products in the presence of a constraint? This question was discussed in Section 20.6(b) as step 2 of the process of ongoing improvement. To correctly rank products, customers, projects, or any other segment, management should measure relative profitability as the contribution margin per unit of the constrained resource.[1]Unfortunately, common practices such as measuring relative profitability in terms of gross margin as a percentage of sales are incorrect.

(f) CONSTRAINT PRICING. According to surveys, managers in most companies try to set prices by marking up some version of full cost. This common practice differs considerably from the price-setting mechanism described in microeconomics. The apparent contradiction between theory and practice has puzzled economists for decades and has provided grist for many articles in economics and accounting that have tried to rationalize full cost pricing. Interestingly, pricing in TOC follows microeconomic theory more closely than does the common practice of marking up full cost. TOC organizations set prices according to what managers believe customers will pay, with an eye to competitive conditions. The organization considers cost only when setting a lower boundary on the price.

Suppose a company already operating at capacity is considering accepting a new order. Clearly, the company should not accept the order if it provides less profit than other potential orders. For illustration, assume that the constraint is labor in process X. Clearly, the company should not accept an order that generates \$10 of contribution margin per labor-hour in process X if it means giving up another order that would generate \$12 per labor-hour. Stated in terms of a formula, the new order is acceptable only if the following holds:

$$\frac{\text{Price} - \text{Variable cost}}{\text{Amount of constrained resource required}} \geq \begin{array}{l} \text{Contribution margin per unit of the} \\ \text{constrained resource for the marginal job} \end{array}$$

The marginal job in this formula refers to the job that the new order would displace. Recall the earlier example of the brass foundry, where the marginal job is gongs. Bells provide more profit per kilogram of molten brass than gongs. Therefore, the workshop would produce bells as long as demand exists and would use the remaining capacity to produce gongs. Since any new order would displace production of gongs, the contribution margin per unit of the constraint for the new order should at least equal the contribution margin per unit of the constraint for the gongs, which is Rup 8,000 per kilogram of molten brass.

Note that fixed costs play no role in the pricing formula. This occurs because the company would be operating at capacity (with presumably the same total fixed costs) whether or not it accepts a new order. The fixed costs should not affect a decision of whether to accept the new order, or what price to charge, since the decision does not affect fixed costs.

---

1. When ranking discrete segments, management should interpret the contribution margin as the difference between the segment's incremental cash inflows and the incremental cash outflows. For example, when the constraint is investment funds, management can rank investment projects by dividing their net present values by the amounts of investment funds they require. The net present value of a project is a way to summarize its incremental cash inflows and outflows.

One can use the preceding inequality to solve for the minimum acceptable price for the new order as follows:

$$\text{Price} \geq \text{Variable cost} + \left(\begin{array}{c} \text{Amount of constrained resource required } \times \\ \text{Contribution margin per unit of the} \\ \text{constrained resource for the marginal job} \end{array} \right)$$

For example, suppose a customer has requested a bid on a set of chimes that would require 100 kilograms of molten brass and that would have a variable cost of Rup 70,000. The minimum acceptable price for the chimes would be Rup 870,000, established as follows:

$$\text{Price} \geq \text{Rup } 70,000 + (100 \text{ kilograms} \times \text{Rup } 8,000 \text{ per kilogram}) = \text{Rup } 870,000$$

The minimum acceptable price for the new order equals Rup 870,000 and consists of two parts: the variable cost of Rup 70,000 and the opportunity cost of Rup 800,000. The opportunity cost is the contribution margin from the gongs that the company would have to give up to accept the new order.

Opportunity cost plays an important role in such decisions. Accepting the new order means that 100 kilograms of molten brass would not be available for making gongs. Since each gong requires 0.5 kilogram of molten brass, accepting the new order for chimes would require reducing the production of gongs by 200 units. Each gong generates contribution margin of Rup 4,000. Therefore, accepting the new order for chimes would require giving up a total contribution margin of Rup 800,000 (= 200 gongs × Rup 4,000 per gong). This reflects the opportunity cost of accepting the new order for chimes. One can also calculate the opportunity cost by multiplying the amount of constrained resource required for the new order (100 kilograms of molten brass) by the contribution margin per unit of the constrained resource for the marginal job (Rup 8,000 per kilogram of molten brass).

When pricing calculations include opportunity costs, the costs often exceed even fully allocated costs. A company that prices its products by applying a markup above its fully absorbed product costs might actually be losing money on some products.

Note that cost does not determine price in TOC; it simply sets a lower bound on price. The market or the value of the product or service to the customer determines the price.

(g) STRATEGIC PRICING IN TOC. Even in markets that one would consider competitive, companies often have some discretion in setting prices. How can a company use pricing to increase its profits?

Taking a variable costing perspective, profit equals the difference between total contribution margin and fixed costs:

$$\text{Profit} = \text{Total contribution margin} - \text{Fixed costs}$$

By dividing and multiplying the total contribution margin by the total amount of the constrained resource used, we get the following equation:

$$\text{Profit} = \left[\left(\frac{\text{Total contribution margin}}{\text{Total amount of constrained resource used}} \right) \times \begin{array}{c} \text{Total amount of constrained} \\ \text{resource used} \end{array} \right] - \text{Fixed costs}$$

We can restate the equation as follows:

$$\text{Profit} = \left[\begin{array}{c} \text{Average contribution margin per} \\ \text{unit of the constrained resource} \end{array} \times \begin{array}{c} \text{Total amount of constrained} \\ \text{resource used} \end{array} \right] - \text{Fixed costs}$$

At this point, we need to ask how the company can use pricing to increase profits. Assuming that capacity is not altered, the company's pricing practices should not affect fixed costs. However, prices can directly affect the average contribution margin per unit of the constrained resource and the total amount of the constrained resource used. For example, a company could increase the prices of all of its products. This would increase the average contribution margin per unit of the constrained resource, but would probably result in a decrease in the total amount of the constrained resource used. This may lead to a decrease in overall profits. The trick in pricing is to somehow increase the average contribution margin per unit of the constrained resource while keeping the company operating at full capacity. How can a company do this?

Assuming that the company operates in competitive markets, with known prices, it can compute the contribution margin per unit of the constrained resource for every product. Some products will prove more profitable than others, according to this profitability index. A company can increase the average contribution margin per unit of the constrained resource by shifting the product mix toward the more profitable products. It can do this by slightly discounting the prices of the more profitable products and charging a premium for any products whose prices otherwise would not cover variable plus opportunity costs. Through the pricing mechanism, the product mix will naturally shift, resulting in a higher average contribution margin per unit of the scarce resource. Of course, this strategy will work only as long as competitors do not retaliate. Competitive conditions in the industry become important in assessing the delicacy with which one should proceed when changing prices.

20.8 SUMMARY

Fundamentally, the Theory of Constraints focuses on the process of solving problems; it is not a collection of solutions to specific problems. Nevertheless, this chapter discusses some generic TOC solutions to common problems encountered in job shops. When the company's constraint is a physical process, management should follow the five steps for ongoing improvement. The five steps work by focusing on the constraint, elevating it through process improvements and other means, and eventually eliminating it. Once the company eliminates one constraint, another will appear and the cycle begins again.

The contribution margin per unit of the constrained resource plays a pivotal role in TOC. This measure is used to prioritize the use of the constraint, to estimate the benefits of elevating the constraint, to assess profitability, and to set prices. TOC regards many cost accounting and management accounting practices—such as absorption costing and standard cost variance reporting—as counterproductive.

BIBLIOGRAPHY

Goldratt, Eliyahu M. *The Haystack Syndrome.* Great Barrington, Mass.: North River Press, 1990.

Goldratt, Eliyahu M., and Jeff Cox. *The Goal: A Process of Ongoing Improvement, Second Revised Edition.* Great Barrington, Mass.: North River Press, 1992.

Goldratt, Eliyahu M. *It's Not Luck.* Great Barrington, Mass.: North River Press, 1995.

Noreen, Eric, Debra Smith, and James T. Mackey. *The Theory of Constraints and Its Implications for Management Accounting.* Great Barrington, Mass.: North River Press, 1995.

CHAPTER **28**

A MANAGERIAL ACCOUNTING GUIDE FOR NONPROFIT MANAGERS*

LESLIE ELDENBURG, PhD
University of Arizona

NAOMI SODERSTROM, PhD
University of Colorado, Boulder

CONTENTS

28.1 INTRODUCTION 697

28.2 COMPARING NONPROFIT AND FOR-PROFIT ORGANIZATIONS 698

  (a) Compensation in Nonprofit Organizations 699
  (b) Tax Status of Nonprofit Organizations 700
  (c) Financial Reporting for Nonprofits 701

28.3 APPLICATION OF CURRENT COST ACCOUNTING PRACTICES IN NONPROFIT ORGANIZATIONS 702

  (a) Activity-Based Costing 703
  (b) Benchmarking 703
  (c) The Balanced Scorecard 704
  (d) Target and Kaizen Costing 704

28.4 ACCOUNTING PRACTICES AND COST ACCOUNTING ISSUES FOR SPECIFIC

TYPES OF NONPROFIT ORGANIZATIONS 705

  (a) Service Organizations 705
  (b) Operating Leverage 706
  (c) Step Down and Reciprocal Methods of Cost Allocation 707

28.5 HOSPITALS 707

28.6 GOVERNMENT ENTITIES AND ENVIRONMENTAL ACCOUNTING REPORTS 710

  (a) Government Accounting—Fund Accounting 710
  (b) Regulatory Reporting Requirements for Government Contracts—CASB Standards 712
  (c) Environmental Accounting 713
  (d) Regulatory Reporting Requirements for Environmental Accounting 714

BIBLIOGRAPHY 718

28.1 INTRODUCTION

This chapter provides a broad overview of accounting for nonprofit organizations. We have designed it for accountants (both for-profit and nonprofit) who wish to understand managerial incentives and cost behavior in nonprofit organizations and for nonprofit managers who want to analyze and reduce costs in their organizations. Section 28.2 discusses

---

* This chapter originally included a discussion of step-down and reciprical methods to allocate service department costs, which the editors moved to the Appendix of Chapter 16.

differences between for-profit and nonprofit organizations and presents managerial incentives and compensation considerations in the nonprofit setting. Section 28.3 applies current managerial accounting techniques to nonprofit organizations. Section 28.4 discusses issues specific to nonprofit organizations. Section 28.5 examines special issues facing hospitals. Section 28.6 presents accounting issues that pertain to government entities, requirements for firms contracting with the government, and information about required environmental accounting reports.

28.2   COMPARING NONPROFIT AND FOR-PROFIT ORGANIZATIONS

Nonprofit organizations differ from for-profit firms on a number of dimensions. To better understand the issues that arise in nonprofits, one should compare the operations within the two types of entities. Nonprofit organizations tend to dominate in areas such as education, religion, and research. Donations frequently support a portion of the operating costs in these types of organizations. Fama and Jensen[1] suggest that nonprofits survive as organizations supported by donors because this type of ownership offers an efficient solution to problems that would arise if private individuals owned the organization. These so-called *agency problems* result from conflicts of interest over efficient use of funds and use of surplus funds generated by organizations.

A for-profit firm with positive net cash flows either reinvests in the organization or distributes to its residual claimants. Residual claimants are those individuals who have contracted with the firm for rights to net cash flows. In privately held firms, these individuals own the firm. In publicly held firms, these individuals are shareholders. In nonprofit organizations, donors prefer that any net cash flows support the mission of the organization, and want more investment in program-related activities and less investment in non-program-related activities, such as perquisites for the managers. The nonprofit ownership structure, therefore, does not include a role for residual claimants such as shareholders. This is the primary difference between nonprofit and other ownership structures.

Over the years, the business environment of nonprofits has changed. Originally, donations provided the only source of funds. For example, prior to 1900, hospitals were charitable organizations founded to provide services for the poor. They did not charge for their services because wealthy donors completely funded hospital costs. Although a large group of nonprofit organizations still rely completely on donations (religious organizations, for example), many others—such as educational institutions and health care providers—receive operating funds from donors, government and other grants, and fees for services provided. As organizations receive increasingly larger proportions of their operating funds from fees, their need for donations diminishes.

Funding sources provide nonprofit organizations with two types of funds: (1) restricted funds that can be used only for purposes specified by the funding source; and (2) unrestricted funds that the organization may use at its discretion. Theoretically, nonprofit organizations use any net cash flows to support their nonprofit missions. Therefore, they use surplus (profit) to deliver products at lower prices, increase the amount of charitable services provided, or increase capacity. These uses of funds eliminate surplus available for distribution to residual claimants.

---

1.   E. Fama and M. Jensen. "Agency Problems and Residual Claims" *Journal of Law and Economics* 26, (June 1983): 327–350.

The absence of residual claims in nonprofits does not mean that nonprofits make no profits or that seeking those profits is risk-free. The organization uses net cash flows to expand outputs or to lower the price of outputs. These organizations need some financial cushion to remain viable, and to the extent the cushion is inadequate, employees, consumers, and suppliers bear some risk. Although nonprofits use their residual cash flows, no one owns the right to share in them. For example, nonprofit hospitals require current medical technology and so may invest surplus funds in assets that provide updated diagnostic and treatment capabilities. Alternatively, nonprofit hospitals with surplus funds might provide more charity care, defer increases in rates, or increase the quality of their services.

Although nonprofit organizations do not have residual claimants, a variety of individuals—referred to as stakeholders—do have expectations for the organization, and these are usually of an implicit nature. These stakeholders include vendors with whom the organizations contract: donors, employees, and the communities served by nonprofits. In a hospital, for example, stakeholders include donors, physicians, employees, suppliers, patients, and the community served by the hospital. Although none of these stakeholders can lay claim to the organization's surplus cash flows, they all expect the hospital to honor some implicit contracts. For example, physicians expect hospitals to provide an adequate number of beds and an appropriate level of technology for patient treatment. Managers of nonprofit organizations may need incentives to align their goals with stakeholder expectations. Compensation packages can provide these types of incentives.

(a) COMPENSATION IN NONPROFIT ORGANIZATIONS. For-profit organizations often use residual claims (compensation in the form of stock or based on stock prices) to link managers' incentives to shareholders' wealth. As managers increase their share of the firm, their preferences become increasingly similar to shareholders' preferences. Because nonprofit organizations have no residual claimants, no comparable incentive schemes can exist. Therefore, to create appropriate incentives, the organization frequently ties a portion of the managers' compensation to performance measures.

Because the mission or objective of a nonprofit organization (by definition) is service rather than earnings, operating surplus (net income) may not appropriately measure success for managers or organizations. Accordingly, many nonprofit organizations use measures of expenses relative to budget. This incentive scheme, however, creates a tendency for managers to add slack to the budget to guarantee that expenses do not exceed budgeted amounts. Because most nonprofit organizations endeavor to deliver services in the most efficient manner possible, other performance measures may more appropriately drive bonus-based compensation. Benchmarks for productivity, or measures of quality of services and client satisfaction, or a combination of performance measures that reflect the organizations' objectives help to align the incentives of nonprofit managers with those of the overall organization.

As financial risk in the nonprofit business environment increases, the need for performance-based compensation increases. For example, hospitals that were relatively inefficient, hence, more adversely affected by Medicare's reimbursement change in 1983, tended to implement bonus contracts more often (see Lambert and Larcker, 1995) than those that were not as adversely affected.[2] This study also found that hospitals closely monitored by either the state or their boards of directors were less likely to use bonus-based compensation.

---

2. R. Lambert and D. Larcker, "The Prospective Payment System, Hospital Efficiency, and Compensation Contracts for Senior-Level Hospital Administrators," *Journal of Accounting and Public Policy* (14) (1995): 1–31.

Organizations with strong visions and clear missions can benefit from using bonus incentives based on measures of financial and nonfinancial performance, such as benchmarks or balanced scorecards, that reflect the organization's values. Chapter 25 discusses these types of performance measures. This chapter briefly discusses them later in Sections 28.3(b) and 28.3(c). When an organization ties the managers' incentives to performance measures that reflect its values, the firm is likely to perform better in those areas measured.

(b) TAX STATUS OF NONPROFIT ORGANIZATIONS.   Nonprofit ownership confers the benefit of tax-exempt status. Although for-profits and nonprofits may operate similarly, nonprofits remain tax-exempt entities as long as no residual claimants exist. In the United States, the Supreme Court and the Internal Revenue Service (IRS) have affirmed a community-benefit standard as the most appropriate for deciding the tax-exempt status for health care providers and other service-oriented nonprofits.

To be tax exempt, organizations apply to the IRS for nonprofit status. Section 501(a) of the Internal Revenue Code explains the requirements for federal income tax exemption. To qualify under Section 501(a), an organization must conform to one of several descriptions listed in the code and must prove that it satisfies all of the requirements. Most organizations qualify under Section 501(c)(3) requirements, which include the following:

- The firm must forbid any form of private benefit or private inurement (laying claim to any surplus) by individuals within the organization.
- The firm must operate exclusively for charitable purposes or for the promotion of social welfare.
- The firm must serve public rather than private interests.
- The firm cannot engage in political or lobbying activities.
- The firm must operate in accordance with established public policy (Fahey and Murphey, 1990).

Nonprofits secure that status under Section 501(c) by filing Form 1023 with the IRS. Once a firm has applied for nonprofit status, the applicant organization may file an annual information return (usually Form 990) for tax-exempt organizations while the application for recognition of tax exemption is pending. Once the IRS has recognized an organization's tax-exempt status, the organization cannot voluntarily relinquish it. Health care organizations such as nonprofit hospitals and homes for the aged or handicapped must provide information to the IRS in addition to that required of charitable organizations in general. For more information, see Hyatt and Hopkins, 1995.[3]

In the United States, tax-exempt organizations may deduct donations from their income when calculating their federal income tax. A nonprofit firm that does not rely on donations, however, may elect to operate without formal recognition as a tax-exempt entity and still achieve the same basic objective—the nonpayment of tax. For example, an organization may operate so that its expenses equal or exceed recognizable income in any taxable year. Cooperatives, other than formally tax-exempt ones, function on this basis without having to pay income tax. Cooperatives issue patronage dividends to reduce any income and avoid paying federal income taxes.[4]

---

3.   T. Hyatt and B. Hopkins, *The Law of Tax-Exempt Healthcare Organizations* (New York: John Wiley, 1995).

4.   Cooperatives do not pay taxes on earnings that are reinvested or distributed as patronage dividends based on individuals' purchases during the fiscal year. However, patrons must declare patronage dividends as income in the year they are received.

Individual states also require that nonprofit organizations file for tax-exempt status. Requirements resemble those of the federal government, but may vary by state. States regulate the process of raising funds for charitable purposes. All but three states (Delaware, Montana, and Wyoming) have some form of statutory structure (termed *a charitable solicitation act*) that regulates fund-raising. Any nonprofit organization that raises funds within a state must abide by the comprehensive charitable solicitation acts established by that state. These regulations usually require annual reports regarding the fund-raising program, describe recordkeeping requirements, list prohibited acts, and detail the sanctions that the state can impose for failure to comply with the law.

Exemption from state and federal taxes may give nonprofits a competitive advantage (lower costs) over for-profit businesses in the same industry. For-profit organizations occasionally complain to government regulators that nonprofits have not provided community benefits in amounts that qualify for tax-exemption. If the tax forms that the organization files reveal, for example, that high-level managers receive excessive compensation, the IRS or state governments could decide that these managers are essentially residual claimants and revoke the nonprofit's tax-exempt status. The organization may also jeopardize its tax-exempt status by not providing adequate community benefit.

(c) FINANCIAL REPORTING FOR NONPROFITS. In addition to preparing information for tax purposes, nonprofit accountants prepare financial statements for various stakeholders. Accounting regulation has traditionally focused on financial reporting for external stakeholders. Financial accounting standards dictate the presentation of financial information for organizations. Over time, nonprofit firms have increasingly depended on the fees they charge for providing service, thereby diminishing the financial accounting differences between nonprofit and for-profit organizations.

Accordingly, during the late 1980s, the Financial Accounting Standards Board (FASB) began to pressure nonprofit organizations to use accounting methods that conformed more with generally accepted accounting principles used by for-profits. In December 1985, the FASB issued the Statement of Financial Accounting Concepts (SFAC) No. 6, Elements of Financial Statements, which replaced SFAC No. 3, Elements of Financial Statements of Business Enterprises (FASB 1994/1995).[5] With SFAC No. 6, FASB extended the concepts and definitions presented in SFAC No. 3 (originally applied only to for-profit entities) to nonprofit organizations. FASB stated that because all organizations have assets and liabilities, the definitions of equity (net assets), revenues, expenses, gains, and losses should fit both for-profit and nonprofit organizations. In response to SFAC No. 6, the AICPA substantially revised the 1987 Audit Guide for Hospitals and issued "Audits of Providers of Health Care Services" in 1990 and updated it in 1994 (AICPA, 1994).[6] The 1994 guide requires health care organizations' financial statements to conform to standards applied to for-profit organizations.

The standards for nonprofit and for-profit firms differ in a few areas, especially for nonprofit health care providers. Recognition of volunteers' time remains one difference. Because nonprofit firms have difficulty placing a monetary value on donated services, they do not usually record value for donated services. The Audit and Accounting Guide for Health Care Services states that if all of the following conditions exist, the firm must

---

5. Financial Accounting Standards Board. *Statements of Financial Accounting Concepts: Accounting Standards.* (New York: Irwin, 1994/1995).
6. AICPA. *Audit and Accounting Guide for Hospitals* (1994).

report the estimated value of donated services as an expense and report a corresponding amount as a contribution:

1. Services performed are significant and form an integral part of the efforts of the entity as it is currently constituted; the services would be performed by salaried personnel if donated services were not available to accomplish its purpose; and the entity would continue this program or activity.

2. The entity controls the employment and duties of the service donor and is able to influence their activities in a way comparable to the control it would exercise of employees with similar responsibilities. This includes control over time, location, and nature and performance of donated or contributed services.

3. The entity has a clearly measurable basis for the amount to be recorded.[7]

FASB Statement No. 116[8] states that a nonprofit firm should recognize contributions of services only if they (a) create or enhance nonfinancial assets; or (b) require specialized skills that are provided by individuals possessing those skills and would typically need to be purchased if not provided by donation. Volunteer participation in philanthropic activities generally does not meet these criteria, however, because no effective employer–employee relation exists (as required in #2, in the list above).

From a managerial accounting perspective, volunteer services may cause significant cost savings for the organization. Organizations with such cost savings should include an estimate of the benefit from volunteer services in cost estimates. Even though measuring these benefits can prove difficult, including rough estimates of their value more accurately reflects operations than ignoring such benefits altogether.

This concludes the general discussion of the difference between nonprofits and for-profits. Many of the accounting practices and innovations introduced in other chapters apply to both for-profits and nonprofits. Section 28.2 briefly introduces relevant information from other chapters and describes any special considerations for nonprofit organizations. From a cost accounting perspective, an important characteristic of nonprofit organizations is their tendency to have relatively high fixed costs. Many for-profit service organizations may have similar cost structures, and the following discussion will apply to them as well.

28.3   APPLICATION OF CURRENT COST ACCOUNTING PRACTICES IN NONPROFIT ORGANIZATIONS

Nonprofits must gather information for regulatory reports. Consequently, they often base their internal accounting systems on the information systems required to produce regulatory reports. Unfortunately, these reporting systems do not provide relevant information for the wide variety of decisions that managers must make. Managers need to consider the types of decisions that they make and develop accounting techniques and systems appropriate to support their decision-making processes.

Development of appropriate accounting techniques requires an understanding of the nature of the organization's costs. For example, many nonprofits have proportionately high fixed costs. These service-oriented firms must often devote a large proportion of their operating expenses to the fixed cost of salaries and benefits. To improve output, the

---

7.   AICPA, *Audit and Accounting Guide for Hospitals* (1994), p. 8.

8.   Financial Accounting Standards Board. *Statements of Financial Accounting Standards No. 116.*

organization needs to analyze these fixed costs, along with output efficiency. Managerial accounting techniques developed for and applied in the for-profit sector do not always directly apply to nonprofit organizations. The following discussion examines several cost accounting techniques developed in the for-profit sector and their relevance and flexibility within the nonprofit sector.

(a) ACTIVITY-BASED COSTING.[9]   When firms use activity-based costing (ABC), they must first analyze production processes to identify a set of activities that drive production costs. ABC aggregates costs in cost pools for specific activities and then identifies cost drivers to measure the activities. For example, a firm could track the cost of purchasing all of its materials and supplies and then designate the number of purchase invoices as the cost driver. This results in a cost per invoice for the activity of purchasing. Once the firm identifies a set of cost pools and drivers, it can set standards and make cost allocations using the cost driver for that activity as an allocation base. (Chapters 6 and 11 discuss ABC).

Early versions of ABC included both fixed and variable costs in each activity cost pool. Information developed in this manner tended to overstate incremental cost, especially for firms with high fixed costs. For example, Noreen and Soderstrom[10] examined a sample of hospital overhead accounts for an average of 108 hospitals over a 15-year period. They found that, on average, 80 percent of costs were fixed and that an activity-based costing model overstated incremental costs by more than 40 percent.

More recent advances in ABC include the development of separate cost pools for flexible and committed costs, as well as categorization of costs into a cost hierarchy, with some categories that do not affect decision making. Implementing these more complex ABC systems, however, can prove time consuming and expensive.

When physicians become part of the team that develops an ABC system, they will more likely believe in the cost information's credibility and consider it in their decision making. In addition, the quality of the cost information improves because those who employ the resources participate in mapping resource usage to cost. Accounting research over the years provides mixed results on the effectiveness of ABC systems in for-profit organizations.

(b) BENCHMARKING.   Analysts use the term benchmarking to refer to the process of measuring products, services and activities against the best levels of performance. One can find these best levels of performance within the organization through internal benchmarking information or through external benchmarking information gathered from competing organizations or from consulting firms that offer benchmarking services.

The hospital industry uses consulting firms that produce benchmark information for departments, service products, and activities undertaken by hospitals. These consultants analyze cost information submitted by hospitals to various U.S. regulatory bodies and generate reports that compare specific hospitals with other similar U.S. hospitals. Hospital administrators use these reports to direct attention to areas with above-average costs. The reliability of individual hospital cost data used in these benchmark reports varies. Hospitals with less refined cost accounting systems may produce unreliable data. In addition, the cost-allocation process affects benchmarking information. Additional factors that

---

9.   See Chapter 6 for a more complete discussion of activity-based costing.

10.   E. Noreen, and N. Soderstrom, "The Accuracy of Proportional Cost Models: Evidence from Hospital Service Departments, *Review of Accounting Studies* (2) (1997): 89–114.

warrant analysis for hospitals include perceived quality of service to patients, success rate of procedures and operations, and satisfaction of employees and physicians.[11]

Benchmarking information has become a valuable source for development of best practices throughout the for-profit and nonprofit sectors. The process of developing benchmarks can promote a dialog among administrators and encourage adoption of identified best practices. Nonprofit organizations that have no counterparts with which to share information can develop internal benchmarks and identify cost-effective practices. For example, nonprofit organizations with numerous branches across the country, such as the YWCA, could gather information from multiple branches and prepare benchmarking information applicable to their branches of similar size and clientele.

(c) **THE BALANCED SCORECARD.**[12]   A balanced scorecard is a set of financial and nonfinancial performance measures and targets that reflect an organization's performance with respect to various stakeholders in the organization, such as its customers, employees, business partners, and the community. For many years, nonprofit firms focused primarily on cost-effective service delivery. During the late 1980s and early 1990s, this focus shifted from the financial perspective to quality or customer concerns. Nonprofits typically have multiple objectives, however, and therefore need to emphasize both financial and other relevant performance measures. Balanced scorecards with multiple financial and nonfinancial performance measures therefore prove especially useful. With a balanced scorecard, nonprofit organizations can balance the weights placed on performance measures associated with nonfinancial objectives against the weights placed on financial measures such as earnings or operating margin and productivity or cost effectiveness measures. Organizations promote multiple objectives by incorporating multiple performance measures into executives' bonus-based compensation plans. Use of performance measures in areas such as the following help organizations fulfill their goals:

- Client or customer expectations and satisfaction
- Cross-departmental teamwork toward a common goal
- Ability to identify waste, such as service delays and errors in decision making, that affect clients or patients
- Ability to identify surplus that the organization can use to increase efficiency
- Ability to accelerate the rate at which the organization learns[13]

As with other types of performance measures, organizations need to ensure that it reinforces only optimal behavior for the organization. For example, if the firm compensates employees for reducing hazardous waste when the organization does not have appropriate environmental policies and procedures in place, employees may pour hazardous chemicals down the drain rather than dispose of them properly, thus exposing the company to legal liability.

(d) **TARGET AND KAIZEN COSTING.**   Japanese manufacturers developed target and kaizen costing. (Chapters 7 and 8 discuss these methods.) Although one usually sees target

---

11.   For further examples of the use of benchmarking information, in general and within a hospital setting, see Horngren, Foster, and Datar (1997), pp. 235–236.

12.   See also Chapter 25, a chapter focused on balanced scorecard issues.

13.   R. Lynch and K. Cross, "Performance Measurement Systems." *Readings and Issues in Cost Management*, edited by James Reeve, (Mason, Ohio: South-Western College Publishing, 1995).

costing in the manufacturing sector, the nonprofit and service sectors can also apply target costing principles. Target costing is a cost control method that occurs at the design phase of new product development. After a market survey, the firm sets a target price and then calculates a target cost, based on its desired profit margin. The firm decides to manufacture the product only if it can meet the target cost. Thus, the method builds cost control into the production process in the development and design phase. As the organization develops a new product, the design team considers tradeoffs in price, functionality, and quality to meet the target cost.

Using techniques that analyze the relevant time and costs to provide a particular service, a nonprofit organization could develop a production plan for a specific service at a predetermined target cost. Because many service organizations have a large proportion of fixed costs, capacity levels affect the variability of their costs. Organizations with ample capacity would not include fixed costs in their estimated product costs. If, however, the firm faces capacity limits, the estimated product cost should include costs to increase capacity or efficiency of throughput. For example, suppose a nonprofit daycare program wanted to add after school care to its program. If the daycare were housed in a building large enough to accommodate increased volume, cost estimates would not include fixed costs related to the building. If the daycare must rent new space, however, the cost estimates should include rent.

Once an organization has established a specific product line, kaizen costing provides an effective method for reducing costs over time.[14] Under kaizen costing, organizations set specific goals for cost reduction (e.g., a 15 percent reduction in labor cost after the first six months of product introduction). These goals anticipate a reduction in market price due to increased competition. As the business environment for nonprofit service providers becomes more competitive, demand becomes more price-sensitive. Kaizen costing builds cost reduction into the product life-cycle plan. Nonprofit firms can use kaizen principles to develop specific cost-reduction goals over time. Because proportionately high fixed costs characterize service firms, if a firm has extra capacity and can reduce costs so that prices fall and volumes increase, increased volumes will likely lead to an increase in profits.

28.4 ACCOUNTING PRACTICES AND COST ACCOUNTING ISSUES FOR SPECIFIC TYPES OF NONPROFIT ORGANIZATIONS

We next examine accounting practices and cost accounting issues for service organizations in general, and for two specific types of service organizations: hospitals and governments.

(a) SERVICE ORGANIZATIONS.   The environment of service organizations (which includes charitable organizations and social service providers) has changed in the past decades. Adequate revenue streams of the past have diminished, and donors and other funding organizations demand increasing accountability with respect to cost. Service organization revenues generally come in four forms:

- Unrestricted lump-sum grants and donations
- Grants or contracts (lump-sum) to develop a program for performance of specific services
- Contracts for performance of specific services priced per unit of service
- Contracts for performance of specific services on a *capitated* basis

---

14.   See Chapter 8 for a more complete discussion of kaizen costing.

Under *capitation,* the organization receives a fixed fee to provide individuals with necessary services for a fixed period of time. In this setting, cost control becomes a critical issue, not only for development of appropriate and competitive bids, but also for the organization to remain viable, because it bears all of the financial risk associated with capitated programs.

As service organizations grapple with more competitive business environments, they face issues associated with managing costs. For example, both internal and external stakeholders request increasing amounts of information about the effectiveness of their donations and grants. Therefore, nonprofit organizations increasingly need to know the percentage of total costs spent on direct service versus administration and fundraising. Charitable donors, in particular, want to know that their funds support the work of the charity and not fund raisers or perquisites for administrators. Abuses of charitable donations abound. In May, 2003, the Supreme Court ruled that a telemarketer could be sued for keeping 85 percent of funds raised while falsely assuring donors that most of their money would go toward charitable activities, such as Thanksgiving food baskets.[15] Tracking the proportion of costs spent on administration not only controls abuses, but also increases the chances for success over time. Consider an organization such as United Way, which raises money through various corporate campaigns using different campaign strategies. Comparing the costs of administering the campaigns to the amount of money raised helps United Way identify effective fundraising methods. Lumping all fundraising activities into administrative costs would make such analysis impossible.

Service organizations also benefit from defining internal benchmarks and tracking performance against these benchmarks. In addition to focusing on cost, organizations need to emphasize service quality. Unfortunately, nonprofit firms frequently face tradeoffs between cost and quality of service, and evaluate performance based on both financial and nonfinancial metrics.

Benchmarking requires development of appropriate metrics. As Section 28.3(b) discussed, the firm should consider the behavioral implications of any performance measure and adjust these measures over time to align employees' incentives with the organization's objectives. Unique service organizations may not have appropriate benchmarks from outside the organization. In this situation, the firm could define areas of the organization—such as accounting and human resources—for which available external benchmarks exist. The firm could also develop internal organization-specific measures and track performance over time. Each organization must also establish the relative weights given to the financial and nonfinancial performance measures.

(b) OPERATING LEVERAGE.   As discussed previously, most social service organizations have a large percentage of fixed costs, which leads to a high degree of operating leverage. The higher the proportion of fixed costs, the higher the operating leverage. Because operating leverage affects an organization's financial risk, social service managers and accountants need to understand it. Some organizations base their fees on cost. For example, a nursing home might charge residents a monthly fee based on their annual operating costs and increase these fees only as operating costs increase. If all of their residents pay based on the monthly fees, operating leverage is unimportant because payments will always exceed costs. If, however, some residents have insurance that pays based on a predetermined daily rate that the nursing home cannot increase, its revenues are based on

---

15.   *Wall Street Journal* (May 6, 2003), D2.

volume rather than cost and its profits become more variable if operating leverage is high. To reduce earnings variability, the degree of operating leverage should be reduced.

Because service organizations increasingly rely on fees rather than donations for revenue, their income depends on volume. Operating leverage becomes important as volumes decrease because by definition, fixed costs do not decrease with decreasing volumes. Many social service organizations attempt to reduce the proportion of fixed cost in their cost structures, thereby reducing their operating leverage. Hospitals typically have a high degree of operating leverage and have suffered decreasing inpatient volumes in the past decade. Accordingly, managers have responded by increasing the proportion of variable costs in their cost structures.[16] Hospitals have several ways to reduce fixed costs: (1) increase the proportion of employees who are compensated on hourly wages instead of a salary; (2) lease equipment on an operating lease basis rather than purchase it; (3) use smaller, mobile equipment rather than large pieces that require a dedicated space; and (4) outsource activities that are not part of their core competencies, such as cafeteria services.

As revenue sources tighten, service organizations seek new funding opportunities. Organizations need to analyze each funding source, not only in terms of the types of available funds, but also for any requirements associated with funding. For example, some funding agencies may require detailed reporting and cost tracking. Such tracking can prove extremely costly to the organization receiving the funds and may actually outweigh the benefits of receiving funds from that source. Organizations also need to understand funding requirements and set up systems to track all expenditures that they can bill to available funding streams.

(c) STEP DOWN AND RECIPROCAL METHODS OF COST ALLOCATION. As part of their cost reporting requirements, funding agencies frequently require service organizations to submit cost reports that require the calculation of a cost per service or cost per client. The required cost is usually a fully allocated cost that reflects use of support services such as accounting, information systems and general administration. The organization therefore needs to assign all costs for these service departments to the departments that either receive revenue or provide charitable services. State and federal regulators often require nonprofits to use the step-down or reciprocal method of allocating costs for reporting purposes. The Appendix to Chapter 16 illustrates these methods.

28.5 HOSPITALS

Hospitals have prominence as social service organizations. Accordingly, we devote this section to special issues that affect hospitals, such as the proliferation of for-profit firms in the industry. The increasing presence of for-profit hospitals has changed the nature of the business environment by increasing competition, particularly for the more profitable services that hospitals provide. For-profit hospitals have no obligation to provide charity care, although to meet federal requirements for Medicare reimbursement, all hospitals—regardless of ownership type—must provide emergency room care for any patient, without consideration of the patient's ability to pay. For-profit hospitals can turn away other charity care patients. This system burdens some nonprofit hospitals with increasing amounts of charity care patients and they must trade off between providing services for

16. L. Eldenburg and S. Kallapur, "Changes in Hospital Cost Structure as a Risk Management Strategy," Working paper, The University of Arizona, 1998.

indigent patients and the hospital's bottom line. Moreover, to remain competitive with for-profit hospitals, nonprofits need to offer appropriate compensation packages to their top executives. Because for-profit organizations can provide compensation packages that include stock options and profit-sharing programs, nonprofits must be able to offer similar types of packages. Performance-based compensation has increasingly become a larger part of the entire compensation package for hospital executives.[17]

To ensure a steady supply of patients, hospitals must attract a large group of physicians with admitting privileges. Since reimbursement has increasingly become either fixed per episode or based on capitation, hospitals must also enlist physicians' cooperation in treating patients in a cost-effective manner. On one hand, hospitals must provide ample resources such as capital equipment, the latest technology and adequate capacity. On the other hand, hospitals must encourage physicians to use these resources in a cost effective manner. Before the era of managed health care, insurers paid patients' bills on the basis of cost, a system that aligned physician with hospital incentives, which did not include cost reduction. Hospitals readily provided whatever treatment physicians ordered for their patients and physicians had no incentive to include cost of treatment in their decisions. During this period, hospitals increased in size and in technological capability. This behavior led to increasing health costs.

These rapidly increasing costs led to changes in reimbursement practices. HMOs and large insurers controlled blocks of patients and began negotiating with hospitals for discounts or capitated services, which has resulted in several problems for hospitals. First, hospital incentives no longer coincide with physicians' incentives. Some physicians build labs and service centers to compete with hospitals. Some hospitals have purchased physicians' practices and put the physicians on a salary in a move to have more control over their practice patterns. When the hospital later sells these practices, the new firm may have completely different capital improvements and compensation for the physicians. Thus, hospitals and physicians have, in some instances, become rivals.[18]

In addition, billing practices have become complex and bill amounts are increasingly unrelated to cost. Large insurers have negotiated discounts, squeezing the industry's profits. Hospitals bill uninsured patients and those insurers without negotiating power at higher rates to compensate for losses on negotiated contracts. Because of these practices, a congressional probe began examining the issue in 2004, first examining the high rates that the nation's top 20 hospital chains charge uninsured patients.[19]

Because cost-based reimbursement was standard for so many years, hospitals tended to focus primarily on enhancing reimbursement. For example, hospitals have traditionally passed the cost of charity care onto paying patients by incorporating the cost of charity cases into hospital prices. When reimbursement schemes began to change, hospitals continued to focus on reimbursement and fine-tuned their ability to adjust their charges to their payor mix to ensure profits. As payors negotiated discounts, hospitals focused on increased efficiency. This focus has had two directions: (1) provision of cost-effective services; and (2) managing patient treatment.

Provision of cost-effective services became the first effort toward cost containment. As hospitals began to examine the cost of providing specific services, a demand for

---

17.   R. Lambert and D. Larcker, "The Prospective Payment System, Hospital Efficiency, and Compensation Contracts for Senior-Level Hospital Administrators," *Journal of Accounting and Public Policy* (14) (1995): 1—31.

18.   *Wall Street Journal* (October 25, 1997), A1 and A14.

19.   *Wall Street Journal* (February 20, 2004), A1.

information about other hospitals' costs of service arose. Benchmarking has thus become well-developed in this industry, to the point of being featured in cost accounting text books.[20] Hospitals can compare the cost of providing specific services with the cost in similar hospitals.

Managing patient treatment poses more problems for hospitals, because physicians make treatment decisions, while the hospital bears the costs of treatment. Because of this dynamic, many hospitals have encouraged physicians to develop practice guidelines for specific diagnoses. The hospital then monitors patient treatment and attempts to hold physicians to the guidelines. A relatively easy and inexpensive alternative exists, however. Hospitals can provide physicians with three sets of information:

1. The cost of any treatment or procedure the physician may order
2. The accumulating costs of treatment per case
3. A benchmark—either hospital, state, or nationwide—of the cost to treat a similar patient

Hospitals that provide all three sets of information tend to have relatively lower average charges, after controlling for other factors.[21] When physicians have this cost information, they use their knowledge of the efficacy of treatment and the patient's response to treatment to make marginal decisions about the cost-effectiveness of additional care. Physicians have access to an increasing amount of information about the cost-effectiveness of different types of treatment, and consultants have established practices to help educate physicians in the most cost-effective ways to treat patients.

Hospitals face a regulatory environment that differs from that of other nonprofit organizations. Because a large percentage of patient revenues result from the treatment of Medicare patients, hospitals must conform to any requirements that the Centers for Medicare & Medicaid Services (CMMS)[22] stipulates as necessary for Medicare reimbursement. For example, CMMS requires hospitals to submit an annual Medicare Cost Report that calculates costs related to Medicare patients. The report first assigns all directly traceable costs for individual departments (e.g., salaries and wages) to those departments as direct costs. Second, it reclassifies costs among departments according to Medicare guidelines. For example, the hospital must reclassify drugs purchased directly by departments such as the operating room to the pharmacy department. The CMMS disallows some costs—such as bad debts and charity care—as not attributable to Medicare patients. The report subtracts these costs at the department level. Third, the report allocates the costs of service departments (such as laundry and linen, housekeeping, and administrative services) to the revenue-generating departments. The guidelines require such calculations to compute the full costs of providing service in the revenue-generating departments.

These allocation methods do not generate absolute per-unit costs. Use of a different allocation base (such as square feet of space instead of hours for housekeeping) changes amounts allocated to each of the departments. Because of this, regulations frequently specify both the allocation bases and the order of allocation for the step-down method. CMMS developed a set of allocation guidelines to prevent manipulation by hospitals. The CMMS

---

20. For example, C.T. Horngren, G. Foster, and S. Datar, *Cost Accounting—A Managerial Emphasis*, 9th ed. (Upper Saddle River, N.J.: Prentice-Hall, 1997).

21. L. Eldenburg, "The Use of Cost Information in Total Cost Management." *The Accounting Review*, 69(1) (1994): 96–121.

22. CMMS was formerly called the Health Care Financing Administration (HCFA).

awards contracts to private intermediaries (e.g., Blue Cross in Washington State) to audit the annual cost reports, as required, and to handle reimbursement for the CMMS.

In addition to Medicare cost reports, many states require that hospitals submit annual budgets as well as annual actual cost information. Reporting requirements for these budgets and cost reports resemble Medicare's requirements, but states want information about all patients, not just a specific group. Some states use this information to evaluate resource allocations, such as whether a hospital should increase its inpatient capacity or purchase new equipment. States also can use this information to monitor hospital prices under rate-setting regulation. In these states, hospitals must conform to profitability limits. The state department of health or the state hospital commission has information about hospital accounting requirements. Details about requirements for individual states lie beyond the scope of this chapter. Although federal and state governments require reports of hospitals and other social service agencies, governments (including municipal) must also provide accounting reports about their own services.

28.6 GOVERNMENT ENTITIES AND ENVIRONMENTAL ACCOUNTING REPORTS

(a) GOVERNMENT ACCOUNTING—FUND ACCOUNTING. Government entities need to demonstrate that they have carried out their functions effectively and efficiently. From an accounting perspective, governments have stewardship responsibilities to serve their constituencies as those who manage other's property or finances, acting as administrators and held accountable for appropriately using resources. To fulfill this stewardship responsibility, these entities use two types of financial controls: fund accounting and budgets. The Government Accounting Standards Board (GASB) Statement of Governmental Accounting Concepts No. 1, issued in 1987, emphasizes governments' accountability to their constituencies. Financial reports must compare actual results with a legally adopted budget, assess financial conditions and results of operations, assist in evaluating compliance with finance-related laws, rules, and regulations, and assist in measuring efficiency and effectiveness.

For internal reporting purposes, governmental entities use fund accounting, a type of accounting frequently used in the nonbusiness sector. Financial management in nonprofit and government organizations focuses on the acquisition and use of financial resources— that is, the flow of funds. In 1979, the National Council on Governmental Accounting issued 12 principles of fund accounting and reporting. In 1984, the GASB adopted these principles and required all government entities to produce financial statements that met these requirements.

Fund financial statements regard state and local governments as combinations of distinctly different fiscal and accounting entities. Each entity should have a separate set of accounts to reflect their independent operations. Whereas business managers use the term *fund* to reflect a portion of the firm's assets, such as a petty cash fund, in government accounting, a *fund* reflects a separate accounting entity. For example, the motor pool for a government entity would have its own fund. Fund accounting uses a modified accrual basis. This method generally recognizes revenues in the accounting period in which they become available and measurable. The method recognizes expenditures in the accounting period in which the entity incurs the fund liability, if measurable. *Available* means that the government entity recognizes revenue during the period of time that it expects collection. For example, property taxes are often due in installments. Revenue recognition occurs on the date the installments are available, that is, during the fiscal year in which the entity will collect them. *Measurable* means the entity knows the amount. The entity cannot predict the timing of payment of some taxes, such as licensing fees, so it recognizes this type of revenue on a cash basis. Government entities classify fund revenues by fund and by source.

Expenditures by government entities include outlays for expenses, retirement of debt, and capital outlays. Entities classify expenditures by fund, function (program), organization unit, activity, the period benefited, or by object (type of items purchased or services obtained). They classify interfund transfers and proceeds of long-term debt issues separately from fund revenues and expenditures.

Some government entities receive proprietary fund revenues and must use the same classifications that a similar business organization would use. For example, a county-owned hospital treats both paying and nonpaying patients and receives patient fees as well as subsidies from the county to cover all costs. Regulations require this hospital to use the same revenue and expense classifications as privately owned nonprofit hospitals would use, and adopt the same accrual accounting methods.

One major difference between fund accounting and business accounting relates to use of Appropriation and Encumbrance accounts. Certain governmental resources receive funds through appropriations laws. Through temporary legislation, governing bodies assign amounts that specific agencies will spend for specific purposes. The appropriation also confers the legal authority to make expenditures from the assigned resources. The governing body sets up an *Appropriation* account to record these resource assignments. Then, as government executives make current expenditures and commitments, the amount of money available in the Appropriations account for further expenditures decreases. To ensure that the agency sets aside cash for expenditures and commitments, it uses an *Encumbrances* account. Journal entries to this account transfer cash balances to restricted asset accounts to honor expenditures and commitments that the agency makes.

Budgets have become another important part of control and planning within government agencies. In addition to these functions, government agencies use budgets to obtain resources by establishing levels of taxation or fees imposed and identifying the level of services to provide. Because budgets are so important in government reporting, GASB has listed the attributes of a legally adopted annual budget in GASB Codification, Section 100.119.[23]

Accounting and business firms have pressured the federal government to provide fiscal information comparable to financial statements prepared according to Generally Accepted Accounting Principles (GAAP). In 1997, the federal government attempted to apply GAAP standards to its books for the first time, with the General Accounting Office acting as outside auditor.[24] The audit was required by the 1994 Government Management Reform Act, one of a series of laws passed to require the federal bureaucracy to more frequently follow private-sector practices. The audit revealed many areas where government agencies violated GAAP, particularly in terms of asset valuation. Individual agencies have since worked toward remedying the deficiencies uncovered by the audit. GASB Statement No. 34 requires state and local governments to issue government-wide financial statements using accrual accounting as well as fund financial statements using a modified accrual method of accounting.

---

23.   For further information on these requirements and government fund accounting, see J. Norvelle, *Introduction to Fund Accounting*, 5th ed., 1994.

24.   *Wall Street Journal* (March 31, 1998), A2.

Public interest has increased regarding the cost-effectiveness of services provided by government and nonprofit organizations. GAAP financial statements, fund accounting and budget reporting do not provide adequate information to calculate a cost per service because they usually include no information about units of service. Choosing an appropriate unit of service or alternative performance measure requires consideration of behavioral implications. For example, suppose a municipal government measures a police department's cost-effectiveness by cost per arrest. Arithmetic dictates that when the number of arrests increases, cost per arrest will decrease—but an increase in arrests may not translate to a safer environment. The change in homeowners' insurance and automobile insurance rates might present a better measure of performance.[25] A decrease in these rates would indicate that fewer thefts had occurred than in the previous period and that the environment has become safer. Hence, the choice of units of service influences both the cost per outcome and the behavioral response to the measure. Government agencies need to consider these effects when implementing self-evaluation programs.

(b) REGULATORY REPORTING REQUIREMENTS FOR GOVERNMENT CONTRACTS—CASB STANDARDS. Governments must also work toward the cost effective use of taxpayer revenues. Because the U.S. government has stewardship of these public funds, it has established a special set of rules for defense contractors who are sometimes reimbursed based on cost. Incentives arise to load expenses onto those contracts or products that the government reimburses based on cost. The government frequently enters into contracts in the defense industry based on cost. To mitigate these cost-increasing incentives, the U.S. Congress established a public-sector board, the Cost Accounting Standards Board (CASB), in 1970 to provide uniform cost accounting standards for defense contractors and federal agencies. Between 1970 and 1980, CASB produced 20 cost accounting standards. Congress terminated the board in 1980, but recreated it in 1988 as an independent board of the Office of Federal Procurement Policy that no longer reports to Congress. The current board's objectives include the following:

- Increase the degree of uniformity in cost accounting practices among government contractors in like circumstances.
- Establish consistency in cost accounting practices in like circumstances by each individual contractor over periods of time.
- Require contractors to disclose their cost accounting practices in writing.[26]

CASB standards are not a comprehensive set of rules. Nevertheless, any companies bidding on or pricing cost-related contracts for the federal government must comply with the standards. Systematic cost tracking and documentation has become important under CASB. Because judgment can alter interpretation of the standards, court records and case outcomes from litigation between the government and various firms has set legal precedence and a "standard interpretation." Firms that contract with the government therefore need to understand this legal history to comply with the rules.

---

25.   R. Todd, and K. Ramanathan, "Perceived Social Needs, Outcomes Measurement, and Budgetary Responsiveness in a Not-for-Profit Setting: Some Empirical Evidence," *The Accounting Review* 69 (1) (1994): 122–137.

26.   R. B. Hubbard, "Return of the Cost Accounting Standards Board," *Management Accounting* (October 1990): 56.

(c) ENVIRONMENTAL ACCOUNTING. The federal government established CASB as part of its stewardship responsibilities. For similar reasons, in 1993, President Clinton signed Executive Order 12856, *Federal Compliance with Right-to-Know Laws and Pollution Prevention Requirements.* This Executive Order requires that each federal agency apply two relatively new managerial accounting tools when evaluating opportunities for pollution prevention: (1) Life-cycle analysis (assessment), a technique designed to measure, at the product level, environmental costs and benefits associated with production and consumption, and (2) Total Cost Accounting, a methodology that the EPA, along with Tellus Institute, developed to facilitate inclusion of environmental costs in evaluation of pollution prevention investments.

We begin our discussion of these methods with a general introduction to environmental accounting. Pollution prevention has become an issue for both for-profit and nonprofit organizations. Most organizations have traditionally ignored or funneled environmental costs into general overhead. As a result, organizations have not included these costs in decision-making processes. Organizations that develop accounting systems to address environmental costs not only reduce environmental costs, but also improve their products and processes. In a two-year period, Dow Chemical realized more than $17 million in savings from its Waste Reduction Always Pays program. Baxter International designed an Environmental Financial Statement that estimates worldwide environmental costs and savings. In 1996, it reported a total benefit from their environmental programs of $104.6 million (in increased income, cost savings and cost avoidance). Using a simplified version of Life Cycle Assessments, Bristol-Myers Squibb identified $3.5 million in potential savings.

Governmental agencies have also realized cost savings. For example, Tinker Air Force Base replaced toxic solvents with high-pressure water blast robotic technology for aircraft component stripping. This single project resulted in numerous benefits, including a financial savings of $1.3 million per year and a 30 percent reduction of worker turnover rate. The base also experienced reductions in turnaround time per aircraft component, occupational illnesses, personal protective equipment requirements, and safety hazards. In addition, the base eliminated each year 140,000 pounds of methylene chloride (a chemical paint stripper), 100,000 pounds of solid waste, and 8.3 million gallons of wastewater.

Standard accounting systems do not accommodate environmental costs. Most systems focus on costs for capital equipment and raw materials and either include environmental costs in corporate overhead or ignore them. The U.S. Environmental Protection Agency (EPA) has identified the following categories of environmental costs that accounting systems should address:[27]

- *Potentially hidden costs,* which result from compliance with environmental laws and regulations (i.e., regulatory costs), or from exceeding regulatory requirements (i.e., voluntary costs)
- *Contingent costs,* which a firm might or might not incur in the future, such as the cost of clean-up following future accidental pollution or victim compensation[28]
- *Image and relation costs,* which a firm incurs either to affect stakeholder perceptions of the organization (such as for production of environmental performance

27. U.S. EPA, *An Introduction to Environmental Accounting as a Business Management Tool: Key Concepts and Terms* (Washington, D.C.: EPA, 1995).

28. The reduction in contingent costs resulting from pollution prevention benefits is one of the significant benefits that has frequently been ignored in cost/benefit analyses of pollution prevention projects.

information), or as a result of poor environmental management (such as the negative public relations effects of an accidental spill)

(d) REGULATORY REPORTING REQUIREMENTS FOR ENVIRONMENTAL ACCOUNTING. Organizations have new accounting tools to facilitate inclusion of environmental costs in managerial decision making. The nonprofit and governmental sectors most often use two such tools:

1. Life cycle assessment (LCA), a technique designed to measure, at the product level, environmental costs and benefits associated with production and consumption

2. Total cost assessment (TCA), a method developed by Tellus Institute for the EPA to facilitate inclusion of environmental costs in evaluation of pollution prevention investments (EPA 1992)[29]

Executive Order 12856 requires that federal agencies develop agencywide pollution prevention strategies. These strategies must deal with the following: pollution prevention, voluntary goals to reduce total releases and offsite transfers of toxic chemicals or toxic pollutants, facility-level pollution prevention plans, and application of LCA and TCA principles when evaluating pollution prevention opportunities. Even though LCA and TCA prove most useful to individuals involved in recommending and evaluating projects, they will benefit any employee involved in procurement. These tools apply outside of the government arena; managers in any organization that has opportunities for pollution prevention should understand them. Several state governments (e.g., Massachusetts, Oregon, and Washington) have implemented requirements for analysis of pollution prevention alternatives by for-profit organizations at the state level.

(i) Life-Cycle Assessment (LCA).   LCA offers a *cradle to grave* approach, which allows analysts to identify areas of potential environmental improvement throughout a product's life cycle. Scientists and engineers originally applied the technique in the 1960s as a mechanism to assess the energy requirements and chemical inputs and outputs of various production systems.[30] In 1990, the Society of Environmental Toxicology and Chemistry (SETAC)[31] established an LCA Advisory Group to facilitate application of LCA to reduce environmental impacts resulting from production processes' product packaging. LCA has become an accepted environmental measurement tool to aid businesses in their decision-making processes. Many diverse organizations have implemented different versions of the technique.

International Standards Organization's (ISO) ISO14000 environmental management standards has incorporated LCA.[32] ISO standards define LCA as a "…compilation and evaluation according to a systematic set of procedures, of the inputs and outputs and the potential environmental impacts of a product system throughout its life cycle."[33] LCA has three stages:

29.   U.S. EPA, *Facility Pollution Prevention Guide* (Washington, D.C.: EPA [EPA/600-R-92-008] 1992).

30.   C. Henn and J. Fava, "Life Cycle Analysis and Resource Management," *Environmental Strategies Handbook* (New York: McGraw-Hill, 1994), pp. 541–641.

31.   SETAC was founded in 1979 and comprises professionals from academic, business, and government organizations who are interested in promoting the uses of multidisciplinary approaches to examining the impacts of chemicals and technology on the environment.

32.   Although ISO standards are voluntary, conformance with them is becoming a condition for doing business across international boundaries (M. Epstein, *Measuring Corporate Environmental Performance* (Montvale, N.J.: IMA Foundation for Applied Research, 1996).

33.   M. J. Bradley, *Applying Life-Cycle Assessment for a Forest Products Company.* Canfor Pulp and Paper Company, March 1996.

1. *Stage one:* In the first stage of an LCA (Inventory), the analyst sets boundaries on the aspects of a product's life cycle that relate to the environment. The analyst decides which environmental aspects to include and omit in the product's evaluation. Even though environmental regulations may drive consideration of some aspects, the analyst has flexibility to limit the analysis according to the purpose of the LCA. For example, the LCA exercise frequently omits environmental impacts associated with transportation or raw material extraction, particularly when the focus is on improvements in the processes inside of a company.

2. *Stage two:* In the second stage (Impact Assessment), the analyst assesses the environmental impacts of the production inputs and outputs. Here the analyst must rely on scientific data or research, or both, to quantify the product's environmental impacts.

3. *Stage three:* In the final stage (Improvement Analysis), the analyst identifies opportunities to reduce the environmental impact (and frequently, associated costs) of the product.

Despite LCA's potential usefulness, it also has some limitations. LCA results heavily depend on the chosen scope and assumptions underlying the analysis. In addition, standardized LCA tools and data sets do not exist. For example, a life-cycle assessment of almost any process entails calculation of the environmental impact of energy usage. The impact will depend on how and where an entity generated that energy. Assessing the full environmental impact can, therefore, become difficult (and expensive), although several organizations are developing databases that provide standardized impacts of various materials.[34] Accordingly, some organizations have limited the scope of their analyses to processes that occur within their walls (including disposal) and have quantified some of the inputs and outputs (such as the amount of energy used) without attempting to definitively assess the environmental impact of those inputs and outputs. This results in a greater focus on LCA as a means of process improvement and cost reduction while continuing to reduce environmental impact.

Evaluating results of LCAs can prove difficult because the environmental impacts do not have common measures. To evaluate different opportunities for environmental improvements, the analysis may trade off reduction in solid waste (measured in pounds or kilograms) with reduction in energy usage (measured in British Thermal Units), and reduction in waterborne wastes (measured in gallons or liters).[35] Analysts can facilitate comparison across categories by assigning a monetary cost to each impact. We call this extension of LCA a *Life-Cycle Cost Analysis.* Some companies use this method to calculate the full environmental cost of their products.[36] Once they have derived the costs, assigning those costs to different life-cycle stages becomes relatively simple. Calculating usage rates, proper valuation of natural resources, and costs of impacts can prove difficult, however. One should view cost estimates derived from such analyses with caution.

---

34. For example, Environment Canada, in partnership with the Canadian Standards Association, has developed a database on environmental impacts of various raw materials to make it easier for Canadian businesses to perform LCAs. The National Renewable Energy Laboratory is also involved in a project to develop such a database.

35. This discussion understates the problem; the same difficulties arise within the environmental impact categories as well. For example, should a kilogram of sulfur dioxide be equivalent to a kilogram of carbon dioxide emissions?

36. See, for example, J. Walsh, and M. Brown. "Pricing Environmental Impacts: A Tale of Two T-Shirts," *Illahe* 11 (3, 4) (1995):. pp. 175–182.

Such analyses not only require assumptions for the basic LCA, but impose additional assumptions to convert impacts into costs. As both LCAs and Life-Cycle Cost Analyses grow in frequency, however, the demand for better cost and impact information should result in better data availability and less subjective analyses.[37]

(ii) Total Cost Assessment.   Total cost assessment (TCA) facilitates inclusion of environmental costs in evaluation of pollution prevention investments. An organization can use this method to evaluate any project involving potential environmental or health and safety impacts. TCA extends the capital budgeting model to include costs that may prove difficult to measure or that accounting systems do not traditionally track.

TCA uses a four-tier hierarchy of costs. The cost tiers follow from EPA's cost categories described in Section 28.6(c): potentially hidden costs, contingent costs, and image and relation costs. The hierarchy progresses from conventional (and certain) costs in Tier 0 to the most difficult to estimate (and least certain) costs in Tier 3.

Identifying costs from the various tiers may prove difficult and costly. Organizations can minimize the cost of a TCA by focusing on one tier at a time, starting with Tier 0 costs. If analysis of Tier 0 costs does not reveal an economic benefit, then the analyst should consider Tier 1 costs, and so on. In this way, organizations will not have to incur the cost and effort involved in analyzing costs in all of the tiers. The EPA suggests the following analysis in each of the tiers:

TIER 0—USUAL COSTS

- Components: Costs that directly link to the project, products, or process under study. These typically include capital expenditures/depreciation cash flows such as buildings and equipment, utility connections, and equipment installation and operating and maintenance expenses such as materials, labor, utilities, and waste management.
- Suggested analysis:
  - Identify pollution prevention alternatives or the project to be analyzed.
  - Estimate the usual costs of current practice and/or proposed project.

TIER 1—HIDDEN COSTS

- Components: Regulatory compliance or other costs that general accounts typically hide. (Managerial decision making frequently ignores hidden costs because they lie obscured in overhead accounts.) Hidden costs include reporting for compliance, permitting, legal support, testing, monitoring, waste manifesting, and closure (decommissioning) costs.
- Suggested analysis:
  - Establish the facility's regulatory status.
  - Estimate hidden capital expenditures.
  - Estimate hidden expenses.

TIER 2—LIABILITY COSTS

- Components: Contingent costs that may result from waste and materials management. In most accounting systems, these costs tend to hide in overhead and general

---

37.   There are numerous resources available concerning LCAs. The EPA has been especially proactive in encouraging organizations to perform LCAs and in providing resources. Examples of resources include, *Life-Cycle Assessment: Inventory Guidelines and Principles* (Washington, D.C.: EPA/600-R-92-245) and SETAC's *A Technical Framework for Life-Cycle Assessment.*

expense accounts. These costs include future compliance costs, penalties and fines, personal injury damage, and legal expenses.

- Suggested analysis:

  ○ Identify regulatory programs under which the firm could incur penalties and/ or fines.

  ○ Estimate expected annual penalties and fines associated with current practice and/or the proposed project.

  ○ Identify waste-management issues with which liabilities can be associated.

  ○ Estimate total expected liabilities.

  ○ Estimate expected years of liability incurrence.

  ○ Estimate the firm's share of total future liabilities.

TIER 3—LESS TANGIBLE COSTS

- Components: Savings for organizations that pursue environmentally beneficial projects. Savings accrue from increases in stakeholder goodwill through increased revenues and decreased expenses. Although analysts may find it difficult to predict the extent of these benefits with certainty, these benefits may be significant for some projects. Benefits can come from improvements in customer relations, employee satisfaction (with corresponding reductions in turnover), relations with regulators, and relations with local communities.

- Suggested analysis:

  ○ Identify qualitatively less tangible benefits of the project.

  ○ Quantify the less tangible costs and benefits of the project.[38]

After managers identify the costs and benefits associated with the tiers, they must analyze them. Managers should give special consideration to evaluation of financial performance when environmental costs exist. For example, many nonprofit organizations and governmental agencies use payback period to evaluate investments. Payback period represents the length of time required before the firm recoups costs of a new project, calculated by the following equation:

Payback period (in years) = Start-up costs/(Annual benefits – Annual costs)

Using this method, the organization funds those investments that recoup their costs within a preestablished period of time (e.g., three years). Although analysts can easily calculate and interpret payback period, it has drawbacks, particularly for projects with environmental costs. Many types of environmental costs occur far into the future (e.g., liability or disposal costs). Because payback analysis ignores any cash flows that occur after the end of the preestablished period, the analyst may not fully consider these costs in the payback calculation. In addition, payback period does not provide for discounting of future costs and benefits. Hence, the method does not properly represent the tradeoff between a dollar today and a dollar in the future. Finally, payback period does not allow consideration of intangible costs and benefits. For costs and benefits to enter into the calculation, the analyst must express them in monetary terms.

---

38. Adapted from U.S. EPA, *Pollution Prevention Benefits Manual* (Washington, D.C.: EPA, [EPA-230-R-89-100]1989).

An alternative metric, Net Present Value (NPV), recognizes that a dollar today is worth more than a dollar in the future. This method reduces (discounts) future cash flows to the sum that the firm would have to invest today to produce that future amount. For federal facilities, the federal Office of Management and Budget (OMB) provides a required discount rate.[39] The analyst sums the discounted annual cash flows (including initial cash outflows) to derive the investment's net present value, calculated by the following equation:

$$NPV = \text{Discounted annual net cash flows} - \text{Initial investment}$$

The higher the NPV, the more desirable the project. Since government and nonprofit projects may not have any revenues, the NPV of the most attractive option will frequently have the smallest negative value.

Although applicable for most types of projects, NPV becomes particularly useful for evaluating projects with associated environmental costs and benefits. Pollution prevention efforts result in annual reductions in costs such as hazardous waste disposal and hazardous materials handling. Although small on an annual basis, if these savings persist for the life of the project, they can become substantial over time.

An organization should consider several issues when applying NPV to projects with environmental aspects. Many environmental projects have long-term horizons, uncertainty, and risk. For example, a firm may enjoy many environmental benefits—such as avoidance of future liability from personal injury, property damage, regulatory fines, and decommissioning costs—long past the usual timeframe included in most capital budgeting exercises. The analyst should therefore choose an appropriate timeframe that fully captures environmental costs and benefits.

The NPV method also has some drawbacks. For example, analysis of environmental risk and intangible costs and benefits can prove difficult. The discount rate for environmental projects should accurately reflect associated risk (or risk reduction). Alternatively, a nonmonetary environmental risk rating in the analysis can reflect the level of risk without specifying monetary effects. The analysis can similarly treat intangible costs and benefits that one cannot quantify.[40]

BIBLIOGRAPHY

Aalbregtse, R. "Target Costing." In *Readings and Issues in Cost Management* edited by James M. Reeve. New York: Warren, Groham & Lamont, South-Western College Publishing, 1995.

American Institute of Certified Public Accountants (AICPA). 1990. Audit Guide.

AICPA. *Audit and Accounting Guide for Hospitals,* 1994.

CCH *Medicare and Medicaid Guide,* Vol. 2. Chicago: Provider Reimbursement Manual. Commerce Clearing House, 1994.

The Center for Environmental Research Information. *A Primer for Financial Analysis of Pollution Prevention Projects.* Washington, D.C.: EPA (EPA/600-R-93-059), 1993.

---

39.   Current rates can be obtained from the OMB's Office of Economic Policy at (202) 395-5873.

40.   Resources for more information on TCA include U.S. EPA, *Pollution Prevention Benefits Manual.* (Washington, D.C.: EPA, 1989); U.S. EPA,. *Facility Pollution Prevention Guide* (Washington, D.C.: EPA [EPA/600-R-92-008], 1992). The Center for Environmental Research Information. *A Primer for Financial Analysis of Pollution Prevention Projects* (Washington, D.C.: EPA (EPA/600-R-93-059), 1993).

Eldenburg, L. "The Use of Cost Information in Total Cost Management". *The Accounting Review*, 69(1) (1994): 96–121.

Eldenburg, L., and S. Kallapur. "Changes in Hospital Cost Structure as a Risk Management Strategy". Working paper, The University of Arizona, 1998.

Environmental Protection Agency (EPA). *Pollution Prevention Benefits Manual,* Washington, D.C.: EPA, 1989.

EPA. *Facility Pollution Prevention Guide.* Washington, D.C.: EPA (EPA/600-R-92-008), 1992.

Epstein, M. *Measuring Corporate Environmental Performance.* Montvale, N.J.: IMA Foundation for Applied Research, 1996.

Fahey, T., and A. Murphey. "Tax Exemption and Charity Care—What Can Hospitals Expect?" *Trustee* (November 1990): 6–8.

Fama, E., and M. Jensen. "Agency Problems and Residual Claims." *Journal of Law and Economics* 26 (June1983): 327–350.

Financial Accounting Standards Board. *Statements Of Financial Accounting Concepts: Accounting Standards.* New York: Irwin, 1994/1995.

Financial Accounting Standards Board. *Statements of Financial Accounting Standards No. 116.*

Henn, C., and J. Fava. "Life Cycle Analysis and Resource Management." *Environmental Strategies Handbook.* New York: McGraw-Hill, 1994., pp. 541–641.

Horngren, C.T., G. Foster, and S. Datar. *Cost Accounting—A Managerial Emphasis*, 9th ed. Upper Saddle River, N.J.: Prentice-Hall, 1997.

Hubbard, R. B. "Return of the Cost Accounting Standards Board." *Management Accounting* (October1990): 56.

Hyatt, T., and B. Hopkins. *The Law of Tax-Exempt Healthcare Organizations.* New York: John Wiley & Sons, 1995.

Lambert, R., and D. Larcker. "The Prospective Payment System, Hospital Efficiency, and Compensation Contracts for Senior-Level Hospital Administrators." *Journal of Accounting and Public Policy*, 14 (1995): 1–31.

Lynch, R., and K. Cross. "Performance Measurement Systems." *Readings and Issues in Cost Management.* Edited by James Reeve. Mason, Ohio: South-western College Publishing, 1995.

Monden, Y., and J. Lee. "How a Japanese Auto Maker Reduces Costs." *Management Accounting,* (August1993): 22–25.

Noreen, E., and N. Soderstrom. "The Accuracy of Proportional Cost Models: Evidence from Hospital Service Departments." *Review of Accounting Studies,* 2 (1997): 89–114.

Norvell, J. *Introduction to Fund Accounting,* 5th ed. Tucson, Ariz.:Thoth Books, 1994.

Seay, J. D. "Community Benefit Prevails." *Health Progress* (Jan.–Feb. 1992): 38–41, 64.

Society of Environmental Toxicology and Chemistry (SETAC). *A Technical Framework for Life-Cycle Assessment.* J. Fava, R. Denison, B. Jones, M. Curran, B. Vigon, S. Selke, and J. Barnum, Eds. SETAC Foundation for Environmental Education, Inc., 1991.

Todd, R., and K. Ramanathan. "Perceived Social Needs, Outcomes Measurement, and Budgetary Responsiveness in a Not-for-Profit Setting: Some Empirical Evidence." *The Accounting Review* 69 (1) (1994): 122–137.

Walsh, J., and M. Brown. "Pricing Environmental Impacts: A Tale of Two T-Shirts." *Illahee* 11 (3, 4) (1995): 175–182.